A Note to Readers

Pirandello's Six Characters in Search of An Author (1921),[1] first read in 1961 by an Architect now turned Storyteller, is the memetic device which haunts this open-ended script Words Made Flesh between LESSONS and CONNECTIVE TISSUES by whispering Building the Unfinished,[2] perhaps framed Between Memory and Amnesia.[3]

This project, as an improvisational spatial script, commenced on the Summer Solstice of 2021,[4] and re-inaugurated self-consciously again on the Solstice of 2023,[5] brings together several individual characters and their work, linked by a multitude of prismatic connections.

It may be a posthuman(ist) project,[6] by a willing removal/disbelief of/in singular self or authorship, when then five strangers each share their unique perspectives on (Peter Waldman's) two pivotal construction sites: Parcel X (1994) and the Eric Goodwin Memorial Pavilion (2004).

The narrator or story teller, Peter Waldman, pivoted strategically from his first person singular, and then plural, tendencies and engaged in a call and response context with these three strangers momentarily, and shortly thereafter embracing a fourth long term witness thus make this a Five Finger Exercise.

Precisely a Lunar Cycle after the catalytic Summer Solstice of 2023, Waldman was introduced to another perfect stranger:[7] David Ireland and his House as Museum, curated by the 500 Capp Street Foundation in San Francisco as we collaboratively changed the Title of this project now to Six Characters in Search of a Spatial Script (and Stage Sets), Critical Improvisations on One Dwelling and One Memorial, (somewhere between Eden and Jerusalem).

IN SEARCH OF SPATIAL SCRIPTS

Introspective Improvisations for Two Construction Sites

Parcel X Encampment (1994) and *The Goodwin Memorial* (2004)

PETER WALDMAN
BEN SMALL
SOFIA KUSPAN
PATRICK SARDO
DAVID IRELAND
DAVID TURNBULL

TABLE OF CONTENTS

FF

He liked making
and threw up his hands
felt
in the earth, and
in the dark,
in search of something.
his subterranean explorations
transforming night
in the trough of the wave,
think of a thing more useless
four inches in length, two inches in width,
he had the 'thing'
of most unusual shape
in hand.
the mixture became
a synthesis of ideas
of labor as a whole.
he never gave it up
His mind was working,
was a condition
a little separate from the world
a human
hand gestured
IN A house in which to live.

thumping and clumping. He reached in his pocket

, and flung

to the ground

some searching questions

A vigorous effort to be something

encounter

THE condition of

what is in his mind."

now

a sense of presence

IN the folded sheet of paper—

in your hand

THE ARTIST'S EYE

a deep blue

Word Pieces by Ann Hamilton from *here • there • then • now* (2023) at 500 Capp Street, San Francisco
(Courtesy of Ann Hamilton Studio)

PROLOGUES FROM STRANGERS

EXCERPTS FROM A CONVERSATION WITH ANN HAMILTON

On December 28th, 2024, Sofia Kuspan & Patrick Sardo met with Ann Hamilton at her studio, discussing background information on the book's origins and describing the connective tissues that unify different characters and voices with the ghost of David Ireland.

Patrick: This is a constant issue we have of explaining this project to other people, and especially if they're not an architect or an artist.

Ann: I understand you're figuring it out, that Peter's work is the *connective tissue* or thread you are weaving through the book.

Sofia: Yes, he uses the term *connective tissues* throughout his teaching; it's also the title of his second book. That's how he describes this idea of collaboration and how all these different references come together, including images that bring together an array of characters and voices.

Ann: Because we're all influenced by every conversation, everything we read, every snippet of everything becomes part of the landscape that work emerges from.

Patrick: And for all the books and projects that he's done, he always references everyone that he worked with. He talks about how indebted he is to these collaborators who brought in other ideas or who left their mark on his projects in different ways.

Sofia: He's also very interested in how an outside stranger might read something in a way that he's never thought about before.

Ann: Exactly… because they don't come out of the same discipline, they bring a different lens to it.

Patrick and Sofia discuss the process of making the plates for the book.

Ann: These are almost like Photoshop collages. How material are they?

Patrick: They're really just made with Photoshop. I would have liked to attempt making them in a tactile way, but we didn't have a lot of the original source material. I wish I could have cut these things up.

Ann: That's kind of one of the problems or challenges with the processes of architecture, isn't it?

Sofia: Yeah, there's a disconnect between working with your hands versus digitally: most of our work is now done on a screen using digital software to simulate the construction of a building.

Ann: And it's scaleless. As an exercise, it might be quite interesting for you to print some of these out to remake them materially as collages. But perhaps that's just an interest of mine how… how has an image become a tactile thing? Because the space is something that you experience viscerally in your body. So, I wonder if your response to some of this might be different if it is a material exercise.

Patrick: Yeah, these images didn't have the chance to become physical. We started working on this project with Peter while we were still in Charlottesville after graduation and then we left to move to Boston.

Sofia: Exactly, and it was a different type of project when we began in the summer of 2023. It transformed over time because Peter doesn't really work in a linear way. He'll see connections between disparate things, and he'll bring other references in. David Ireland wasn't part of the project at the beginning. Once he had visited the house later in the summer, he had this realization where he saw so many connections between 500 Capp Street and Parcel X along with his interests and David's interests. We didn't know initially how we would weave that in with everything else we were working with.

Ann: So partly you're also really following a design structure and visuality that's been laid out by these other two books.

Sofia: Exactly. And a lot of Peter's terminology is closely defined and referenced from his other books and from his teaching.

Ann: Right. It's a very evolved vocabulary that has very specific meaning relative to his practice.

Patrick: It's referenced in his teaching, drawing from other architects and artists. He's very well-read so there's a lot of references that we don't know, but he alludes to books, poems, plays, even paintings or sculptures often.

Ann: But, isn't that multiplicity the origins for thinking and making in all fields, architecture included.

Reflecting on Parcel X; showing Ann photographs from GA Houses 51.

Patrick: We were asked to house-sit for him while he was visiting his daughter in San Francisco. And that's how he ended up seeing the David Ireland house for the first time.

Sofia: After the initial tour from Peter, we were able to revisit the house and explore it on our own terms. It's unusual to get that type of experience in a space as intimate as someone else's home.

Ann: The vocabulary is industrial. I like how the curtain sections the space without walls.

Patrick: Peter's roots are in designing stage sets for theater performances, so it's mostly open and it has veils and scrims all throughout.

Sofia: He's a collector of many things and artifacts. The house is filled with all these bits and pieces from different eras that he's collected throughout his life. There's so much art all over the walls.

Patrick: We both enjoyed photography, so we took lots of pictures while we house-sat, seeing how the light changed the space.

Sofia: And not with the intention that these would be part of a book or published. But they were photos we took because the space was incredible to be in. As the project progressed, one of the themes that we became interested in was the act of construction and how a building or space is built rather than focusing on a final product.

Ann: The image.

Sofia: Right. We wanted to celebrate the process of how something is built by making the ideas surrounding labor visible, highlighting how people leave their mark on it. And the idea that the building isn't just a static object that exists only as some beautiful, pristine thing, but is lived in and shaped by those experiences.

Ann: How it's a handmade thing that continues to be made and remade over time.

Sofia: It's lived in and subject to weathering and decay. It's the whole narrative and process of building architecture.

Ann: Which is how artists work. It's not like a design happens and then is executed; its invention is ongoing in the process. I can hand-make an object, but the building and logistical practices of architecture mitigate against someone going in and saying, okay, we actually want the wall or beam or whatever over here. Where is it that you can have process that is still very mutable? I imagine it is a huge challenge in the practice.

But from the point of view as an artist, I find it hard to work in what I would call conventional museum spaces. I can more easily work responsively with spaces that have some other history, some former youth or hand that it gives me something to respond to.

Patrick: When I spoke with Henry Moss about the project, we were talking about MASS MoCA and that big hall that your project *corpus* was installed in. There's a point in the wall where it's painted pink and he says, "Well, we weren't going to take that off. That's where the women's bathroom used to be." So, it has such a history to it, and it offers a lot to an artist who's installing something there to say there's so much history just to this room, and everything didn't get sandblasted off the walls and covered.

Ann: He didn't pretend it was something that it wasn't.

Patrick: Henry spoke of how David influenced his way of approaching these types of projects.

Ann: Of understanding how to let that be part of the building rather than going and asserting something on top of it.

Patrick: Yeah. When I spoke with Jock Reynolds, he mentioned that David didn't want to obliterate the history of things.

Ann: I think that would be something that was probably a huge influence, consciously or unconsciously, for me approaching making installations; I am always are working with what is given in a space. That can mean a lot of different things. *With* is the operative word. My approach is to respond and amplify. Part of what I try to do is bring out or make more visible, what I find. David influenced my thinking about how, why, something has to be of the wall and of the architecture, rather than on it.

Patrick: Henry spoke of that while working with David for the artist's apartment at Phillips Academy. David wanted a certain way of finishing the wall so the edges would be exposed, the little metal corners. And people who normally build stuff don't think about that because they're not thinking about it from an artist's perspective. They're just building it how you would build anything else.

Ann: Your collage of Capp Street has the accordion text from the window. That's what I responded to when I was there. My project was very minimal. I wanted to inhabit the space *with* David rather than make something *on* David. And that's a real fine line.

Patrick: You had worked with David before and known him for some time. And then you came back to this house. And after looking at his objects and revisiting them, what drew you to go back?

Ann: It was a joint anniversary invitation from Capp Street project and the Marin Headlands. I had renovated their kitchen in 1990 and in the process, I lived in the work that David and Mark Thompson had done there. This was a chance to work in the space David actually lived in but my approach, learned from David, was the same: How do you respond to a situation or a condition? How do you listen to it? Because that's essential to what will lead and inform a project. And that's really distinctive in David's practice.

Patrick: That's why we wanted to talk with you about the project and about David specifically, to get the perspective of someone who's worked with him before also. You spoke about his presence.

Ann: Well, he was kind of a trickster.

Patrick: You could see it in the house.

Ann: I just remembered, there was a project, it was an exhibition somewhere in Spain, it must have been in Madrid. David and I were both in a group show and I remember the morning after the opening he was there cooking pancakes in the gallery. I loved how the smell turned the museum into a kitchen, how David was always playing with and inverting categories and our expectations. I think that's something you can do as an artist in a really different way than you can as an architect. You know, there's a fleetness… a lightness of hand to a lot of what David did like the dumballs, made passing wet concrete back and forth between his two hands until it set as ball. It takes discipline and rigor and commitment but of a kind so different than making a building.

Ann: We did a project with the flour at the Walker Art Center in two side-by-side galleries. A big pile of flour in "his" gallery was augered up to sift over a table in mine. David wasn't a big talker about what we were doing, but he definitely had a clear vocabulary and approach. You learned from being with him. I wouldn't say I really knew David. But I think what's probably important for your book, as far as I'm understanding, is its ethos of process and approach. How do you ask a question? How do you gather what you need to respond to?

It seems to me the collages are similarly a condition of response. Art and architecture have different work to do. I would suspect, although I don't know for Peter, that he might have sensed in David or David's approach, even though they didn't know each other, a kind of freedom that is very hard to have. David's freedom came by going into the cave.

David lived his dedication; it manifested in his house. His house wasn't an image, it was a being. Processes can take a really long time and need a lot of support. Taking a long time feels radical in this time of fast paced consumption, delivery, and product. There is immense pressure on the architectural practice to deliver models and images. I sense in this project you are exploring, through Peter's work and teaching and now perhaps David's, what kind of processes will support the practice you want to grow and develop.

I've always said, trust the process, because the process will get you there, which is something you've had to do with the book itself, right? You have to trust the process of its long coming-together.

Sofia: You don't know where it's going either. It could go in any direction, and you can't think about the process as an end result. You have to look at your material to figure out the connections and see where that will lead you.

Ann: It's really wonderful that his process makes room for your work in a way that's not a postscript or footnote, but meaningfully invites you in to take part. There is no greater generosity.

Ann Hamilton is a visual artist internationally acclaimed for her large-scale multimedia installations, public projects, and performance collaborations. Her site-responsive process works with common materials to invoke particular places, collective voices, and communities of labor. She has previously collaborated with David Ireland at the Walker Art Center and the Fabric Workshop and Museum. In 1989, she completed a residency at the Headlands Center for the Arts, where she created a permanent installation that referenced David's 1986 Headlands project, the Rodeo Room and Eastwing by transforming the Mess Hall into a gathering space. Her exhibit at 500 Capp Street in 2023, *here • there • then • now*, draws from the history of the house and David's materially unique works.

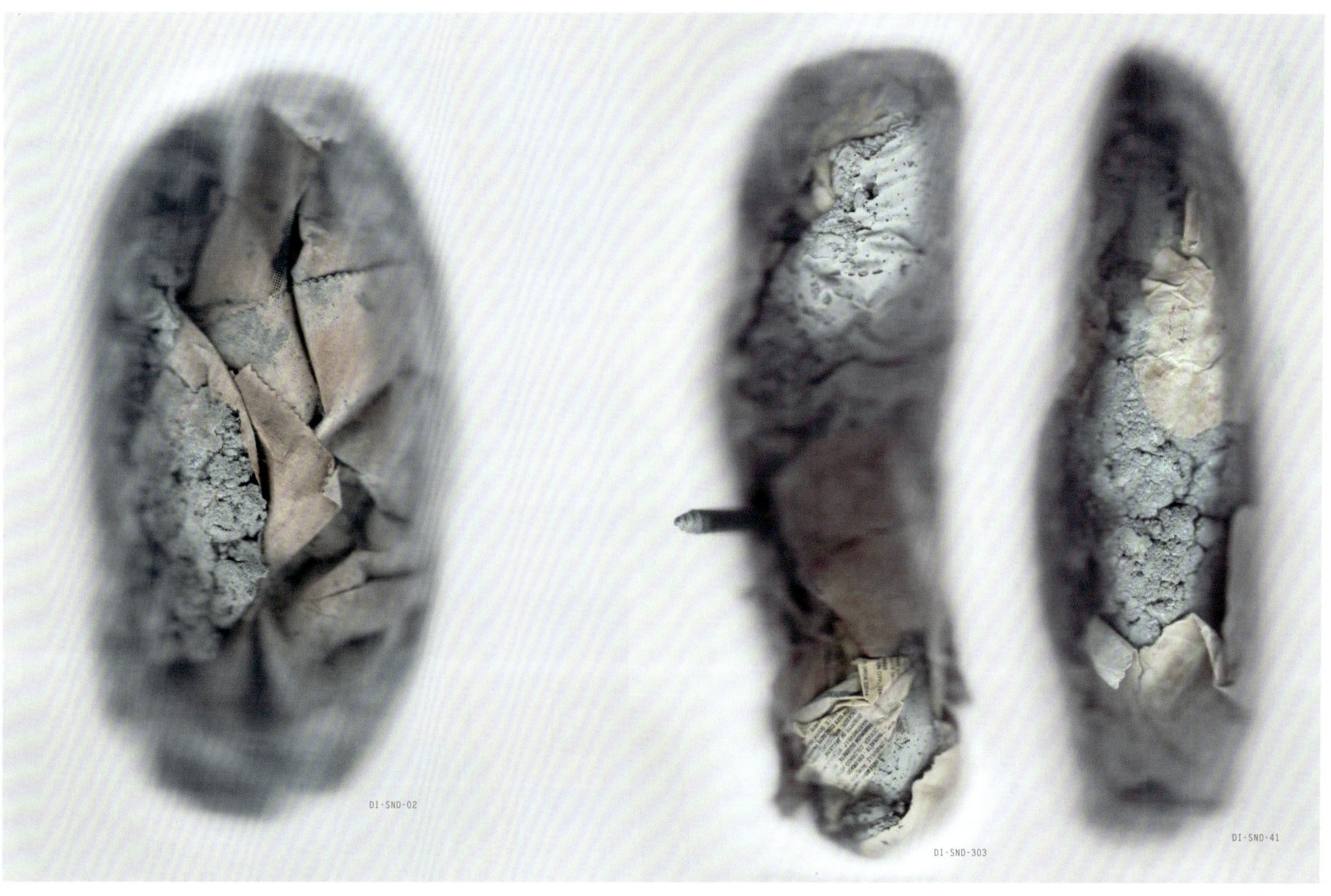

Scans of David Ireland's Concrete "Torpedoes" by Ann Hamilton from *here • there • then • now* (2023) at 500 Capp Street, San Francisco (Courtesy of Ann Hamilton Studio)

PROLOGUES FROM STRANGERS

HENRY MOSS

David Ireland's Headlands project came across my world through large illustrations in an architectural magazine. Wall surfaces broke with corporate sterility. Disconnected toilets without reference to Duchamp. Magazine text erased itself as I read it, but the images stayed. The Headlands was in Marin, and I was stuck in Boston. I considered all of California's coastlines to be imaginary places. Not long afterwards, while my colleagues and I were developing the master plan and first visualizations of MASS MoCA, and I was rehabilitating an 1829 academic building at Phillips Academy in Andover, Massachusetts, the director of the Addison Gallery of American Art introduced us to David Ireland, with whom we would work to convert a derelict attic and 19th-century observatory to an apartment for visiting artists.

Conversion of the attic was a challenging construction task. By contrast, convergence of our imaginations into material decisions and their visual outcomes was almost automatic. David's vision was paramount. Part of my role was to help him avoid doing anything that architects might be expected to do. Instead—shiny steel floors, Masonite finished to look like leather, stair handrails made of 12/8 rebar that extend to resemble elephant ears, a stainless steel toilet developed for prison use, light fixtures assembled from rough electrical hardware. These surfaces and artifacts converged within 170-year-old spatial constraints of the attic's timber framing. David visited the site frequently during construction (red-eye flights from San Francisco) and communicated critical formal decisions directly without drawings. He wanted to expose metal edges at changes of plane where attic ceilings converged, citing white piping on cowboy shirts. Plasterers were too set in their ways to comply. Public health code required a toilet seat. Attic and observatory remained uninsulated. David designed uncomfortable chairs. He designed furniture which he derived from the patterns of prisoners' tattoos, for a California prison's waiting area. The correctional authority sent that furniture to a landfill.

Jock Reynolds was director of the Addison Gallery. He contributed ideas to our design for the apartment and studio for visiting artists. In addition, he organized trips with David to visit Jim Magee's *The Hill*, between El Paso and Marfa, to Walter De Maria's *The Lightning Field*, and to David's house at 500 Capp Street in San Francisco. While the house is a masterpiece of installation art, the integrity of its collection gained depth from his radiant treatments that resurfaced plaster walls along with David's overlay of stories about each object. Concrete juggler spheres. Rhinoceros skull. Semi-conceptual canvas pieces impregnated with smeared concrete. Partially-excavated basement with swinging light bulb and worn chair. Later, it became clear to me that the nontransportable nature of David's signature pieces would reduce the number of people who could experience his work. I visited his incomplete (and now derelict) generator plant interior at the Boott Mill in Lowell, Massachusetts, to witness once again his obsession with hardware—this time on the vast scale of multilevel boilers and steam distribution.

David's anti-sleek grasp of existing materials ties directly to Peter Waldman's Parcel X Encampment and Sofia Kuspan's spolia compositions. It is consistent with brutalist architecture's acceptance of surfaces that alter over time as an emphatic expansion of materiality in late modernism's aesthetic. At 500 Capp Street, a prior owner's collection of worn-out brooms provided spolia for David's sculpture, but that piece is highly contextual. It would read very differently in Hancock Shaker Village, Massachusetts, where flat household brooms were invented, or isolated, in a commercial gallery. The prior owner retains a somewhat ghostly presence through the medium of David's contextual sculpture. Patrick Sardo's posthuman architecture resonates conceptually because of the physical absence of its original creators. I now begin to imagine how AI and robots might engage aesthetically with spolia and canvases smeared with hand-mixed *béton brut*.

Henry Moss

Henry Moss is an architect with a half-century immersion in the shifting worlds of historic structures, and mesmerized by scattered collisions among building design, city sites, contemporary art, and our natural worlds. As an architect at Bruner/Cott for the last 38 years, Henry has changed architectural discourse around transformative reuse and renovation of historic and modernist buildings. He leads Bruner/Cott's historic preservation team, responsible for award-winning projects such as MASS MoCA Phases 1–3, Harvard's Smith Campus Center, and Boston University's School of Law.

Attic of Abbot Hall before transformation, Phillips Academy in Andover, MA

Abbot Hall Artist Apartment at the Addison Gallery, Phillips Academy in Andover, MA, by Henry Moss of Bruner/Cott, David Ireland, and John Sirois (1996) (Courtesy of Jock Reynolds, 2021)

FOREWORDS BY FAMILIAR WITNESSES

KAREN VAN LENGEN

Having a conversation with Peter Waldman is akin to having one's first sip of champagne—the bubbles excite the palate and the mind. And so it goes, a summary of any encounter with Peter includes an infinite number of references and allusions that stimulate a whirlwind of ideas, which become collaged into our everyday experiences. A devotee of Gaston Bachelard, Peter lives in the Poetics of Space. In a conversation with him, one might find oneself in one of Bachelard's reveries or walking into a Grimm fairy-tale forest or seated at the dinner table of Babette's Feast. These delightful musings are part and parcel of knowing Peter Waldman.

If Peter's first book, *Lessons From the Lawn: The Word Made Flesh: Dialogues Between Citizens and Strangers*, focused on his legendary course on the University of Virginia's Academical Village, this book brings us into Peter's inner world to discover the sanctum of his imaginations and musings.

I first met Peter Waldman when I moved to Charlottesville, Virginia, to become the dean of the School of Architecture. He immediately invited me to review the work of his summer studio that had designed a myriad of possibilities to add to our Campbell Hall building. As the new dean, I was charged to complete these renovations and additions, and this one-hour review was a pivotal opening into the possibilities of this new adventure. This was the first act in our Campbell Constructions Project that lasted for the next 10 years. Using our own design faculty to create 11 different projects, we transformed our school into a completely different environment, one that reflects the values and intentions of our mission. Peter's project, the Eric Goodwin Memorial, located on the north courtyard of the school, is first and foremost a celebration of Eric Goodwin's life, cut short just months before he was to graduate from the school. This heartfelt space, designed and built by Peter and his students, is a celebratory piece. Its sloping concrete wall has been arrested in the act of rising up, and yet it still provides enclosure for contemplation, conversation, and creative occupations on its eastern side. Its central cut into the ground locates its place in the earth and commemorates the changing of the seasons as it fills with rainwater or fall leaves. Its western side gives pause to consider the constellation of our celestial enclosure as its oculus aligns with the setting sun. Its design is alive and open-ended, attending to the seasons, the celestial alignments, to Eric's memory that unites the sky with our everyday hopes and dreams.

And then there is the Parcel X Encampment, Peter's home in North Garden, Virginia, with a magical interior space filled with wonder and unexpected discoveries. Here he can retreat from the public realm into his own imagination because he has constructed the space to do so. Many architects strive to create the perfect place, one to be photographed and promoted as such. Peter's home is a reverie of Peter, always changing, always engaging, always filled with discovery. In his cabinet of curiosities, one is reminded of Sir John Soane's home in London or the original Dr. Barnes collection of paintings in his residence in Merion, Pennsylvania, where uncanny and original relationships drive the adjacencies of the pieces on display. Peter's world is made in this way and taking a trip to his home is to enter into an original wonderland of ideas and emotions. During one evening dinner there, it was raining very hard, so Peter showed me the manhole cover located in the middle of his open living loft space. The gushing sound of water passing under the house that evening filled the entire volume and reminded us that even in this safe and nurturing interior, larger forces lurked beyond.

This book, with its presentation of three acts, reminds us of Peter's theatrical underpinnings and his desire to be part of a coterie of inventive people and situations, in live action. From his own directed design projects to his deep appreciation of others' designs and writings, we are brought into the wonderful world of Peter—an extraordinary one that should not be missed. When he draws a section of a small rural barn in a Virginia landscape, he includes its expanded section all the way around the globe and we are reminded of where we are on Earth. It may seem extreme, but it will change our perception of that barn forever. When he recounts one of his New York City childhood memories of riding up a distance of 100 feet in the subway elevator from the platform at the 168th Street station to the street level while clutching his cage of hamsters, we are there. What did he think about in that ride up to the street with his hamster friends? What did the hamsters experience during their trip upwards, what did the other passengers think standing alongside Peter and what did the elevator know as it moved upwards to deliver its passengers from the bowels of this station through the deep bedrock of upper Manhattan to the lights and life of the street? These are the many musings of Peter Waldman and well worth our visit into his world.

Karen Van Lengen, FAIA

Karen Van Lengen, FAIA, is an architect, and the Kenan Professor of Architecture and former dean (1999–2009) of the School of Architecture at the University of Virginia. Her current research focuses on the exploration of sound and communication as an integral part of the architectural design process. With artist Jim Welty, they have created interpretive visual animations of the soundscapes of iconic buildings and landscapes. Their work is included in the permanent collections of several international museums. Van Lengen has authored several books and articles related to themes of sonic spaces and landscapes. Van Lengen began her professional career as an Associate of I. M. Pei & Partners before founding her own award-winning firm in New York City, Karen Van Lengen Architects.

Cover of *Urgent Matters: Designing the School of Architecture at Jefferson's University* (University of Virginia, 2009) by Karen Van Lengen

ERIC GOODWIN

MEMORIAL PASSAGE

ARCHITECT: PETER WALDMAN
COMPLETED: 2004

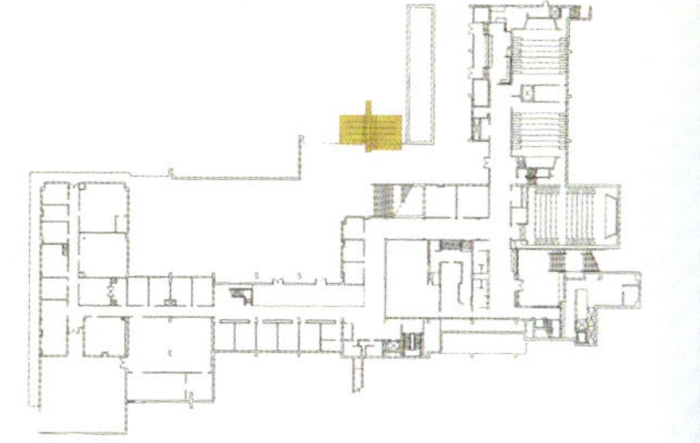

A pair of outdoor classroom spaces designed and built by Professor of Architecture Peter Waldman and his students, led by alumni Sam Beall, Jennifer Finley, and Justin Walton, in collaboration with other faculty members was constructed in August, 2004. "The Eric Goodwin Passage" is located adjacent to the north terrace, aligned on one side with an interior corridor of Campbell Hall and on the other with the tree memorializing Carlo Pelliccia, a much admired professor at the School. Eric Goodwin was a member of the Class of 2002 who passed away during his final year of study at the School of Architecture. Prof. Waldman and his students incorporated two walls with circular openings, on either side of a slim passage. In part, the larger grey wall is positioned short of vertical to recall the tilt-concrete method by which the walls were poured, set, and later raised from the ground. In between the walls, the narrow passage floor is lined with oyster shells to recall Eric Goodwin's love of the beach.

– Peter Waldman

Night Study of west facing elevation, by Justin Walton, BSArch '04

Eric Goodwin Memorial Passage from *Urgent Matters* by Karen Van Lengen

FOREWORDS BY FAMILIAR WITNESSES

ON COLLAGE—WG CLARK

Architecture is often thought of—and its design approached—as if it were an object: a singular, perfect, pure, alone thing.

I believe that is fundamentally wrong.

Architecture is about the intersection of many things and is better thought of as an armature of their connection.

Architecture joins a place on this Earth with use, people, times, ideas, materials.

It connects, frankly, the spiritual and the material.

It is the art of connection.

Even more interesting to me, it is the intersection of opposites. Opposites conspiring to be one. *It's a collage.*

One of our best teachers, Peter Waldman, always introduces his design projects, to my jealousy, as collages. He starts projects by saying, put all your thoughts, ideas, places, considerations, references, and allusions, put them together and let's see them.

It is the proper way I've decided to begin because, to a lot of people, this looks like an extra exercise. It looks like fun, but *what does that have to do with the program? What does that have to do with the place? What's the point?* The point is *everything*, because when you are designing a building, you are not just packaging a program—heaven help us—you are connecting use to the Earth. All your thoughts and all your associations that run through your mind when you're thinking you're pulling them all together, corralling them and seeing how they influence one another and how wonderful they are together. It's wild and it's just stuff all over the place, and it is weird and wonderful. I'm not so sure any other people do what we do. It is not just problem solving, as Le Corbusier said:

". . . Art enters in."

Furthermore, it is not just naming all the things that one might consider in words, it is the transformation of those ideas and words into images. Shifting from a thought or an idea to a piece of paper, to something that can be realized through a graphic image, is a big deal. It occurs to me that your mind forms thoughts that are related to each other like a shish kebab, as axes of alliance of things that relate to each other. It further strikes me that when two of those lines of ideas related to different subjects cross like an intersection, there's a collision or collusion. And all of a sudden that is called an idea, when two thoughts collide. Design is making those lines of thoughts into *a diagram of a building*.

So, the theme of this lecture and the theme of next semester is that architecture is never one, it's **two.** Two or more, it is multiples conspiring to make something. I think that's the real way to think of design. Not having a single idea, whittling it, polishing it, carving it, and making it perfect. *That's not the point; the point is that it's a joint, not a thing.*

I'll show you an example. Carlo Scarpa built an entrance to the College of Architecture in Venice, and I show it to you because it's hardly a building. It's just the beginning of a building, just the conception, if you will.

IUAV Main Gate in Venice, Italy, by Carlo Scarpa (1966–1972/1985)

It's a collage, isn't it?

It begins as a juncture of two axes, x and y, one being the streets of Venice and one being the path into this institution. It's a pause, a moment of *do I want to come in here? Do I want to turn left and go in this thing?* I'm not sure–it is a critical decision.

And then I look at it some more: this thin building is not just the connection of a path and a street, it's the connection of oppositions. It is both a gate, meaning a barrier: *keep out*. It is also an invitation: *come in*. Two ideas collide in this building, *go away* and *come in*, depending on whether that

Alternate Book Cover as suggested by W.G. Clark, with the 2021 collage by Ben Small drawn out and "etched" into David Turnbull's photo of *Three Transformations or Totem to Tomb* (1988) by Peter Waldman, Christopher Genik, and Edward Wilson in Parcel X.

glass door slides. It's a combination of the kinetic and the static. The door moves, it slides on those wonderful wheels and closes dramatically to say *you can look in, but you can't come in*. It's both a shelter if it's raining, and a threat. It looks very tentative and scary—Mr Scarpa is suggesting something might fall on you, but it's also keeping the rain off you while you pause. It is also the portal itself, turned into concrete and lifted to become a roof, a wall becoming a roof. It's all these things, all these joinings, to say nothing of the old and the new.

In that piece of white stone that is carved and brought there is a fragment of antiquity. And the new is the concrete formed to specific duty at that location. It's metal, it's glass, it's concrete. It is modern technology with ancient technology and ancient inscription in stone while you realize you're looking at a very modern thing. For people entering the gate, it's the beginning of new ideas, and a new profession. It's quite something. Inscribed on that piece of white stone is *Verum esse ipsum factum*. The truth is itself made, from Giambattista Vico. Scarpa uses it to say that architecture or making proves the truth. But herein, we don't mess around with falseness, we are looking for truth and we're looking to build truth. What an admonition to an entry to a school: *truth and making*. The bottom line is that architecture is a joint of use and place. It's not a thing and it's not a program. It's the juncture of a program and site. When you design, begin by taking an idea, an inspiration, from both. Architecture, after all, is a conspiracy between a room and a place.

WG Clark

WG Clark was born in Louisa, VA, and studied architecture at the University of Virginia. After working for Venturi Rauch in Philadelphia, he began an architectural practice in Charleston, SC, in 1974. In 1989 he was appointed chairman of architecture at the University of Virginia and named Edmund Schureman Campbell Professor. He has earned three AIA National Design awards for the Middleton Inn, the Reid House, and the Croffead House, and was a recipient of the Brunner Prize by the American Academy in Rome.

This foreword is an edited transcription of a lecture given by WG Clark to second-year architecture students at the University of Virginia in 2024 for Peter Waldman's introductory course, Lessons of the Lawn.

EXCAVATING PROJECT ORIGINS

I remember being on Thesis Reviews at the University of Cambridge in 1983 when I commented early on a student's project, and immediately Dalibor Vesely responded emphatically, "Well Peter, that is certainly amusing."

Offended, I responded, "But Dalibor I am deadly serious and not trying to be missing the point and nor trying to be offhanded."

He responded, "But dear Peter, it seems you do not understand the power of the verb to muse, and thanks to you, you have now made me rethink the entire heretofore familiar debate Peter Carl and Alvin Boyarsky and I have had for years."

This short dialogue now recalled from four decades ago made me appreciate the intensity of acting as a stranger, seeing things in a new light, if not the role of the Lunatic in the Post-Enlightenment Age.

This evolving project, didactically termed in elemental incipient terms A Five Finger Exercise, commenced on our recent summer solstice 2023 and began with a photo-shoot exercise on the role of light in Parcel X, our dwelling since 1994 in rural North Garden, Virginia. Two recent Master of Architecture graduates, Sofia Kuspan and Patrick Sardo, teamed up initially to collaborate with me on another first-person singular project juxtaposing two projects two decades apart: *Parcel X Encampment* (1994) and the *Eric Goodwin Memorial Pavilion* (2004) at the University of Virginia. When they shared their photos, I was "amused" by how they "read" my house and asked them to show me their recent thesis presentations, to see from where they were coming.

Sofia's was on the role of spolia, an adaptive reuse of a former abandoned Packard Factory in Detroit; and Patrick's thesis was on the immensity of current and future non-specific construction sites of data centers, server storage, fulfillment centers, and vast agricultural plantations without the need for the sun and human interaction, all entitled *Posthuman Architectures*.

As a result of that initial interaction, I found their points of view opened scales of thought, reconsiderations, or pentimenti so distinct from my two small construction sites already two decades old, if not familiar.

The project now evolved from singular to Collective; a collaboration, if not a chorus of singular voices, charged with documenting my work through their theses, photos, and collages, following a previous exploratory project with another graduate student, Ben Small, in the Era of the Cicada of 2021,[9] and a blog of texts of David Turnbull, another conceptual soulmate of mine for four decades, as well. Thus, we settled on Pirandello's postwar *Six Characters in Search of an Author*, the sixth being David Ireland.

DIDACTIC INTENTIONS

There are a number of ways to read this journal, which deciphers, through dialogues, the construction of ideas. Ambiguity is appreciated as multiple meanings and not understood as confusion. The scripts of this journal are fleshed out through the step-by-step layers of the didactic collage plates.

This project is framed by the coordinates of Julio Cortázar's *Hopscotch* (1963) and the meanders of Rebecca Solnit's *A Field Guide to Getting Lost* (2005).

This book is structured around the beginning and the end, with in-between adolescent conditions, sequencing scripted dialogues of surveyors, nomads, and lunatics in response to the spatial stage sets of collage plates where fallow grounds are inseminated to generate spatial tales of resilience.[10]

This book acts as a postscript to *Lessons From the Lawn* and *Connective Tissues*, borrowing the structure of Pirandello's *Six Characters in Search of an Author* as inspiration for how each of the six individuals think and see things in the world.

THE CHARACTERS OF THE PLAY IN THE MAKING

Peter Waldman the William R. Kenan Professor of Architecture at the University of Virginia narrates Spatial Tales of Origin through Specifications for Construction. Educated at Princeton, and then a Peace Corps Architect in Arequipa, Peru, he became infected by the poetics and pragmatics of the construction site. For more than 50 years he has taught and practiced, first at Princeton, then Rice in Texas, and he finally commenced his Piedmont Condition in 1992 in the Oasis of North Garden where he has grasped connective tissues first found in Mica Mines in Manhattan. He is a Fellow of the American Academy in Rome and author of *Lessons From the Lawn* and *Connective Tissues: Essays by Ten Kenan Fellows 2001–2016*, both previously published by ORO Editions. Peter Waldman is a character who clearly cannot act, sing, or dance, but his love of theater commenced in his adolescence at Grey Gables Theatrical Workshop intentionally out of sight, backstage constructing scrims and flats and masks while exploring the magic of pre-digital light boards.

Ben Small was a surrogate Kenan Fellow as a M.Arch graduate student and then teaching colleague at the University of Virginia in recent years. He collaborated with me on a residential project at the shore of Lake Anna on "a self-reflective architecture of almost not there," as another simpatico student of mine Scott Bernhard would muse. It involved precise calculations in plan of cut and fill operations on the steeply sloping lakeside site in a sequence of *bas-relief* models with a reflexive kaleidoscope of diaphanous veils yielding aqueous landscapes in the vertical plane.

Sofia Kuspan grew up in Frank Lloyd Wright apprentice-designed houses and came to the Master of Architecture graduate program at the University of Virginia from an undergraduate degree BSArch program from Ohio State University. Her master's thesis was on the subject of *Spolia* evidenced in the transformation of a Packard Assembly Plant in Detroit, Michigan. She was selected to be a Kenan Fellow discussion leader for Waldman's foundation course, Letters of the Lawn, in her first year and then served in her final year as his research assistant on evolving InDesign syllabi for Lessons as well as Waldman's Undergraduate Transfer Studio. It was during that latter collaboration that Sofia photographed Parcel X with her classmate Patrick Sardo, which foray consequently sustained in 2023 this collaborative project. She is now working with Schwartz/Silver in Boston.

Patrick Sardo came to the Master of Architecture graduate program at the University of Virginia from the undergraduate BSArch degree program at Ohio State University. Patrick's thesis was focused on *A Posthuman Architecture* (of data centers, fulfillment centers, power plants, etc.). When Patrick joined Sofia to photograph Parcel X on the summer solstice in 2023, I realized their insights were "amusing" to me and I asked them to join this once familiar first-person project to become a collaborative dialogue provoked by another exceptional graduate student Ben Small two years previously. Patrick is now working with Henry Moss at Bruner/Cott in Boston.

David Ireland (1930–2009) was a nationally significant Bay Area conceptual artist and collaborative architect. His House as Museum at the 500 Capp Street Foundation still serves this spatial script as a catalyst to bring the Forewords by long-term collaborators Ann Hamilton and Henry Moss to contextualize the parallel sensibilities of the original Cast of Characters improvisationally assembled around two construction sites as oases in Virginia's Piedmont. David Ireland came late to the attention of the Stage Manager and remains as a haunting figure, a deus ex machina of sorts.

David Turnbull an educator and architect, and I met when he served as an early collaborator with James Stirling who designed, in 1981, the additions to Anderson Hall, the School of Architecture at Rice University. He has been a witness to my teaching and practice through his blogs on the Internet for more than four decades and has collaborated with me on thesis reviews at the University of Virginia for three decades now. David was very much a part of my evolution on *Lessons From the Lawn* and *Connective Tissues* as we would meet over the past 10 years in the Mudhouse Café in Crozet, VA, on intermittent early mornings. He advised me to write A Note to the Readers and to structure my stream of consciousness tendencies with a chronological frame, commencing with my collages at the American Academy in Rome and ending with an essay on the 8/11 White Nationalist Invasion in Charlottesville revealing Landscapes of Aggression. When I commenced with this project with Sofia and Patrick and their photo revisions, I realized Ben Small had helped me see these projects anew two years earlier and that David Turnbull had been helping me see my work over many, many decades of blogs when I gifted him my archive of the Hurricane House drawings developed with yet another then student collaborator Christopher Genik.

THE SAME TALE TOLD TWICE

I find myself again and again pausing in the Goodwin Passage specifically as Surveyor, Nomad, and Lunatic,[1] not disengaged as nowhere but now here in Virginia. I find myself in my mind simultaneously in two recurrent New World Oases: New York City and Arequipa, Peru.

The first oasis was revealed to me as a child growing up on the East Coast of North America as well as on the West Side of Manhattan in an introverted cavernous maze of digitally accountable 10 huge double-hung windows facing North of merely reflected light by day, but reliably anchored to the North Star by night. However, a singular dining room window facing south to a courtyard became the daily frictional hierophany of visceral light, as I would force dust up into the air by stomping on the carpeted floor. I could play in light for one brief moment by my own instrumental actions and the sun's predictability. But the sun moved all too swiftly to this disoriented child, and I would need to wait until another sunny day to reconfirm this magical moment, again.

The same psyche recalls the second oasis encountered during my Peace Corps service in Peru where sensibilities were to be reborn in shade, revealing rather the power of moving shadows and resultant coolness, indeed in the darkness revealed in an altiplano Andean settlement, Arequipa, at the Ceja de la Sierra (eyebrow of the mountains) at the western edge of the Pacific.

The same magical windows were to be intentionally flooded with sunrise and sunset decades later (1994) in yet another collaboration at the scale of dwelling, Parcel X, obsessed now with numbers in the night, a preoccupation with envisioning the world anew with my eyes almost closed.

Now a decade later (2004) and a stone's throw from my current place of work, I return again and again to the same haunted oases in this modest memorial passage from south to north, disciplined daily by the accountable rising and setting of the sun.

I have come full circle now from the child who hit the ground to see the sun so long ago in suspended space in New York City to now a site not quite out of mind, indeed two meters away from where I have mused for the last 32 years. Times Square is the vision of a public domain revealed on an annual basis with a ritual at the scale of citizens; Parcel X is another public domain revealed for Nomads who encounter a lost paradise in North Garden through the routines of daily life; and the Goodwin Passage is the secret oasis of the next generation, another collaboration yet with young fresh-faced students, lunatics all perhaps as we stride to polish *Mirrors for the Moon*.[2]

Here and Now another site looms close at hand for me teaching at Mr. Jefferson's university in the shadow of the Academical Village. The projects presented herein are also imprinted by the *Lessons of the Lawn* as an ethical strategy for the collaboration of distinct generations of *citizens and strangers*[3] alike to envision common ground.

ACT ONE:

INTROSPECTIVE IMPROVISATIONS FOR TWO CONSTRUCTION SITES

IN THE BEGINNING

This kaleidoscopic project, both an Atlas and an Almanac, commenced with a recounting of Spatial Tales of Origins[4] of two ongoing construction sites by Peter Waldman, architect, conceived a decade apart 1994–2004.

It commenced with a singular authoritative voice and became a magical unfolding scripting of at least *Six Characters* (and counting) *in Search of an Author*, inspired by Pirandello.

The intention of this revision is to reveal and to share regenerative lessons as an epilogue to two previous publications by ORO Editions: *Lessons From the Lawn* (by a self-appointed guide) and *Connective Tissues*. Both construction sites are singular and collaborative and share a memetic device of a kaleidoscope, which is both telescopic and microscopic in scale and some say magical. The pedagogic consequence is the enduring utility of Recurrent Dualities, and in their synthetic temporal conjunction, the value of spatial connective tissues.

Commenced in 1994, Parcel X in North Garden, VA is the familial encampment of this late-20th-Century Nomad with roots somewhere between Manhattan and the Piedmont Condition, Princeton and Peru.

In 2004, Waldman led a fourth-year design-build studio for a collaborative memorial to a classmate who passed away in his last semester, resulting in the Eric Goodwin Pavilion in the foreground of the School of Architecture at the University of Virginia. These initial two projects, however, are no longer being reconsidered as a self-indulgent first-person singular set of insights, rather they have become instruments to recount *Mirrors for the Moon*.

Now in the COVID years, 2021–2024, marking two decades since the Goodwin construction, Peter was provoked again and again to review these two projects from the recent photographic insights first of a vital, catalytic sequence of short-term student assistants, Ben Small in 2021 and then Sofia Kuspan and Patrick Sardo in 2023, forcing the self-evident inclusion of the insights of David Turnbull, a multi-decades long blogger of Waldman's work, and was then finally haunted by an introduction to David Ireland's 500 Capp Street House as Museum in San Francisco midsummer 2023.

In 1943, Peter Waldman commenced his architectural practice of self-help in the Mica Mines of Manhattan, then in 1953 constructed Peter's Pitiful Pine Pond at the edge of the Kitchawan Preserve, in New York.

In 1967–1969, Waldman served as a US Peace Corps volunteer architect in the Altiplano City of Arequipa, Peru, on *ayuda mutua* civic projects across scales, and in 1969 initiated a four-year apprenticeship with Michael Graves' one-man office in Princeton.

Finally, in 1974, he commenced his own practice, first licensed in New Jersey and in 1984 then in Texas with coincident NCARB national accreditation, working on climatic dwellings and urban competitions, until 1992 when he joined the University of Virginia faculty where he focused on these two pivotal construction projects and on coming to terms with his parallel sensibilities with the larger-than-life elephant in the room.

Michael Graves and Peter Eisenman conducting a studio critique at Princeton in 1970, Peter Waldman seated to the far right. (Courtesy of Princeton School of Architecture)

Contemporary Art Museum, Peter Waldman, Houston, TX (1981)

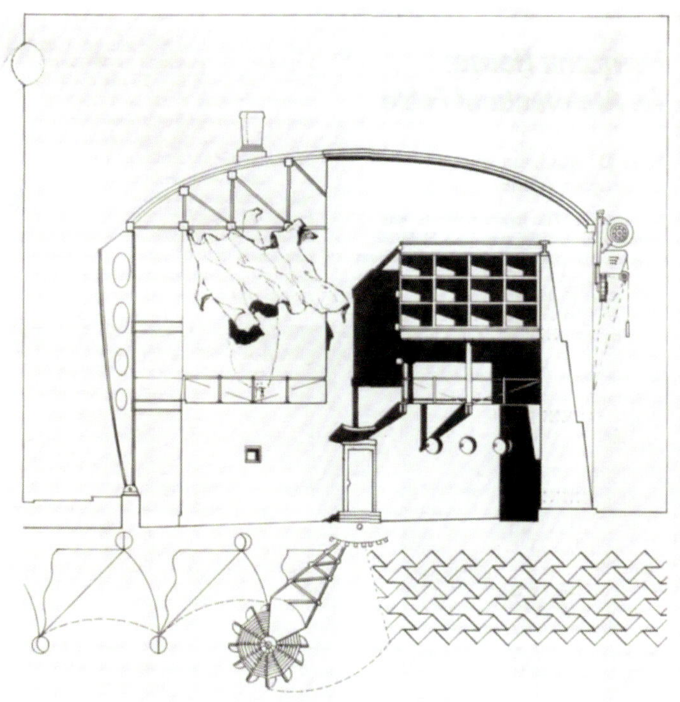

Hurricane House, Peter Waldman and Christopher Genik (1985)

A portion of the Southern Gallery Wall of Parcel X (2023)

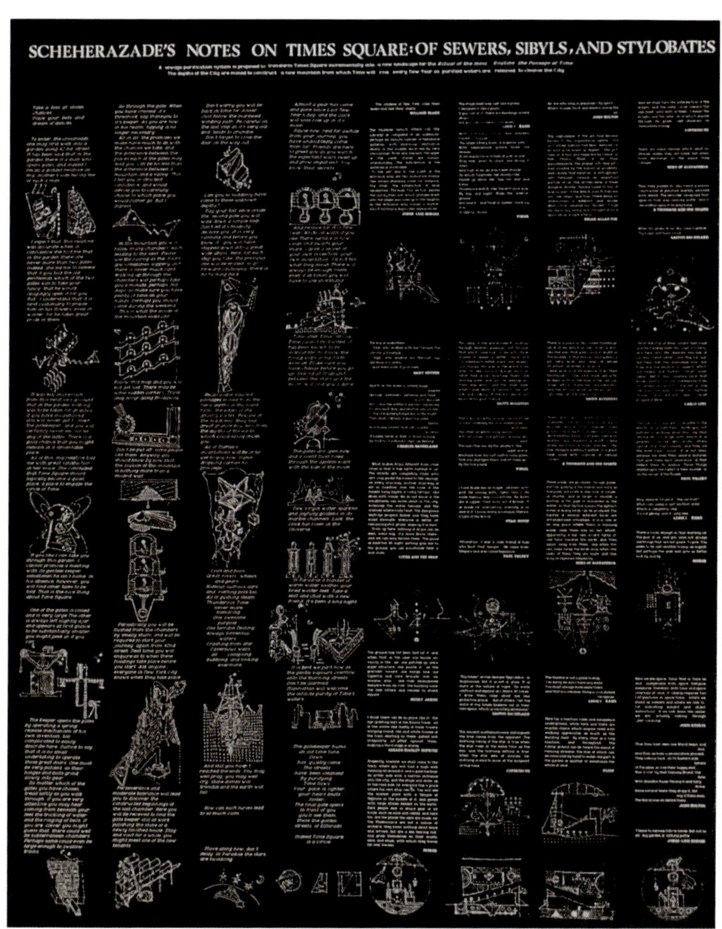

Times Square Competition, Peter Waldman and Christopher Genik (1983)

Plate XXII from *Lessons From the Lawn* (2019)

HERE AND NOW (1994–2021)

Simultaneously, in the summer of the last Cicada Emergence 2021, I was asked to document an inventory of my 100'+ Gallery Salon Wall for the Spatial Tales of Origin they might narrate as my nomadic narrative. I asked Ben Small to photograph these interior landscapes with their glass shields or lenses set within thin gilt frames.

He chose to make a connective set of literal tissues between the Lake Anna *bas-relief* and the glass sheets that simultaneously reflected the predominant glass block grid to the hillside northern facade.

I had asked for an inventory of content, and Ben Small offered me a looking glass into a more expansive perspective, within and without, of these two projects a decade apart. Ben Small in large part helped me see both projects as one guardian or shepherd of a flock of spatial postures.

Mirroring each other that summer, we decided to see the same framing by layering a collage of an Eric Goodwin Memorial photo by colleague Kirk Martini with a linework etching of a Cicada's anatomical structure all superimposed on a section of Bramante's Tempietto (1502).

I need to repeat, Ben Small in large part helped me see both projects as one, as we mirrored in syncopation a flock of spatial scripts and a template for stage sets between memory and amnesia. I am indebted to this brief summer of insights into our sustained dialogue, which initiated this evolving collaborative project.

To make clear this evolving intent, I asked Ben Small, a former M.Arch student and then new faculty colleague, to start photographing the framed content of artwork on the Summer Solstice of June 21st, 2021. From his insights I then determined to open up my understanding of not only Parcel X but now the Eric Goodwin Memorial as a dialogue of *Connective Tissues*, call and response to be repeated with the 2023 solstice photographic insights of Sofia Kuspan and Patrick Sardo, to be echoed I then realized in their recent theses and as I now realize haunted as well by David Turnbull over previous decades. I find I must step out, all too often perhaps, as the nameless narrator to make clear the nature of a third-person observer on an ever-expanding collaboration that is inherent in my pedagogy and practice, and I suggest the Architect resonates in the character roles of Surveyor, Nomad, and Lunatic.

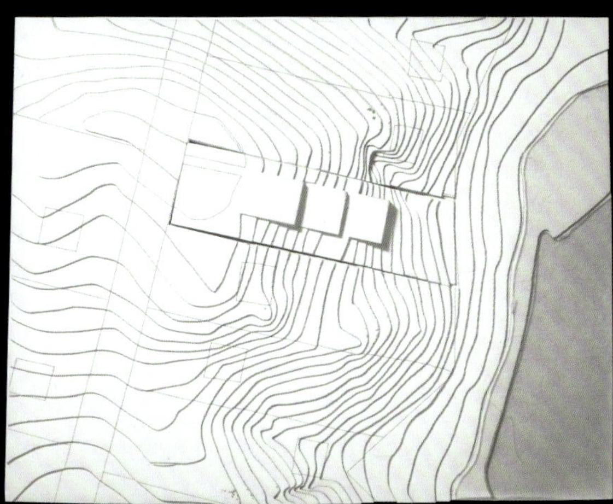

Lake Anna House *bas-relief* model (2021)

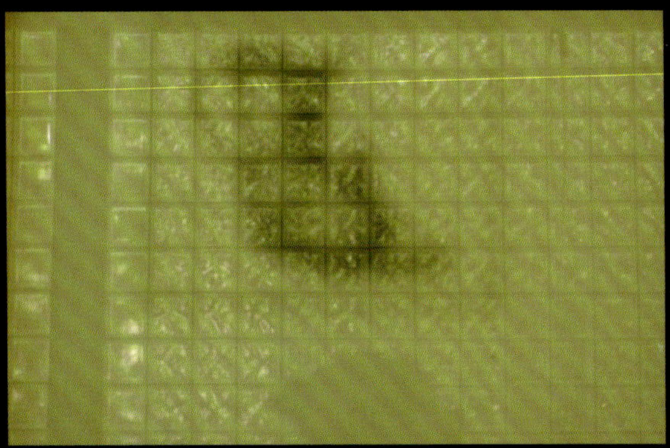

Glass Block reflections of a gilded frame print in Parcel X

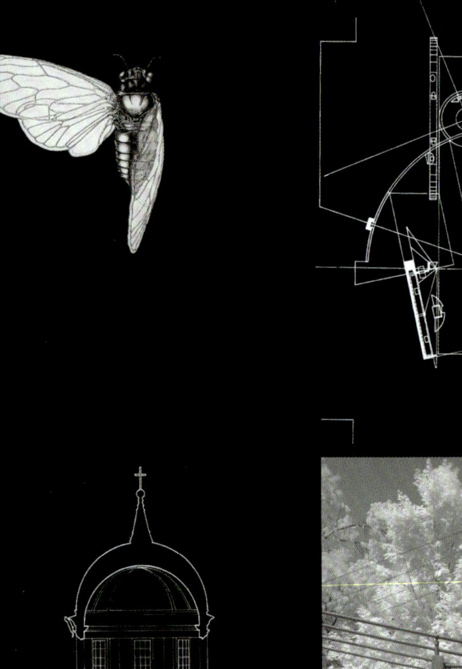

Elements of Ben Small's catalytic 2021 collage

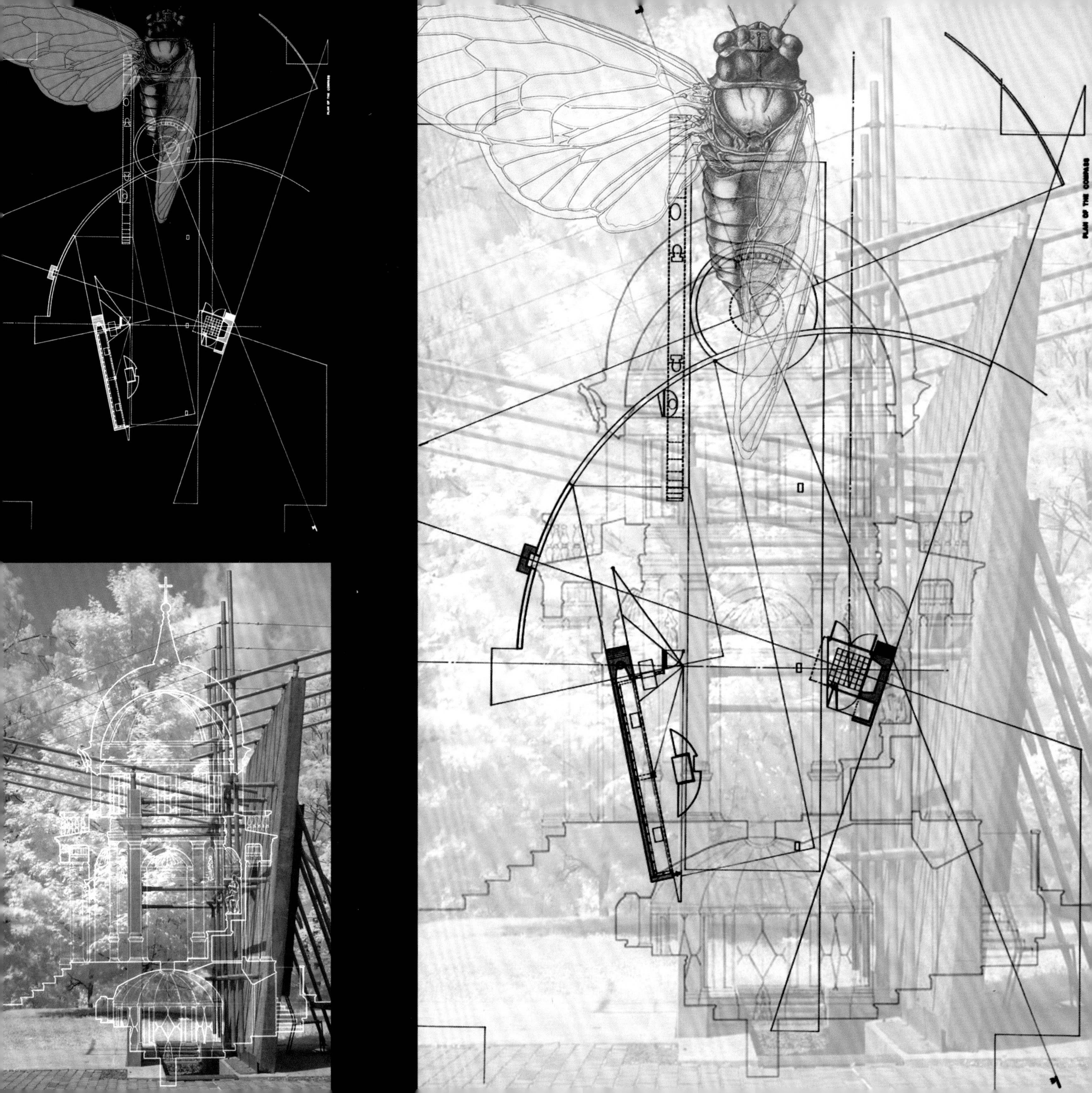
PLAN OF THE COMPASS
PLAN OF THE COMPASS

CHOREOGRAPHED SEQUENCING: THE CAST OF CHARACTERS IN SEARCH OF A SPATIAL SCRIPT

Ann Hamilton and **Henry Moss** first offer prologues to the script through conversations with the Edenic Catalytic characters.

Karen Van Lengen and **WG Clark** offer forewords as Familiar Witnesses to the two construction sites.

The Curtain opens on the First Stage Set of Two Superimposed Scrims set a decade apart. The Sun and the Moon are in cahoots to choreograph a Long Day's Journey into Night where Parcel X and the Goodwin Memorial with Secret Lives of their Own await Scrutiny by Strangers.

The First Character, a Pilgrim of Sorts, appears holding Specifications for Construction and a Shard of Mica, seeking answers from an Oracle. This ancient **Narrator**, He who has no name, is a mere storyteller of *Spatial Tales of Origin*.

Ben Small is then called upon initially and briefly between the scrims, short-term as the instrumental lens of a photographic hunter and gatherer, as agent of change emerging with the coincidental Cicada cycles and recalling/fusing through collage the magic of Bramante's Tempietto section in the Goodwin Memorial fused to Parcel X.

Sofia Kuspan and **Patrick Sardo** enter next and cultivate the potential of this sustained improvisational dialogue. They serve as Edenic Catalysts, who now enter briskly from stage left and stage right and linger as pillars that never leave the stage. They provide additional insightful readings framed by their photography and then enduring scaffolding, contextualizing Spolia and the immutable *systems within* of an enigmatic Posthuman Architecture.

David Turnbull has been waiting in the wings for decades now and is, then, a long-term familiar witness of recurrent dualities promised by agricultural cycles. David Turnbull hovers behind the scenes, and around the world, patiently witnessing from a balcony (higher ground) the evolution of this authorless Script and Collages of improvisational forays amidst *Mirrors for the Moon*.

The sixth character emerged offstage first in July 2023 when Beth Davila Waldman introduced the ancient pilgrim to 500 Capp Street, San Francisco, The House as Museum of David Ireland.

David Ireland is the Serpent who embodies haunted Archaic knowledge as we relate to Carl Sagan's *The Dragons of Eden*.[5]

Raphael, *The School of Athens* (1509–1511)

FIRST IMPRESSIONS OF THE PRECONDITIONS OF THE SITES FOR A NOMADIC ENCAMPMENT AND A STUDENT MEMORIAL

If Parcel X is a temporal shelter for Nomads of the late 20th-Century, tentatively breaking the ground as Semper demands,[6] and glacial rock outcroppings and massive, ancient First-Growth Tulip Poplars testify and trace the haunted indigenous pre-Anthropocene campsites of flora and fauna proceeding The First People, then the site is not just pristine as an idyllic Wilderness of massive First-Growth trees and glacial outcroppings, but is read now as full of the frictions, blisters, and scars of ecological and cultural landscapes.

As previous cultures used this site for annual hunting grounds, what might be termed primordial Landscapes of Aggression,[7] so this project is akin to both the found ruin and defacement in Detroit and this project's reanimation with Court and Gardens, of Pentimenti to mark and erase, but not too well, of the persistence of Jefferson's Cartesian grid confronting the animate aggregations of figural graffiti.

The wild fig seed will destroy the Marbles of Marcellus resonates here.[8]

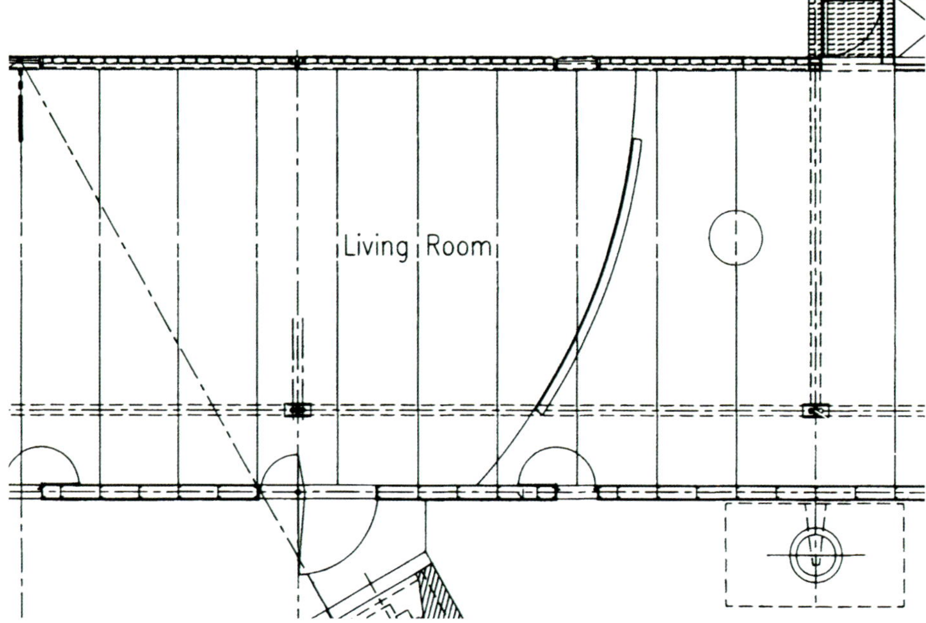

Parcel X Main Floor Plan Detail (1994)

North Garden, VA (2023)

But Parcel X, I realize now, is also the direct result of the *Tyranny of Reason* resonant in Patrick's nonhuman architecture of rigorous Specifications for Construction, with an inventory of material and dimensional accountability determined by 4' × 8' plywood formwork/shuttering, to be reused on the interior as Cabinets commenced in the *Hurricane House* as Packing Crates.

The steel frame follows as a correspondent syntax of structure corresponding to Calvino's demand now for Lightness and Exactitude[9] at the 4' × 20' module of the heavy embedded Concrete Retaining Walls and echoed in the 20' bar joists on a 4' module, the meter of which is inscribed into the concrete floor slabs.

All electrical and plumbing systems are exposed on a correspondent but diminished scale of the 8" span of a hand as persistent wire frames throughout the space, with fittings and modules following the codes and craft covenants exactly. There were no cut-offs, no waste to be hauled from the site.

The issue of nonhuman architecture as predetermined by off-the-shelf products, systems within systems of the industrial, and engineering evidenced-based design as BIM was an economic decision by *inventories in cahoots with ethics*.

Parcel X framing, piping, and spotlights (2023)

The only figural exceptions were the curved kitchen wall, which followed the path of the sun, and two slits, the first on the lower-level kitchen wall to the SW, which marks sunset on the Winter solstice, which proceeds diagonally through the slit in the NE elevated retaining wall on the upper level, which marks the emergence of the sunrise on the summer solstice. A massive primal hearth rises from this curved wall and pivots to high noon on the summer solstice and serves as an anchor approximating Stonehenge in this North Garden oasis.

The only exceptions to the *Tyranny of Reason*, or systems within inclusive systems, are the Archaic practices of early human tendencies to pay attention to the preconditions of human curiosity, that is the power of forces beyond human control, that is the Sun, the self-reflective Moon apparent to so-called Lunatics and correspondent Celestial soffits that mark, stain, and scar the human imagination found in Sanford Kwinter's provocation: *What is more Modern than the Archaic?*[10] and/or Hildner's Cabalist secret posture of *Architecture is a Game of Chess.*[11]

Parcel X Solstice Markers (2023)

Parcel X Hearth Chimneys (2023)

CRITICAL PATH METHOD

Pirandello's *Six Characters in Search of an Author*, written in 1921, was assigned in 1961.

Kingsley Erwin, my mentor at Horace Mann, gifted this text as a Field Guide on my way to Princeton, his former alma mater.

Spatial Tales of Origin have been crafted for some time now by me through *Specifications for Construction*.

Eugene O'Neill's *Long Day's Journey into Night*[12] was the first text assigned at Princeton.

1961 was a pivotal year for me moving from Manhattan to this Oasis of the Garden State.

Genesis and *Exodus* frame the *Five Books of Moses*, the Beginning & the End in Six Days.

Genesis specifies the generative chaos yielding an Oasis for the Characters: Adam & Eve, a Serpent, Cain & Abel, and an unspecified narrator, *he who has no name*.

Parcel X is a timeline without end from sunrise to sunset, framed by a Nomadic Teepee.

The Goodwin Memorial is charged, as was Stonehenge, with Approximating the North Star.

Parcel X & the Goodwin Memorial are Two Stage Sets framing the decade: 1994–2004.

One Stage Set midway down a hillside facing South on Sutherland Road, North Garden, Virginia.

Another Stage Set at the top of a crest facing North on the edge of Carr's Hill Fine Arts Precinct.

Nomads approach Parcel X turning West off an ancient Ridgeline of The Seminole Trail.

Lunatics approach the Goodwin Memorial from the thickened edge of the North Terrace.

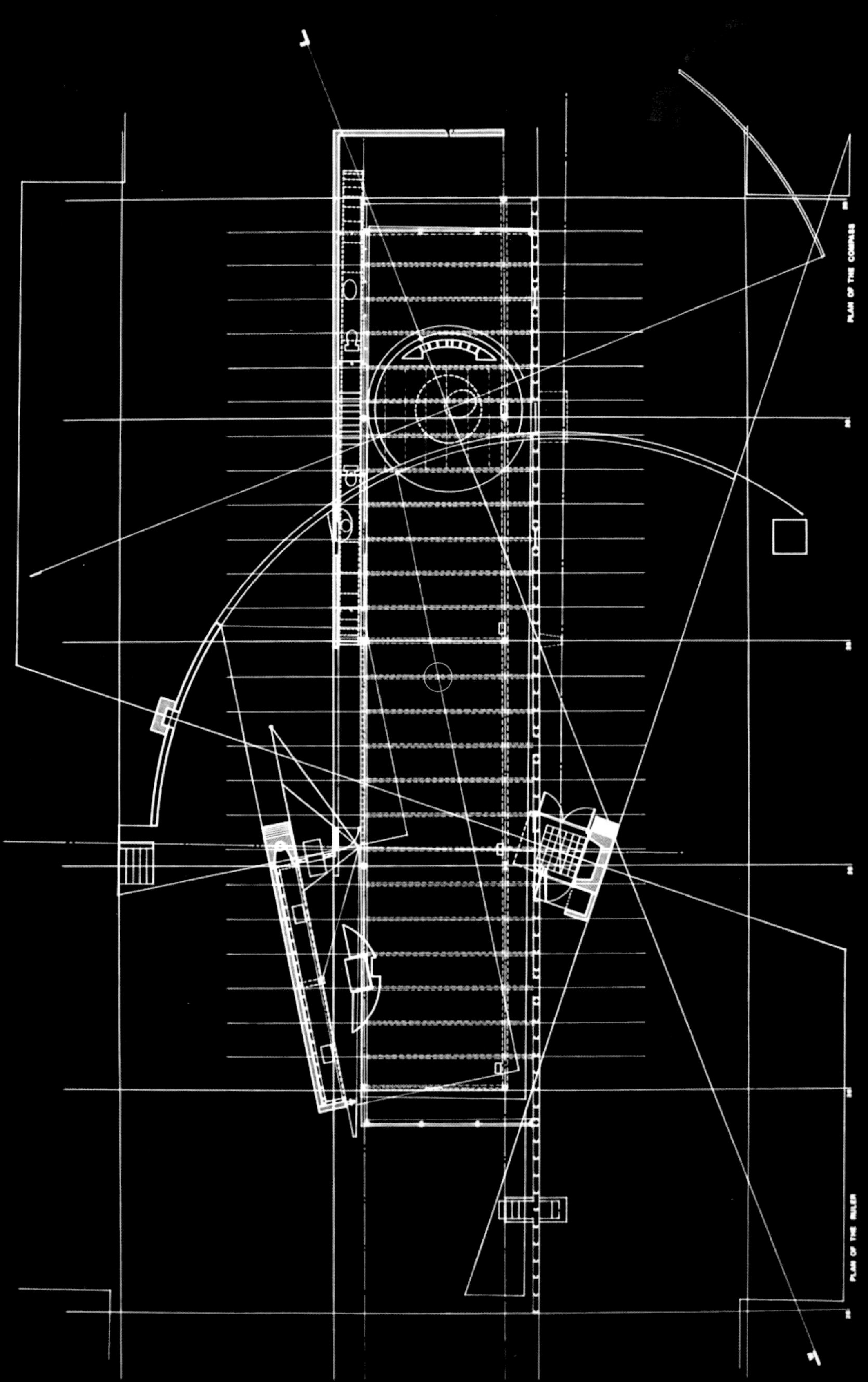

Parcel X Composite Plan (1994)

PARCEL X (1994)
PETER WALDMAN
NORTH GARDEN, VA

When I committed to join the faculty of the School of Architecture at UVA in 1990, I stated I needed two years to finish up my academic and professional commitments at Rice. One of the intentions in coming to Virginia was to commence an unfinished construction site as dwelling with the preconditions of a wild frictional nature so unlike the synthetic toxic cultural landscapes of Texas. Thus, with an ongoing thriving practice and several former graduate students now in my office in Houston as collaborators, we embarked on alternative schemes for alternative sites. Philippe Baumann, whose Strasbourg-derived origin translates as *building man*, was my primary collaborator on this self-generated project, which was an essential motive to leave Houston and my wealthy client-indulgent practice for this Piedmont Condition, seeking an architecture of almost nothing.[13]

For a year, we prepared a bidding documents set for a barn-like structure for upscale Free Union township to the east of Charlottesville with a Cook House and Garden appendage tenuously attached as a 270-degree observatory tumbling down the hill. The bids came in high, given the expectations of the conservative developer of this highly desirable tract, and I got cold feet.

Soon thereafter I found the Parcel X site, on the tax map in a most rural southwest part of Albemarle at the crossroads of Albemarle County, as the last almost unbuildable remnant of a century's old subdivision of an 18th-century tract. Philippe and I visited it on December 19th, 1990, and we developed a three-level observatory cranked to the orientation of an adjacent cherry orchard across from a *hullah*[14] and the rising sun. Engaged with the ascending hill, a huge hearth shelters a grotto for a descending stair cranked on the north, to be built from construction debris serving as a Temple to the Vestal Virgins. Adjacent to the buttressing hearth, a long 24'-high concrete retaining wall descends as a shadow maker to the west. Bracketed along this wall, an equally long, slender catwalk marks the setting of the sun through repeatedly framed views of Long Arm Mountain to the west, emerging from a bedroom retreat as mezzanine overlooking a double-height Collective Hall below. This hall contains only one collective table, set within one huge prerequisite bay window to the southeast. The Kitchen is located within the Grotto/Bowels of the earth, some call Family Room, excavated to the north, and monumental stair and hearth but on grade level to the south where the house is entered modestly to the west and more monumentally past an outrigger washhouse/baptismal font to the southeast, which becomes an observatory terrace off the major collective *piano nobile* above. We developed this in my Houston Studio for the next 18 months and I arrived to teach in Summer of 1992 with a full bid set in hand. Shortly thereafter, I received a totally acceptable bid to build this pretentious tower observatory, a chess piece of strangely Knight or Bishop-like figural pretentions.

I was teaching a summer studio for incoming graduate students and my teaching assistant, a landscape architect, asked to see the site out in rural North Garden. It was a midsummer day and the heavily wooded and generously leafy canopies speckled the steep site as glacial rocky ridges cleaved the site, giving us coordinates to stabilize our climb to the top ridge to command a 360-degree view. Halfway up, Sarah said why attempt the summit, all the site needs is a straight line or pausing level in plan and in section against the cacophony of the topographic setting, millions of years in the making. The site had such good bones it did not need the pretensions of a vertical tower to own a vista. An all-too-immediate response to this first interrogation was that the preconditions of the site were already powerfully embodied by the context of this crossroads location, and it was the task of the architect to reveal that which was already there.

This was the process that caused me to begin again, once again collaborating with a new crop of perfect and imperfect strangers as new graduate students, initially Joe Atkins, my first semester teaching assistant, and thereafter Robert Corser substantially for the next two years in my now Charlottesville basement studio. With a contract in hand in 1994 from the Pitts Brothers of ACE Construction, we commenced on building the present unfinished shell suitable for archaic dwelling practices of a Nomadic family with roots on both sides of the Equator.

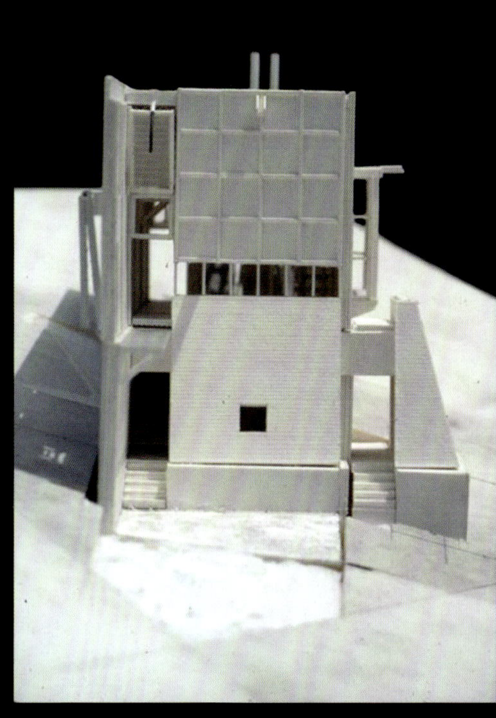

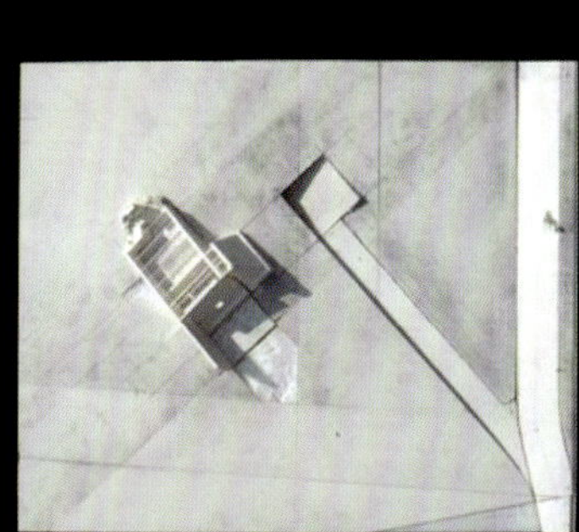

Baumann House—Initial design for North Garden House (1991)

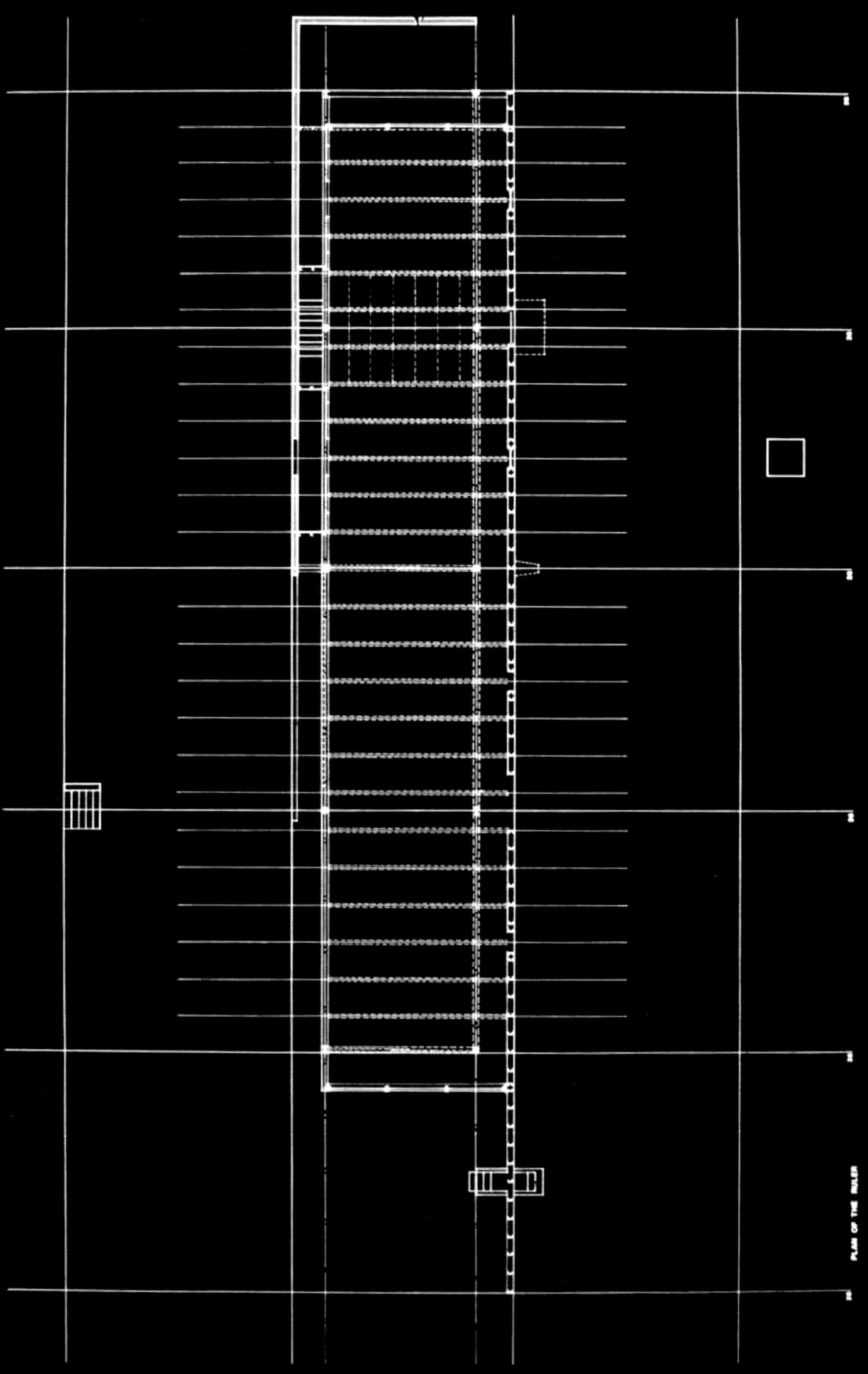

Parcel X Plan of the Ruler (1994)

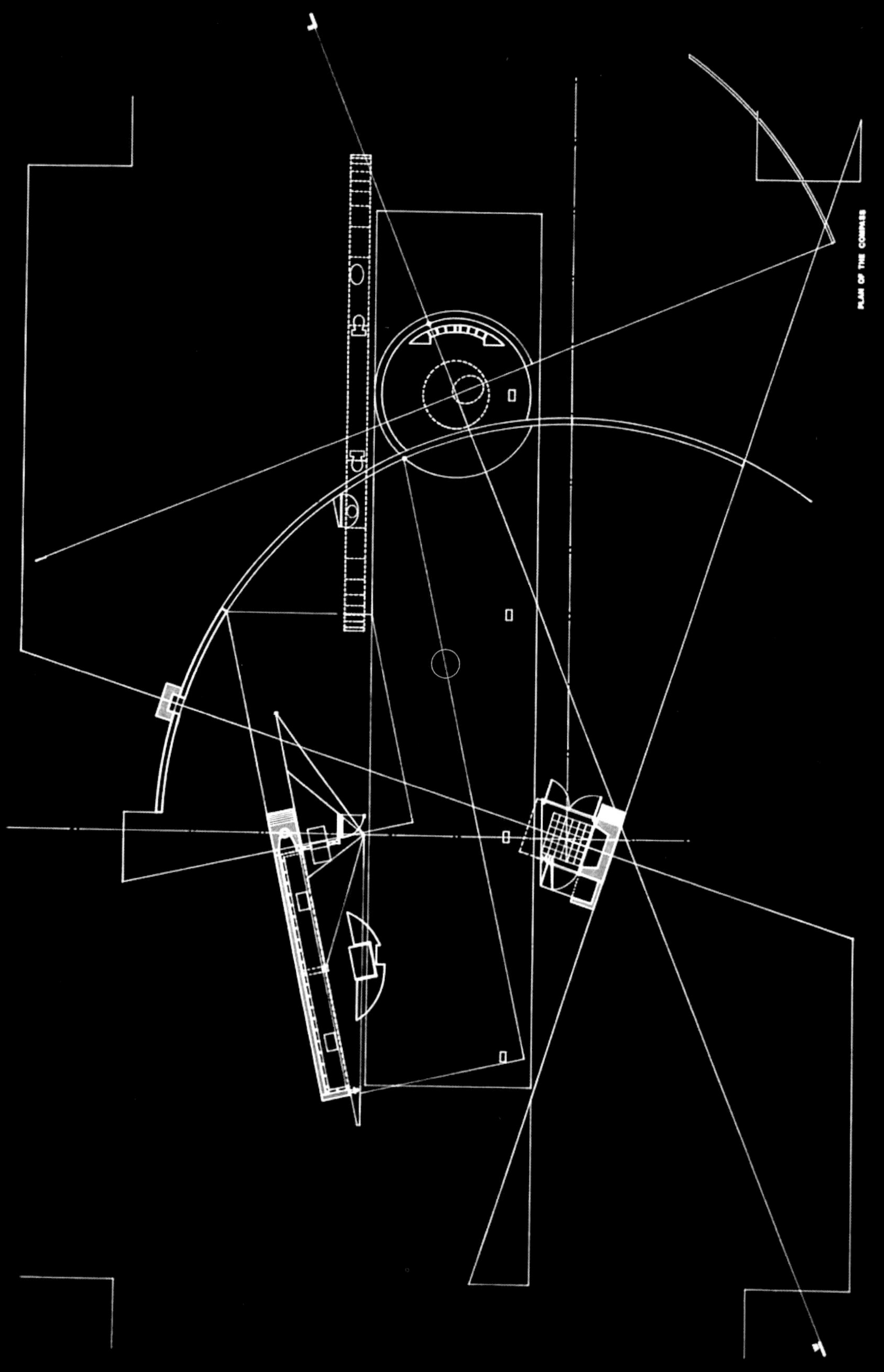

Parcel X Plan of the Compass (1994)

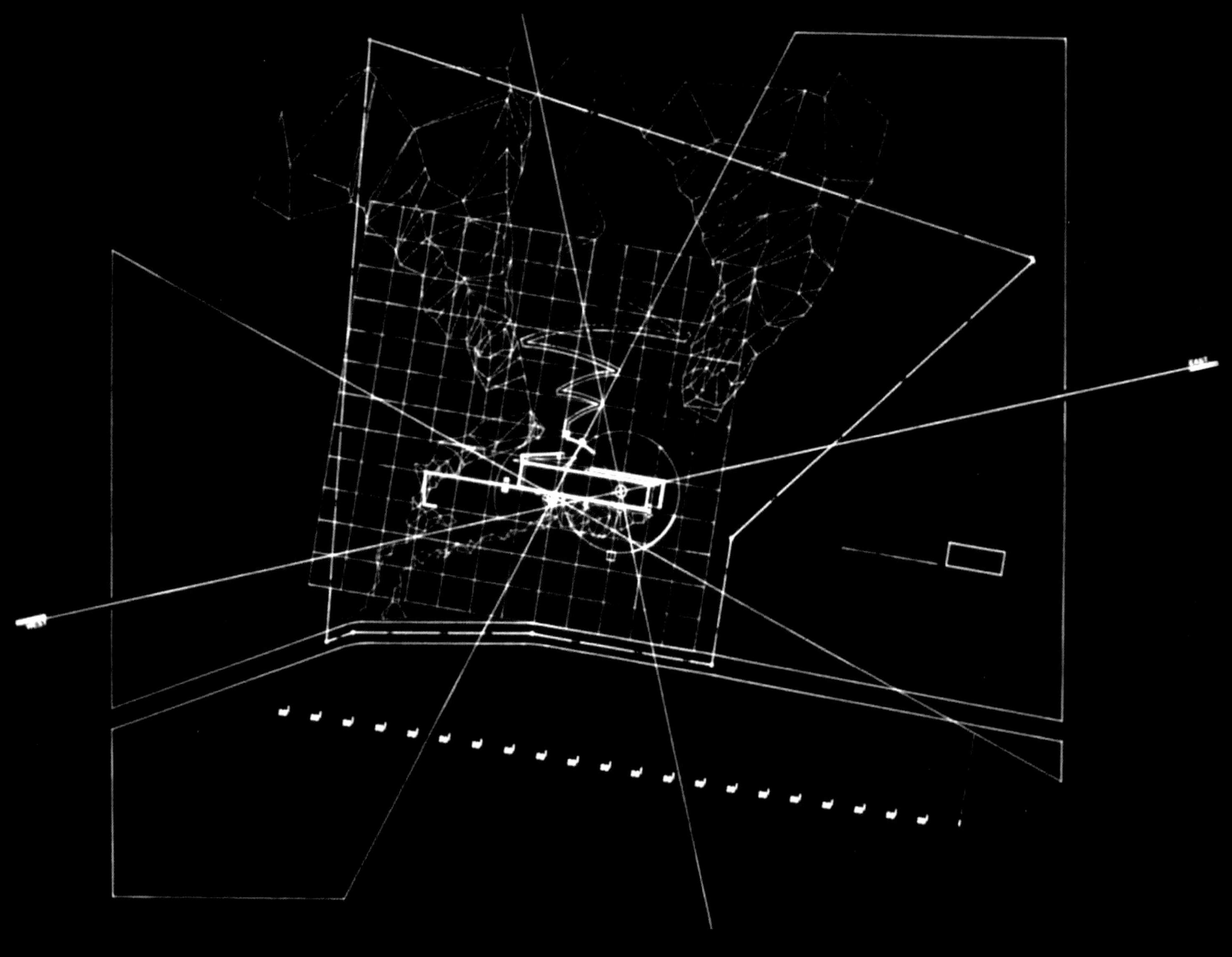

Parcel X Site Plan (1994)

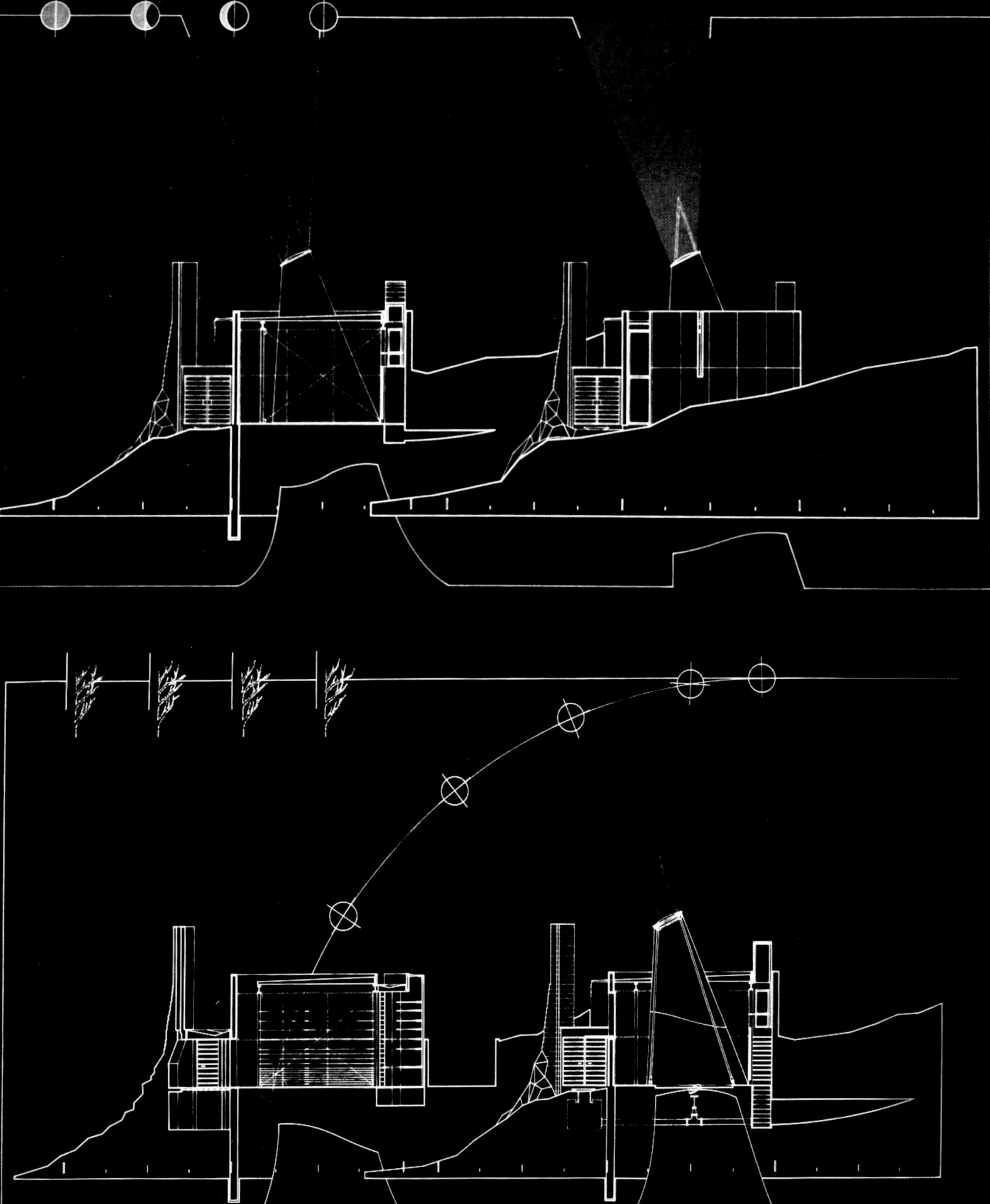

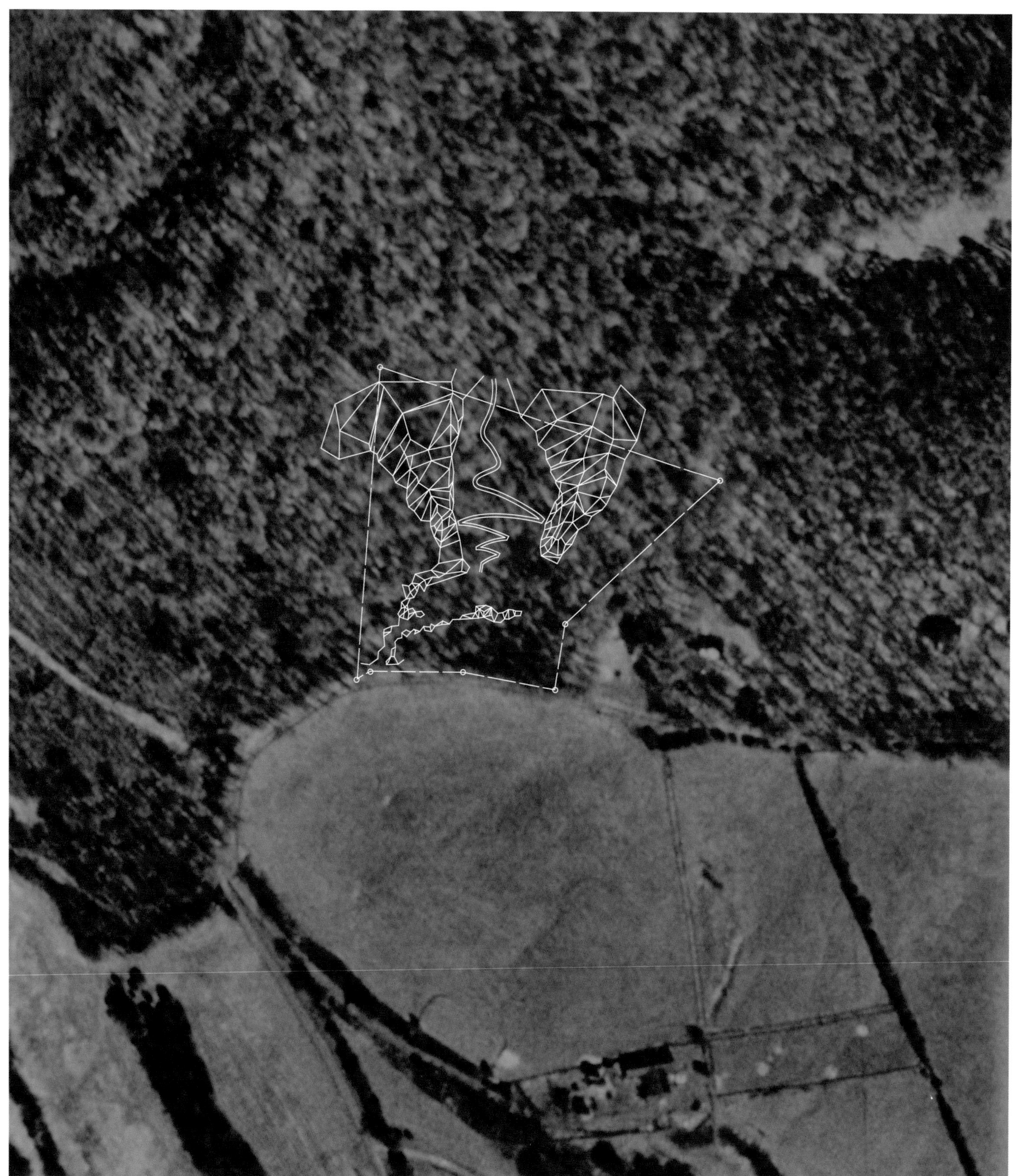

Parcel X, North Garden, VA (1994)

Parcel X, North Garden, VA (2021)

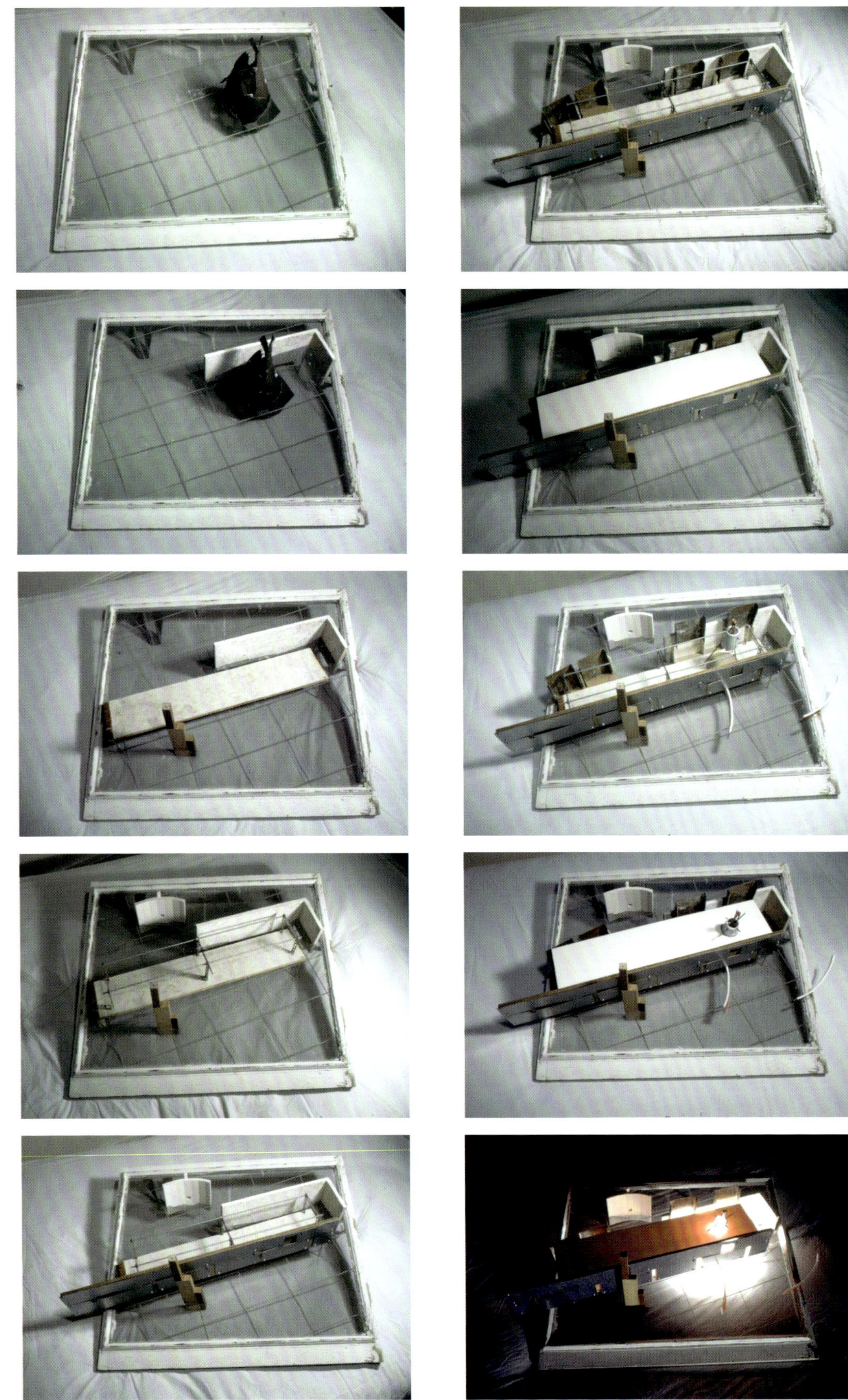

Parcel X Process Models (1992)

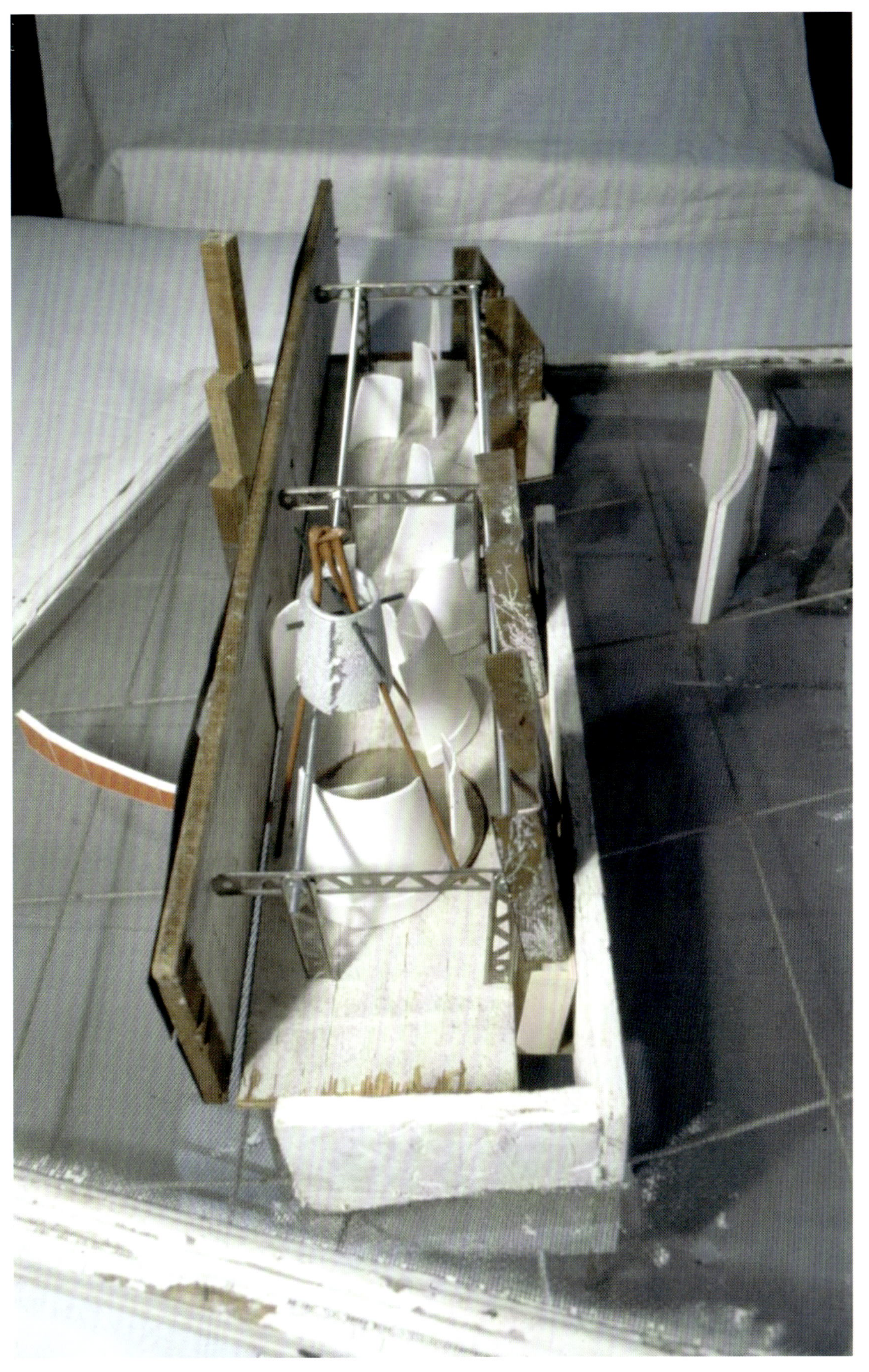

Parcel X Process Model (1992)

NUMBERS IN THE NIGHT: STRUCTURE AS THE SYNCOPATION OF GRAVITY AND ORIENTATION

Interpolated From *Perspecta*: The Yale Architectural Journal 31, "Reading Structures" (2000) by Peter Waldman

In the beginning God created Heaven and Earth, and all was without form.
Genesis 1:1–2

1. *Reading Structures* is read routinely herein as a gerund, an ongoing activity to which one returns to trespass again and again throughout the construction process in the anticipation of ruin.

2. *Numbers in the Night* is the specific speculation of an Architect as Surveyor and Cabalist who presupposes two simultaneous conditions necessary to Reading Structures.

One condition (*Numbers*) presupposes *accountability*: the meters derived from the precision of the physics of Gravity.

The other condition (*in the Night*) is the myriad of *permutations* of *Orientation* associated with evident fragments of several temporal logics resisting, in the dark, the absolute resolution of Cartesian thinking while making space for the coincidental rush of the nightmare, which others more discretely call the warehouse of the imagination.

Subtext (1+2)

An architecture may be simultaneously rendered accessible to the Surveyor by the diagrammatic clarity of its archetypal structural paradigms determined by *gravity* (Caves/Tents), as well as rendered *magical* to the Cabalist by the permutations of distinct cultural orientations (the Megaron).

Parcel X Construction (1995)

On Repositioning

The first architectural act is to break the ground;
The second is to raise structure vertically to the sky.
Gottfried Semper

3. *On Repositioning* begins with a tale of a surrogate structural member: the *metamorphic body at the end of the day* whose dynamic reorientations, commencing with one center and one flagellating line, go on to retrace patterns of the spiral through the contrast of diurnal and the nocturnal postures, coming finally to rest, ultimately, in the ruinous condition of dust and ashes.

   On Repositioning presupposes that every architectural project since Genesis *repeats* the text of *Reading* Structures into this world by rules first determined by the Sun, and then inverted time and again by the Mirrors of the Moon.

   On Repositioning presupposes reflectivity, a reflexive predictable cycle that regulates us by day and amazes us by night. Since the labyrinth of Knossos, the role of architecture has not only been to ground us *here and now*, but to take us to terrific realms where no one has been before.

4. *On Landscapes of Aggression* assumes the construction site over time is the only possible location from which to witness the dual readings of structure (Gravity and Orientation) by distinct bodies now repositioning themselves with one another as collaborative and constructive citizens. The additive benchmarks of the Surveyor are always followed by the subtractive excavations of the Cabalist, and through these double-crossed territories there is to be found on occasion the mender of the Nomad in search of *other* oases.

Parcel X Construction (1995)

Subtext (3+4)

The Surveyor and the Cabalist establish two distinct yet syncopated meters for the construction site. The Nomad, another kind of structuralist beyond the scope of this essay, reminds the other two of resources within the earth as evidence of geological and cultural structures beyond those of the geometry and mathematics of an ideal villa.

There are successive logics projected here, *Reading Structures*, as the Mapping of a Spatial Tale of Origin and identifying Landscapes of Aggression as a changing, reflexive *repositioning of the construction site,* which is neither a passive armature nor a singularly linear process. The subject of this subtext is the frictional union of an endurant syntax of structure, as a chess game played out through the permutations of a topographic imagination.

I read *Specifications for Construction* as instructions for alchemy: strategizing the soiling of foundations before burnishing eschatological finishes, defining architecture as the collaboration of the Gardener and the Engineer.

Structure as a visceral conjunction of sequential frictions is appreciated most

Parcel X (1996)

emphatically in terms of the lingering construction site in the revelation and representation of geological and historical evidence first, then appreciating the elemental acts of ordinary individuals repeating routine, familiar tasks. Reading structure is literally reading each spatial project, whether garden, dwelling, or civic theater, as a Spatial Tale of Origin, as an Architecture read as a Covenant with the World, Again.

Structure as Armature meters the spatial realm where citizen and stranger move with distinct rhythms, where lunatics leverage light levels, and weathering obscures some measures and accentuates others. If the warehouse of the imagination is illuminated by darkness, the armatures of structure, the inventory of caves and tents, the preconditions of dark labyrinths and shadow-full forests, all provide for an architecture that transposes authoritative orders associated with the bright light of day. Tanizaki's *In Praise of Shadows* (1933) and Picasso's *Guernica* (1937) both identify the light bulb as the phenomenal plague of the pre-enlightenment imagination where now nothing is hidden, and *terra incognita*[15] is erased from all world maps.

Parcel X (2023)

Landscapes of Aggression

Structure-before-enclosure is a precondition of dwelling within Architecture and provides the last evidence of the post-occupation ruin.

Building as a verb, as an instrumental deformative act, is manifested through successive territorial transformations, Semperian Landscapes of Aggression, conventionally conceived as the short-term construction site, and resistively perceived as the long-term scarred territory of repositioned topographic engagements.

Starting with the foundations of Parcel X, structure is the festering frictional determinant of a spatial tale of origin negotiating the territory defined by both concentric gravity and eccentric orientation. The initial retaining wall splits to frame a gap as it emerges from the ground to permit the oblique ray of summer solstice morning light to enter the basement of Parcel X. Next, glowing steel studs of equal meter cast magical shadows for a brief moment in collaboration with the adjacent stand of ancient tulip poplars before they were enrobed with a copper skin. This magic is merely represented now by

Parcel X (1996)

the regular markings of the burnished standing seam sleeves that meter the copper shield from sunrise to sunset.

It is not the point of this essay to assume that architecture and structure began as one condition of harmony. Petrarch had to flee the city to appreciate the ameliorative condition of the countryside. Rather, by bracketing the debate with Genesis and then Exodus, I am suggesting that *the world as construction site* was primal place before human-conceived gardens, buildings, or cities. Construction in its incompleteness was there first in its *progressive* state. The moment the task was finished, e.g., *Paradise* as a walled-in garden was abandoned as subsequently were the cities of Sodom and Gomorrah. Structure mediates with the world of nature first. Only then does architecture fix, no, posits a world within. Something might be suggested by the Lachaise cave paintings within, the tomb paintings of Gizeh within, the rise of the pastoral narratives of Giorgione's *Tempesta* (1506–1508) and Tiepolo's *Ai Nani Foresteria* series (1757).

Parcel X (2023)

Parcel X is an ancient and familiar tale, an architectural primer recounting the enduring codes and components of our discipline, demonstrating a syntax of structure all too often forgotten in the current amnesia where nothing endures for the contemporary. The preconditions of Parcel X record a site already full, not empty: of geological fissures and colluvial soil where ancient forests of vertical tulip poplar trees are metered by cattle fences and punctuated by camping sites of nomadic origins. Building as a verb, as an ongoing phenomenal process, is in crisis if one also accepts the notion of substantial completion, with the assemblage of a checklist with the assumption that structures are invariant and thus should not creak or leak. There are alternatives to an impoverished and pretentious architecture that conventionally values more the resolution or stabilization of structure over the vitality of stress scars and watermarks.

I suggest an architecture that celebrates the instrumentality of structure as progressive. The Spatial Tales of Origin recounted in Specifications for Construction should begin and end with yet another eschatological beginning, always found in water and watermarks, soil and stain, in darkness

Parcel X (1996)

Parcel X (2023)

and encrusted patina, in fire and in ash, in secret springs as well as manholes and finally, lightning rods. The insistent horizons of the floor and roof planes contrast with the oblique section of the site as dynamic ground. The copper shield is an unrelenting ruler with the character of a fine-tooth comb. The Volcano is also a tent encamped once again upon the site. The hearth is a grotto, the outrigger ark beneath the kaleidoscopic box, which merely frames the sun and the moon. Parcel X is an apology for the temporary encampment of those in search of a New World Arcadia, where the steel frame audibly creaks in the wind, the concrete displays stress cracks seasonally, and the rain shield does not leak (too much).

Parcel X (2023)

FOOTNOTES FROM THE STAGE MANAGER

The Eric Goodwin Passage

What follows are a series of diary entries which mark the evolving re-conception of this project; first in the light of a symposium Sites out of Mind, next a reconsideration of scope and site, then onto the approval process, a site work onto itself, and finally the extensive documentation of construction.

A footnote may be useful about the context of my teaching some call foundational research; others term exploration of an architecture of enduring connections, perhaps recurrent dualities. The Eric Goodwin Memorial Passage/Pavilion at the University of Virginia evidences one overlapping/haunted site out of mind, as both ever-present Lessons of the Lawn and equally demonstrations of Architecture as a Covenant with the World. Again. Both courses I coincidentally teach, some say, in the basements, grottoes, and foundations of our school.

Spring Equinox 2004
Preface to the Project by Student Design-Build Team:
Samuel Beall and Justin Walton

Founded in the context of a final semester project of the undergraduate studio sequence at the University of Virginia, this project began as a design-build challenge for specifying both a temporary installation to transform space for the Phoebe Crisman Site Out Of Mind Symposium Spring 2004 as well as constructing a more permanent space for the celebration of graduation in the same place of daily collaborations between faculty and students. The students provided a three-ring circus of sorts, with tents and centipedes; bonfires emerging from freshly excavated grottoes, and a flimsy fence or two. The symposium endured for three days, then disappeared from memory, but it is still rumored that the fingerprints of recent resultant ashen citizens still claim Goodwin's Walls.

Following the studio's final review, circumstances changed, forcing us to modify our final approach. The adoption of a new international building code by the University meant that touching the existing building or bracing a structure near it would not be permitted. Our focus is now onto a slight cut into the ground with two butterfly wings emerging with the nurturing help of the Sun.

The site of the Eric Goodwin Memorial Pavilion, now referred to as The Passage, concerns itself with an interesting edge condition of brick meeting grass and spatially between a raised planter and a retaining wall. It is along this edge that we have focused our energy, attempting to clarify this boundary between the building and its environs in articulating an axis from the exterior nature and interior character of Campbell Hall. Several years ago, a maple tree was planted in memory of Carlo Pellicia, a principal professor of the school for many years. This tree begins a dialogue along an axis that fundamentally relates to a primary interior circulation path. In the tradition of remembrance, and the Lawn's legacy of student-teacher interaction, this project aims to provide a structure for both remembering those lost, but also celebrating daily life and its change throughout the seasons.

Summer Solstice 2004
Contextual Issues and Design Intent

This student/faculty collaboration is a demonstration of the enduring principles of the Lessons of the Lawn (as well as Stonehenge) as part of the teaching agenda for all the Citizens and Strangers who come to this pivotal location on Carr's Hill. It seeks to reconfirm orientation at the time of Solstice and Equinox and provide an appreciation of ritual and routine as essential for contemporary life in this public university.

One pavilion of juxtaposed outdoor instructional spaces is projected to occupy the transitional space between the brick pavers of the North Terrace of the School of Architecture and the residual landscape of Carr's Hill dominated by Centennial Oaks and the singular Carlo Pellicia Memorial tree. At the end of a major circulation corridor on the ground floor of Campbell Hall, an existing window frames the new Pellicia Tree about 50 feet to the North directly on axis with the centered threshold of the projected memorial project.

Between these two pavilions of Light and Shadow that are furnished with singular bench on one side and a seminar table on the other, is a place of passage into the earth and out again for contemplation at the scale of the human body where the student may appreciate the encounter of both one generous mentor, Carlo Pellicia, and a recent genuine newcomer, Eric Goodwin, who loved this School as an ongoing construction site and who passed away shortly before graduation in 2002.

Fall Equinox 2004
On the Necessity for Ruins

The Aeneid recounts the arduous journey of Aeneas, with his father and son, escaping from the ruins of ancient Troy to found the new city of Rome as a consequence and triumph of test and toil.

Around here, conventional wisdom has it that Troy fell on April 30th 2004 (at the end of spring semester's final review)… A few days later, the expanded vision of a Circus Maximus that was just out there and now disbanded, there emerged ancient Anchises to seek out the future of his seed to recommence with a compressed vision, a more modest first move based on a pre-existing condition, a gap in a wall, an aperture clearly set on the Carlo Pellicia Memorial now forgotten so soon and known as the pleasant young shade tree out there. With one stroke, ancient Anchises scratched in the ground a path from tree to crack in Campbell Hall's North-South axis. With his two young traveling companions they set a course the day after graduation to envision and to communicate their determination to begin to build within the evolving culture of this place here and now. No 9/11 paralysis now here. To build well in the face of external devastation is the prerequisite task of those who survive to leave ruins to tell the tale.

FOOTNOTES FROM THE STAGE MANAGER

The Eric Goodwin Passage

What follows are a series of diary entries which mark the evolving re-conception of this project; first in the light of a symposium *Sites out of Mind*, next a reconsideration of scope and site, then onto the approval process, a site work onto itself, and finally the extensive documentation of construction.

A footnote may be useful about the context of my teaching some call foundational research; others term exploration of an architecture of enduring connections, perhaps recurrent dualities. The Eric Goodwin Memorial Passage/Pavilion at the University of Virginia evidences one overlapping/haunted site out of mind, as both ever-present *Lessons of the Lawn* and equally demonstrations of *Architecture as a Covenant with the World, Again*. Both courses I coincidentally teach, some say, in the basements, grottoes, and foundations of our school.

Spring Equinox 2004
Preface to the Project by Student Design-Build Team:
Samuel Beall and Justin Walton

Founded in the context of a final semester project of the undergraduate studio sequence at the University of Virginia, this project began as a design-build challenge for specifying both a temporary installation to transform space for the Phoebe Crisman Site Out Of Mind Symposium Spring 2004 as well as constructing a more permanent space for the celebration of graduation in the same place of daily collaborations between faculty and students. The students provided a three-ring circus of sorts, with tents and centipedes; bonfires emerging from freshly excavated grottoes, and a flimsy fence or two. The symposium endured for three days, then disappeared from memory, but it is still rumored that the fingerprints of recent resultant ashen citizens still claim Goodwin's Walls.

Following the studio's final review, circumstances changed, forcing us to modify our final approach. The adoption of a new international building code by the University meant that touching the existing building or bracing a structure near it would not be permitted. Our focus is now onto a slight cut into the ground with two butterfly wings emerging with the nurturing help of the Sun.

The site of the Eric Goodwin Memorial Pavilion, now referred to as The Passage, concerns itself with an interesting edge condition of brick meeting grass and spatially between a raised planter and a retaining wall. It is along this edge that we have focused our energy, attempting to clarify this boundary between the building and its environs in articulating an axis from the exterior nature and interior character of Campbell Hall. Several years ago, a maple tree was planted in memory of Carlo Pelliccia, a principal professor of the school for many years. This tree begins a dialogue along an axis that fundamentally relates to a primary interior circulation path. In the tradition of remembrance, and the Lawn's legacy of student-teacher interaction, this project aims to provide a structure for both remembering those lost, but also celebrating daily life and its change throughout the seasons.

Summer Solstice 2004
Contextual Issues and Design Intent

This student/faculty collaboration is a demonstration of the enduring principles of the *Lessons of the Lawn* (as well as Stonehenge) as part of the teaching agenda for all the Citizens and Strangers who come to this pivotal location on Carr's Hill. It seeks to reconfirm *orientation* at the time of Solstice and Equinox and provide an appreciation of *ritual and routine* as essential for contemporary life in this public university.

One pavilion of juxtaposed outdoor instructional spaces is projected to occupy the transitional space between the brick pavers of the North Terrace of the School of Architecture and the residual landscape of Carr's Hill dominated by Centennial Oaks and the singular Carlo Pelliccia Memorial tree. At the end of a major circulation corridor on the ground floor of Campbell Hall, an existing window frames the new Pelliccia Tree about 50 feet to the North directly on axis with the centered threshold of the projected memorial project.

Between these two pavilions of Light and Shadow that are furnished with singular bench on one side and a seminar table on the other, is a place of passage into the earth and out again for contemplation at the scale of the human body where the student may appreciate the encounter of both one generous mentor, Carlo Pelliccia, and a recent genuine newcomer, Eric Goodwin, who loved this School as an ongoing construction site and who passed away shortly before graduation in 2002.

Fall Equinox 2004
On the Necessity for Ruins

The Aeneid recounts the arduous journey of Aeneas, with his father and son, escaping from the ruins of ancient Troy to found the new city of Rome as a consequence and triumph of test and toil.

Around here, conventional wisdom has it that Troy fell on April 30th 2004 (at the end of spring semester's final review)… A few days later, the expanded vision of a Circus Maximus that was just out there and now disbanded, there emerged ancient Anchises to seek out the future of his seed to recommence with a compressed vision, a more modest first move based on a pre-existing condition, a gap in a wall, an aperture clearly set on the Carlo Pelliccia Memorial now forgotten so soon and known as the pleasant young shade tree out there. With one stroke, ancient Anchises scratched in the ground a path from tree to crack in Campbell Hall's North-South axis. With his two young traveling companions they set a course the day after graduation to envision and to communicate their determination to begin to build within the evolving culture of this place *here and now*. No 9/11 paralysis now here. To build well in the face of external devastation is the prerequisite task of those who survive to leave ruins to tell the tale.

On Two Journeys in a Land Where Approvals Proceed Construction

The first journey recorded the approval process: *Was this architecture or was it art? Declare one not two entries. Is this project temporary and/or permanent? Surely it is set into a landscape in the end, or is it a garden turned inside out? Is it a private memorial to one of our own, or a public domain for citizens and strangers to share?*

The second journey retraces the steps of construction, the emergence of natural and man-made consequential situations, the meander and recalculation; so much for linear timelines and critical path methods, of guarantees and the strange concept of *contingencies*.

Sometimes cultures gather under the cover of a new moon for the youngest to repeat ancient questions wanting only for the eldest to reply. *This happened here, let me tell you on this thickened edge between hillside and terrace not so long, long, ago*.

This is a tale of an approval process that took exactly as long as the construction process. *Was this project architecture or art or merely a landscape?* Again and again, they asked. No one was sure. We needed approval as all three. The journey took us through the labyrinth of the university grounds from center to edge and back again. A model of the Section of Campbell Hall and Carr's Hill to the North journeyed from the top-floor studios to reunions with faculty down to the Office of the Dean on the *piano nobile* one high noon only to descend minutes later on site just out there; after all, at the end of the day the real site was just out there. We staked out the site as if we could determine scale that way on the ground, we questioned dimensions and proportions, we expanded the context model to see our project in the context of Campbell Hall and the adjacent Fiske Kimball library as the garden walls of this then larger-than-life Summer House (Aalto). We now understood the project less as a Pavilion as it shrank in scale in our self-confident vertical descent. We journeyed next west late that afternoon onto the gurus/engineers, all of the Facilities Management compound, and next morning, requirements in hand, over the mountains we went to consult with our own Licensed Civil Engineer. The Journey of a Model from Campbell Hall to Carr's Hill by way of Richmond and Afton onto Ohio and back in 40 days is the stuff of both Odysseys and mythic legends recovering broken pieces of the Ark.

Another 40 Days Later
Construction Comes to a Pause when Floods Endure and the Moon Stood Still on 09/21/04

Around a forbidden campfire and under tarps out of sight but within earshot of Campbell Hall, tales are recounted of a construction site some call *The Best Little Place in the World*. Several young master-builders share the stories with newcomers to this school of 40 days of construction when the world came to a halt and then resurrected itself yet again, a camera rolled all this time as a witness capturing the site of chaos and chorus, of topsoil reconstructed as a mound and then a schist mountain revealed.

15 tons were lifted with ease, *within 15 minutes* shout some; then, 32 tons were tilted and dropped, tilted again and again until a mountain was constructed and magical anchor plates flown in. The school came out to witness on a Monday applauded; at noon shrank back in horror repeatedly that afternoon. Anchors popped, the larger slab cracked from suction and collapsed, soon to be bound by a splint. Temporary braces were inserted only briefly under our second full moon. Justin and Barrett, Tim and Anthony inserted three permanent braces and added two more for good measure.

We began this tale not with a hole in the ground but with journeys made to wise gurus at Facilities Management, student presentations to the Arboretum Committee, midnight journeys to Virginia Beach to collect oyster shells and to model crustacean antennae, then back to Facilities Management to accommodate *ten drunken fraternity brothers suspended until Sunday dawn's early light* from the angel wing sombrero, back down to Richmond to present the Commonwealth's smallest Permanent Art Piece to the Design Review Committee, and back to Facilities Management to re-specify forensic couplers, finally hunting down the Engineer's approval over Afton Mountain in a Ravine for Seismic Review. Three wise men came from Maryland, Pennsylvania, and as far west as Dayton, Ohio, bearing gifts of advice, bracing hardware, and release mediums and rare pigments as watermark disguised against the sun and the moon. The President's committee gave the final blessing, insisting that this space could not possibly be called a Pavilion at Mr. Jefferson's university, but rather a Passage. *All right with us*. It was a rite of passage only forty days long for heroic young students and yet another test for ancient Anchises.

The Next 40 Days
Excavate
Form slab
Pour
Form again
Pour
Raise 15
Raise 32
Resurrect 32
Brace
Brace quickly again
Oyster shells
Steps
Table
Now bench
Good Night Moon

On Two Journeys in a Land Where Approvals Proceed Construction

The first journey recorded the approval process: Was this architecture or was it art? Declare one not two entries. Is this project temporary and/or permanent? Surely it is set into a landscape in the end, or is it a garden turned inside out? Is it a private memorial to one of our own, or a public domain for citizens and strangers to share?

The second journey retraces the steps of construction, the emergence of natural and man-made consequential situations, the meander and recalculation; so much for linear timelines and critical path methods, of guarantees and the strange concept of contingencies.

Sometimes cultures gather under the cover of a new moon for the youngest to repeat ancient questions wanting only for the eldest to reply. This happened here, let me tell you on this thickened edge between hillside and terrace not so long, long, ago.

This is a tale of an approval process that took exactly as long as the construction process. Was this project architecture or art or merely a landscape? Again and again, they asked. No one was sure. We needed approval as all three. The journey took us through the labyrinth of the university grounds from center to edge and back again. A model of the Section of Campbell Hall and Carr's Hill to the North journeyed from the top-floor studios to reunions with faculty down to the Office of the Dean on the piano nobile one high noon only to descend minutes later on site just out there; after all, at the end of the day the real site was just out there. We staked out the site as if we could determine scale that way on the ground, we questioned dimensions and proportions, we expanded the context model to see our project in the context of Campbell Hall and the adjacent Fiske Kimball library as the garden walls of this then larger-than-life Summer House (Aalto). We now understood the project less as a Pavilion as it shrank in scale in our self-confident vertical descent. We journeyed next west late that afternoon onto the gurus/engineers, all of the Facilities Management compound, and next morning, requirements in hand, over the mountains we went to consult with our own Licensed Civil Engineer. The Journey of a Model from Campbell Hall to Carr's Hill by way of Richmond and Afton onto Ohio and back in 40 days is the stuff of both Odysseys and mythic legends recovering broken pieces of the Ark.

Another 40 Days Later
Construction Comes to a Pause when Floods Endure and the Moon Stood Still on 09/21/04

Around a forbidden campfire and under tarps out of sight but within earshot of Campbell Hall, tales are recounted of a construction site some call The Best Little Place in the World. Several young master-builders share the stories with newcomers to this school of 40 days of construction when the world came to a halt and then resurrected itself yet again, a camera rolled all this time as a witness capturing the site of chaos and chorus, of topsoil reconstructed as a mound and then a schist mountain revealed.

15 tons were lifted with ease, within 15 minutes shout some; then, 32 tons were tilted and dropped, tilted again and again until a mountain was constructed and magical anchor plates flown in. The school came out to witness on a Monday applauded; at noon shrank back in horror repeatedly that afternoon. Anchors popped, the larger slab cracked from suction and collapsed, soon to be bound by a splint. Temporary braces were inserted only briefly under our second full moon. Justin and Barrett, Tim and Anthony inserted three permanent braces and added two more for good measure.

We began this tale not with a hole in the ground but with journeys made to wise gurus at Facilities Management, student presentations to the Arboretum Committee, midnight journeys to Virginia Beach to collect oyster shells and to model crustacean antennae, then back to Facilities Management to accommodate ten drunken fraternity brothers suspended until Sunday dawn's early light from the angel wing sombrero, back down to Richmond to present the Commonwealth's smallest Permanent Art Piece to the Design Review Committee, and back to Facilities Management to re-specify forensic couplers, finally hunting down the Engineer's approval over Afton Mountain in a Ravine for Seismic Review. Three wise men came from Maryland, Pennsylvania, and as far west as Dayton, Ohio, bearing gifts of advice, bracing hardware, and release mediums and rare pigments as watermark disguised against the sun and the moon. The President's committee gave the final blessing, insisting that this space could not possibly be called a Pavilion at Mr. Jefferson's university, but rather a Passage. All right with us. It was a rite of passage only forty days long for heroic young students and yet another test for ancient Anchises.

The Next 40 Days
Excavate
Form slab
Pour
Form again
Pour
Raise 15
Raise 32
Resurrect 32
Brace
Brace quickly again
Oyster shells
Steps
Table
Now bench
Good Night Moon

THE ERIC GOODWIN MEMORIAL PAVILION (2004) AS SPECIFICATIONS FOR CONSTRUCTION

PETER WALDMAN
CHARLOTTESVILLE, VA

Our current School's reconsideration of *Material Realities* marks a significant anniversary of a previous generational cycle of a design-build project of a memorial to an architecture school student commenced in the spring of 2004. Then dean Karen Van Lengen provided the opportunity for a fourth-year undergraduate studio to realize a memorial to a fellow classmate who passed away earlier that year.

Eric loved the poetics and pragmatics of the construction site, and an alumni donation suddenly made this a fast-tracked demonstration project of material realities as a self-activated culture of collaboration within this (*Yes, we can-do it*) A-School.

In March of 2004, mock-ups were prepared by this studio for Phoebe Crisman's and Sanda Iliescu's Symposium *Site out of Mind*, and the thickened edge of the North Terrace between Artifice and Nature was identified as the site between *Memory and Amnesia* dedicated to Approximating Stonehenge (*Finding North*).

Allied Concrete intentionally funded this memorial of *gravitas* on the condition that it demonstrate innovations in tilt-slab construction, an economical alternative to redundant formwork, to which this studio critically responded with the counterpart of light tubular scaffolding and tensioned steel cables to reframe the celestial soffit by day and by night.

Partners
Peter Waldman, Arch 4020 Studio Critic, Spring Semester 2004
Sam Beall, Jennifer Findley, and Justin Walton, Design-Build Team

Eric Goodwin Memorial Pavilion Watercolor by Justin Walton (2004)

APPROXIMATING STONEHENGE

On Specifications for Construction: North Porch, Campbell Hall

On the Collaboration of Allied Concrete and A Swarm of Spiders

On the Utility and Transformative Qualities of Tilt Slab Construction

On Sequential Markings of the Memorable Horizon and the Totemic Vertex

On the Strategic Responsibilities of Surveyors, Nomads, and Occasional Lunatics

A remarkable architecture student passed away suddenly before graduation; his peers rose up to erect a memorial at the thickened edge between architecture and landscape. These outdoor classrooms were a student/faculty design-build operation to be used routinely to mark time for seminars and studios and to celebrate the annual Ritual of Commencement.

Our Site, the North Face of Carr's Hill, might not be easily described as Level Ground. A review of the archive of maps of Carr's Hill since Jefferson's inception reveals numerous fictions as to the location of True North. Thus, with Eric's passing and his peers scattering to the winds shortly thereafter, we Citizens of Campbell Hall who remained were not certain where North might be precisely located.

We needed to use the strategies of construction to orient ourselves. That summer, we proposed to construct one by one with each New Moon concrete slabs determined by the meter of the structure of Campbell Hall. The first slab became the formwork for the next as one proceeds from east to west. With each sequential pour, the previous one was tilted to the sky; then each totem braced. Shadows danced, implying a village of teepees.

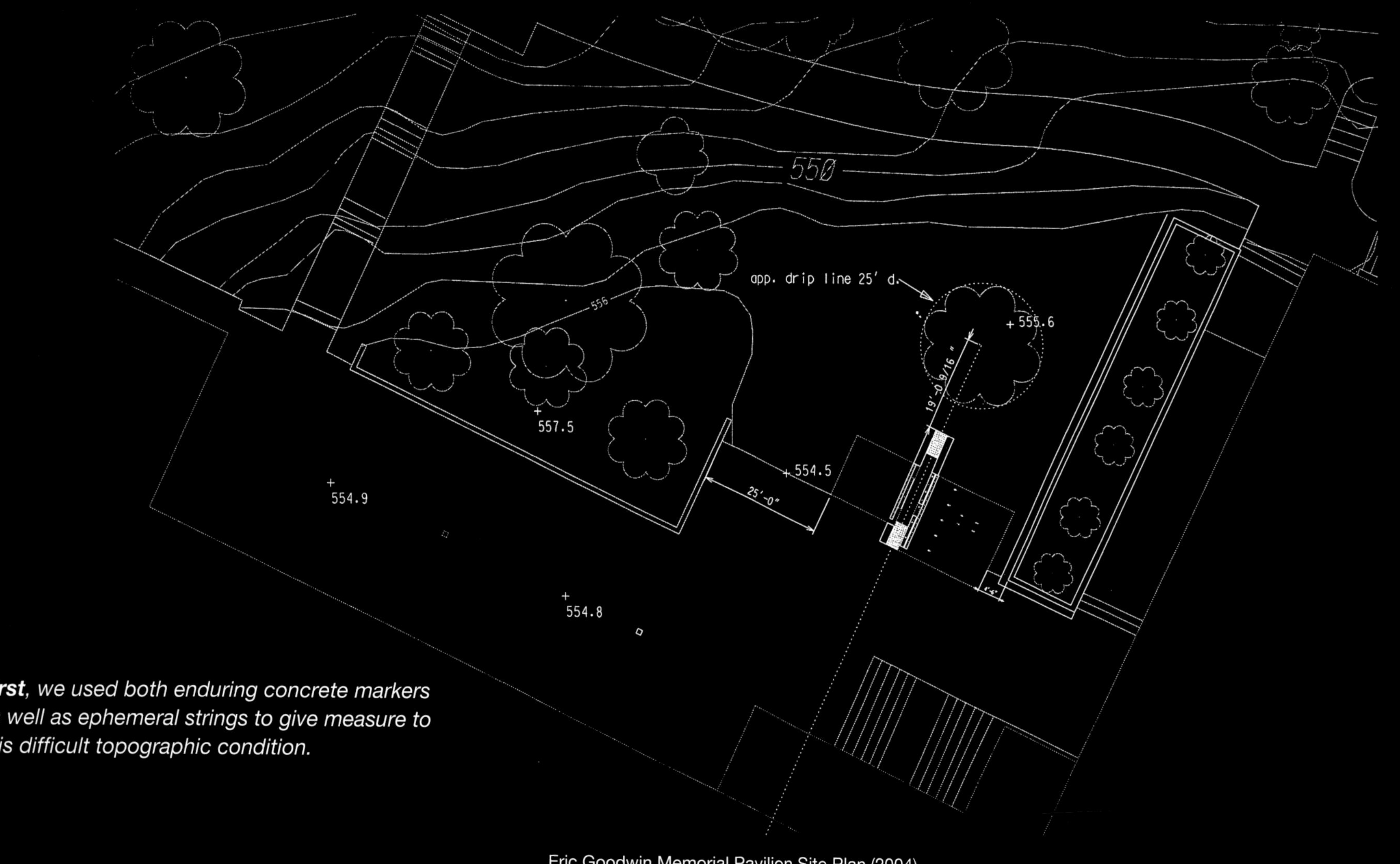

***First**, we used both enduring concrete markers as well as ephemeral strings to give measure to this difficult topographic condition.*

Eric Goodwin Memorial Pavilion Site Plan (2004)

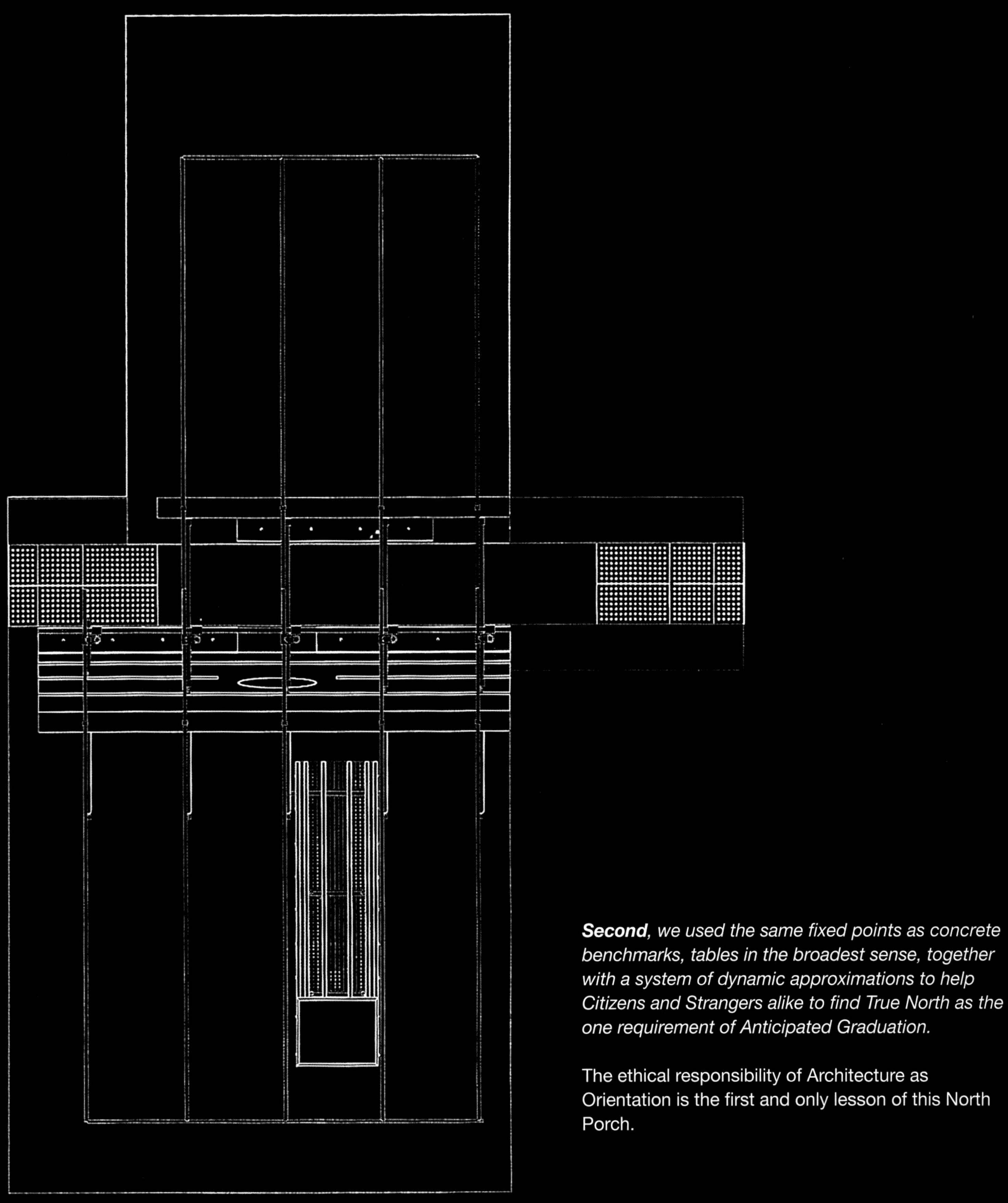

Eric Goodwin Memorial Pavilion Plan (2004)

***Second**, we used the same fixed points as concrete benchmarks, tables in the broadest sense, together with a system of dynamic approximations to help Citizens and Strangers alike to find True North as the one requirement of Anticipated Graduation.*

The ethical responsibility of Architecture as Orientation is the first and only lesson of this North Porch.

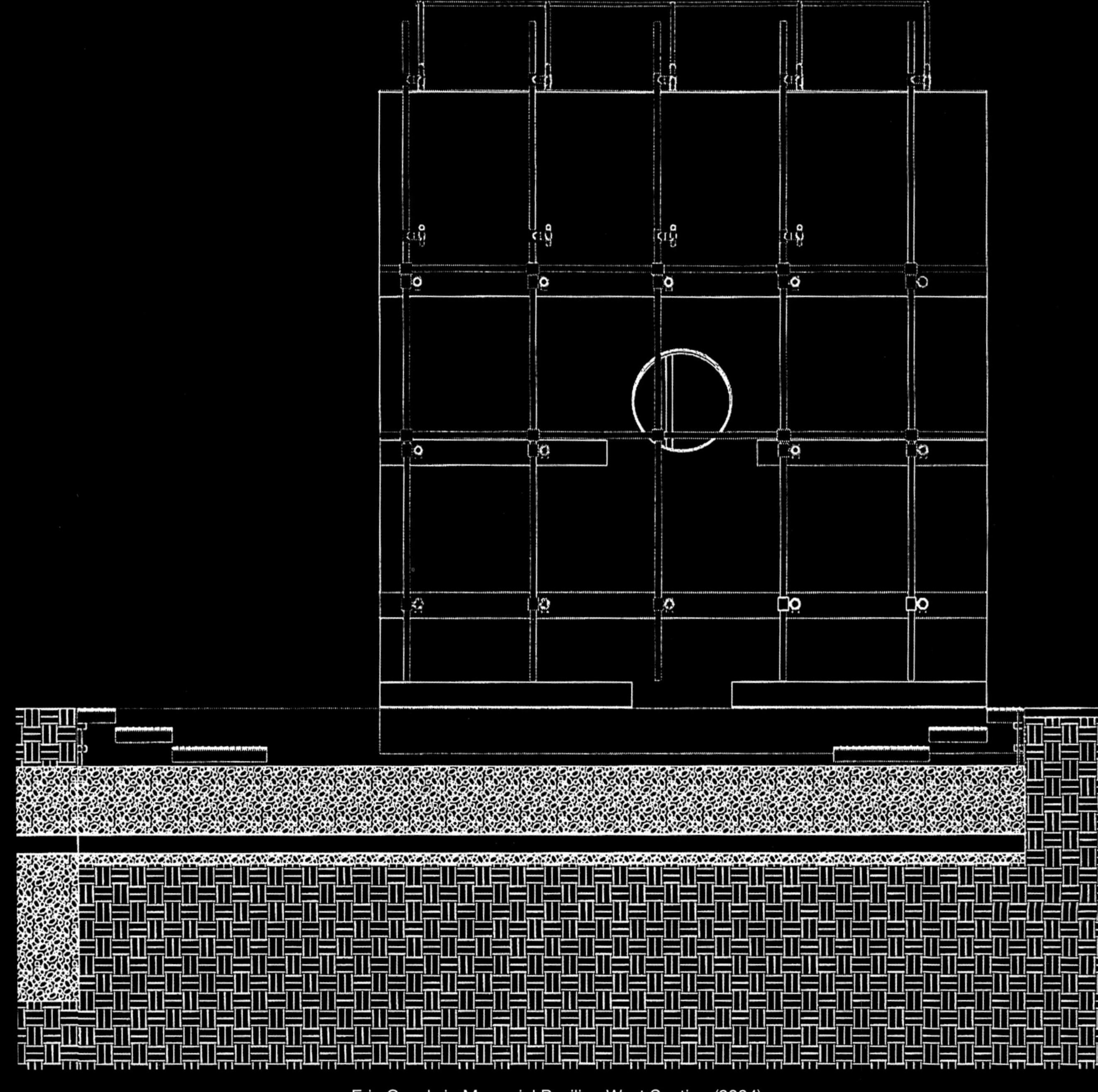

Eric Goodwin Memorial Pavilion West Section (2004)

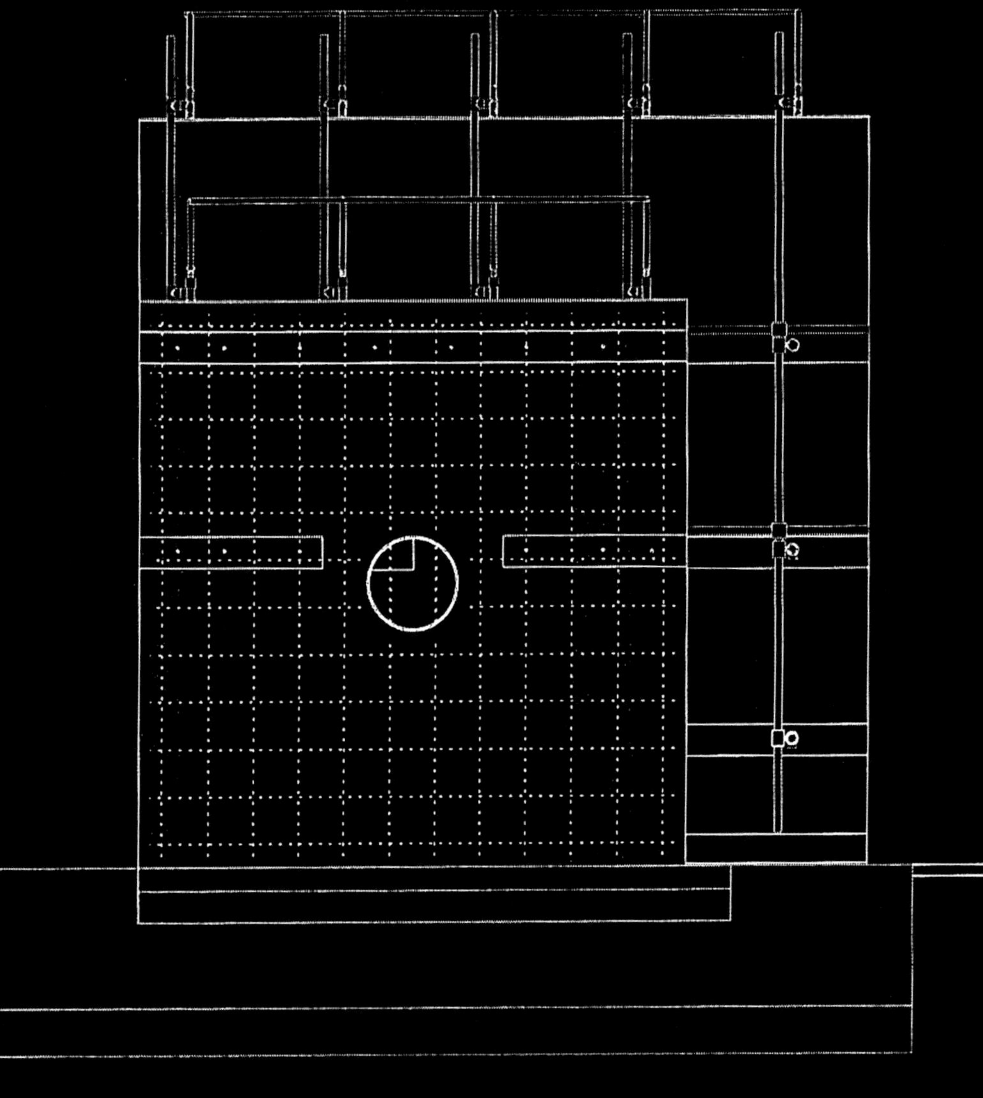

Eric Goodwin Memorial Pavilion West Elevation (2004)

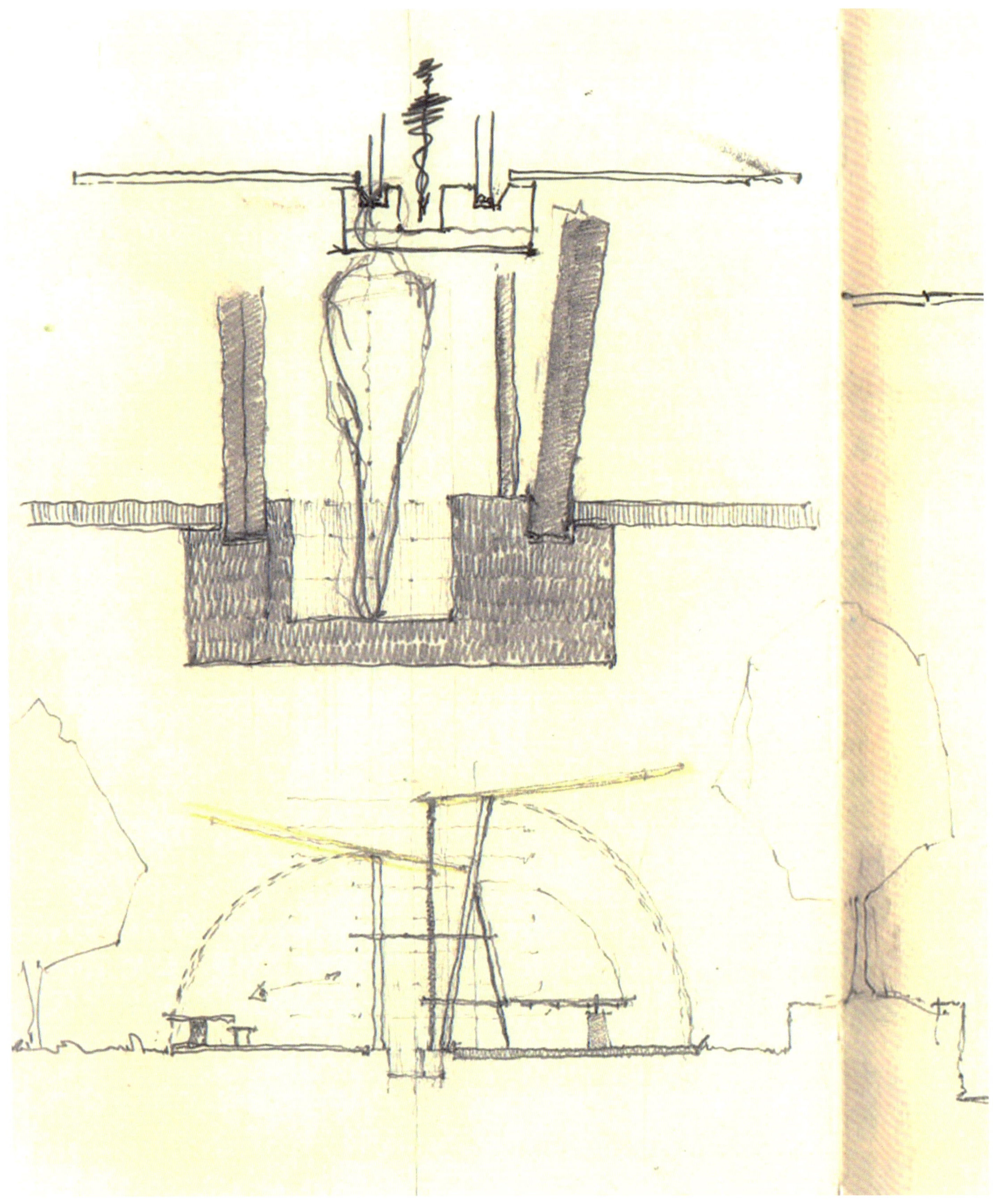

Eric Goodwin Memorial Pavilion Preliminary Design Sketches (2004)

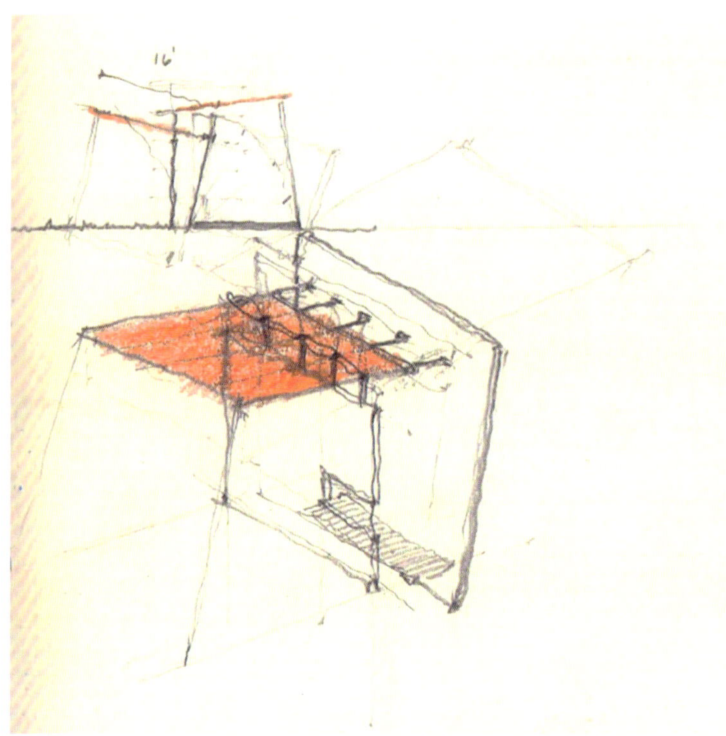

Third, *Nomads were to project experimental theaters and landscapes for a Tent, a Table or two, and a myriad of commemorative and transformative Tablets at the scales of both bricks as well as civic mirages.*

The spatial setting of the North Porch was to be nothing less than the construction site of the intersecting *lessons of civic literacy* commencing with the ABCs of the Acropolis, onto Bilbao, then the Campidoglio, with the Ise Shrine as pivotal, and ending, no doubt, in Zurich at the threshold of a tent perched between the Mountain and the Zee.

Eric Goodwin Memorial Pavilion Preliminary Design Sketches (2004)

Fourth, *Surveyors constructed concrete Markers to measure the Horizon first from Ground to Mountain Ridge.*

Fifth, *Lunatics provide upon these foundation plinths additional pours of progressive dimensions now to give measure to the Hill as they are then tilted Vertically to Frame a Window to the Sky.*

Eric Goodwin Memorial Pavilion Construction (2004)

***Sixth,** with time, the tilt slab panels will be incised with the names of departed students and faculty, generous donors, and legendary caretakers alike as a prerequisite of citizenship.*

Eric Goodwin Memorial Pavilion (2004)

Seventh, *upon these Window plinths a swarm of spiders insert telescoping poles and cables as stanchions for the eventful tent reliably erected by a band of meandering Nomads in the midst of May.*

Eric Goodwin Memorial Pavilion (2004)

***Eighth,** it is rumored that another Lunatic in the ruins of an ancient fraternity site has supervised a Deep Casting Pit that is quarried as formwork for incubating Groundhogs to sustain the stress of tent-induced wind loads.*

Eric Goodwin Memorial Pavilion (2004)

Ninth, *a Forest of Pylons and Correspondent Water Runnels syncopate the Hill.*

Eric Goodwin Memorial Pavilion (2024)

Tenth, *Fires burn.* ***Eleventh,*** *Columns begin to Dance.*

Eric Goodwin Memorial Pavilion (2024)

Eric Goodwin Memorial Pavilion (2024)

Eric Goodwin Memorial Pavilion (2024)

THE OFFSTAGE MANAGER RECOUNTS

Sofia and Patrick were given the Keys to Parcel X to water the gardens and to photograph the interior contents at will.

It seemed natural to them to record not only the self-reflective interior, but to trespass to the exterior flanks of both North Garden and then onto the North Terrace of Campbell Hall as well.

Their positions on *Spolia*, a version of the not-so-*Secret Life of Buildings*,[1] and a semantically mute *Posthuman Architecture* were evidenced first through their camera lenses and later through oppositional voices contained in ACT TWO.

Sofia's engagements with *The Necessity for Ruins*[2] were tactile, left us sensing frictions, blisters, and eventually scars, while Patrick's Scripted Codified Systems left no possibility of recording *Fingerprints in the Act of Making*. Their observations revealed, however, both conditions of recurrent dualities lingering in these improvisational settings.

Both remain stabilizing pillars on center stage left and right in this project as their own two domestic pilasters weekly mirrored the central spine of our Sunday Zoom sessions for more than a year, connecting their East Boston loft (right) to our North Garden observatory.

This stage manager observed them wandering through the distinct boundaries of two distinct self-reflected Paradisical Gardens, the straight/strait jackets of Parcel X reiterated a decade later in the tilt-slab Goodwin Memorial.

In the reflected light of these now two central characters who commenced as strangers, is now revealed and is invoked in a new sense of collaborative citizenship, a call and response relationship animated by improvisation.

Fire was a catalyst for Vitruvius as was Water, a catalytic memetic device in both Genesis and again in Noah's Great Flood.

Herein, this so-called stage manager guides us now in this ACT TWO by blowing on the still blazing embers of the Temple of the Vestal Virgins and is still refreshed again and again by the Fountains of Rome.

Here and Now Sofia and Patrick have recovered from these still blazing embers, reflective metallic shields, concrete planes and cartesian scrims, the counterparts to the Paradisical walls of Eden.

This second act reflects on the first sparks of a catalytic/kaleidoscopic appreciation of the insights of the next generation reviewed through their own genesis of haunting work.

ACT TWO:
WELCOME STRANGERS

WASTELAND SPOLIA (2023)
SOFIA KUSPAN

Wasteland Spolia is informed by the *connective tissues*[3] of past inquiries, travels, and curiosities about history, fragments, and piles of construction materials that have deteriorated, been neglected, and forgotten. This proposal is informed by the concept of spolia, the ancient practice of material recycling, as a foundation for a sustainable design and preservation method that emphasizes the fragment rather than the whole. Partially deconstructed structures remain in place as remnants and relics, as scattered building pieces can be reconstructed into walls, pathways, and sculptural piles. They form a distinct landscape filled with cultural artifacts rather than a singular building restored to its pristine beginnings. This method builds upon an existing discourse and practice that challenges the notion of erasing the complex histories of degraded "postindustrial" sites across the United States, which are often slated for demolition or prone to the remanufacturing of their perceived gritty image.[4] By advocating for a rigorous circular design method that seeks to embrace the reuse of spolia as integral to the site's evolving legacy, this proposal presents both a critique of and an alternative to the architect's tendency to design for a blank slate, leading to the practical and pedagogical inclination to ignore the context, history, and material realities of historic yet degraded sites.[5]

The project develops a design and preservation approach that can be adapted to specific site conditions across the post-industrial typology. *Wasteland Spolia* experiments with the Packard Plant, a dilapidated yet historically significant former manufacturing site located in Detroit, Michigan, to offer a process-based design method that seeks to *not obliterate the history of things*.[6] The site's current state exists in the cultural apparatus as a wasteland—a barren and neglected plot of land filled with building remnants that seem to deserve no more than a slated demolition order. Upon further introspection, the site is filled with a valuable material history that manifests itself as crumbling bricks, shards of glass, and concrete mushroom columns with exposed rebar. This material can be cataloged and evaluated, leading to its careful disassembly that then can be sorted, tested, designed, reconstructed, and exported into further acts of rebuilding. These acts of reassigning material value redirect the former plant's trajectory away from a state of decay and inevitable descent into erasure, and instead create a series of landscape and architectural interventions that produce tectonically rich moments in wall and ground assemblies. Their vitality embodies a design method informed by the present idiosyncratic site conditions that have arisen due to a lack of maintenance, leading to material degradation.

The Packard Plant is one of several former manufacturing sites that exemplify an American form of spolia: materials that are no longer defined by previous acts of large-scale construction that served as industrial repositories, but rather by their present form that blends into a landscape defined by degrading materials.[7] An integral event in the site's story is the takeover by ecological forces, present in the spontaneous vegetation emerging in the various ecological niches of the decaying structures' cracks and crevices. These novel plantings generate a synergy between the landscape and building debris that should continue to evolve. The Packard Plant and other historically significant postindustrial sites should be recognized and protected as cultural landscapes, offering ample opportunities for design interventions that reuse materials with positive cultural and ecological value that deserve a second chance. It is essential to build upon the existing narratives of these places through acts of both site and material reuse and preservation by embracing the site's spolia to evoke its cultural memory.

Wasteland Spolia (2023)

The project falls somewhere between the loose spatial explorations of David Ireland's artistic practice and the more solution-oriented goals of an architect. The Packard Plant is explored as an ongoing construction site, with visuals that layer the unique histories and realities of construction, deconstruction, and reconstruction. These acts unfold as a narrative directed by the enactment of spolia, which revives the wasteland and beyond.

The site planning and design strategies for the Packard Plant's future are influenced by both the contemporary practices of architectural material reuse, along with landscape projects that have transformed industrial wastelands into public parks. These precedents informed specific opportunities to enact positive change on the Packard Plant site. The outline includes space for artists to create and display their work, an area for visitors to reflect upon the site's trajectory, and a place of ecological respite for flora and fauna. The conceptual framework of the project outlines a vision for the former plant's overall transformation into a public park for the surrounding community, including the ecological need to remediate and rewild a majority of the site's footprint. The center point is reimagined as an activated courtyard defined by the largely intact remnants of the buildings' structural grid—a place for artists to experiment with the building remnants on-site to create site-specific installations. The existing building components are partially deconstructed and then reconstructed to enrich the complex historical narratives of production and decay, using an aesthetic language of juxtaposition and a structural assembly logic that encourages the reuse of available site materials. Since there is no longer a need for much of the overall building complex footprint, the components that are no longer relevant to the site's future trajectory can be repurposed as exports for reuse to construct relevant art, architecture, and landscape projects across the city.

The site was selected for experimentation with past encounters in mind. I first visited the Packard Plant in 2015 while exploring abandoned buildings in Detroit. The building complex was filled with shards of broken glass, rusty factory equipment past its prime, vibrant graffiti paintings, and spontaneous plant growth, all far away from the comfort of the places I knew that were planned, ordered, and cared for. There were piles of debris that were no longer needed or usable in their fragmented form. Some openings surfaced in the crumbling brick walls, suggesting battle scars that beckoned those with curiosity, taking in the trespassers of this once vibrant place of making. As I explored the stripped-away surfaces, I was careful not to disturb the uneven floors and debris and discovered a secret garden in the unexpected patches of flora that spread out across any claimable territory. These images and memories remained as a visceral ghost haunting me over the years. I remained disheartened by the Packard Plant's decrepit state, unconvinced by the discourse of lofty redevelopment goals.

Packard Automotive Plant, Detroit, MI (2015)

Marble lintels and reliefs at Basilica of Santa Maria in Trastevere, Rome (2018)

I became captivated by spolia after my initial encounter with the concept while studying in Rome. Spolia as an ancient practice took on several roles: as a display of acts of political conquest, reappropriation of past religious iconography, and in fulfilling construction needs as raw materials during material shortages. I learned that much of Rome has been continually reconstructed using spolia—in the columns, bricks, and architectural details from former sites that were partially deconstructed for new building projects. Spolia can be seen in the granite columns of Bramante's Tempietto, the reliefs on the Arch of Constantine, and the columns of St. Peter's Basilica. While sketching inside the Basilica of Santa Maria in Trastevere, I admired a colonnade reconstructed with an array of disparate columns. These columns featured repurposed capitals hauled away from the ruins of the Baths of Caracalla.[8] The church's facade was covered in marble lintels and reliefs from the once grandiose bathhouse, seemingly pasted onto the wall like a gallery of past triumphs and downfalls. I imagined how each pasted element represented a past life and thought about how history isn't so linear or strictly focused on the past. The endurance of these fragments throughout the eras contributed to my fascination with how a vast array of buildings throughout Rome resulted from continual evolution, reuse, and reconstruction. The mighty forces of spolia that constituted much of the city's fabric challenged the view that a building is one complete object, from its construction to its eventual demolition. Rather, the building's components reconstruct a narrative bound by deliberate change, which has led to an evolving use of fragmented materials and imagery.

Watercolor sketch of spoliated columns at Basilica of Santa Maria in Trastevere, Rome (2018)

Collage of ancient and contemporary Spolia (2023)

Four years later, while visiting Berlin, I encountered former industrial wasteland sites that had been transformed into public parks. I observed an urban fabric shaped by a contemporary spolia that is very recent when compared to Rome in the collective memory of a place, as Berlin was no stranger to significant rebuilding during the postwar era. I visited sites such as Natur-Park Südgelände and Mauerpark. These sites were populated with their own spolia—remnants of past industrial lives, piles of building materials, and the scars of former train tracks. Most of the spolia were left out to slowly deteriorate and return to the earth, forgetting the purposes they once served in the dignified act of forming a wall assembly. This informed my realization that the definition and purposes of spolia can be expanded to incorporate the scattered remnants across a site as a new form of preservation, one that doesn't require a strict readaptation to fulfill its original purposes.

Natur-Park Südgelände is a nature preserve that demonstrates how the Packard Plant could be reimagined. Once an active railyard, the area was abandoned after its closure in 1952 and succumbed to the forces of ecological succession. This generated a new life for the site—a place with rare flora and fauna that could seek refuge from the surrounding encroachment of urbanization. It has become a place for making and exhibiting art as well, which is also manifested in the Packard Plant's vibrant ad hoc display of graffiti art.

Spolia and wasteland merge a dialogue between the history of a material and of a site. Spolia is an artifact of material memory. It can be extrapolated from one deconstructed site and reused in multiple locations. On the other hand, wasteland is fixed and bound by the memory of a site. It is inherently tied to the industrial processes that have scarred the land. These formerly industrial wastelands offer an alternative view of nature by breaking down the conventional divide between humans and nature. The human scars are abundantly marked through architectural and infrastructural remnants, which arise as an alternative form of spolia. They tell the story of places that have been degraded by industrial capitalism. The final act appears to be one where humans do not control the narrative. It can be reclaimed to enact positive and transformational change for all future site occupants, including people, plants, and animals.

Industrial artifacts in Natur-Park Südgelände, Berlin (2022)

The story of the Packard Plant resembles the rise and fall of former empires that have historically produced spolia. Once the largest automobile factory in the United States, it embodied the ideals of prewar-era American manufacturing at the peak of industrial capitalism. Designed by American industrial architect Albert Kahn, the factory produced Packard Cars from 1903 to 1956. The design was notable for introducing steel-reinforced concrete, thus shaping the future of how factories were constructed. After the production of Packard automobiles ceased in 1956, the buildings began to slowly deteriorate. Piles of material began to form, scavengers hauled away material, and the site's conditions slowly degraded. Despite this state of decay, the site's function, use, and meaning were being transformed by the alternative activities of taggers, squatters, and urban explorers.

Although it became a haven for urban explorers, it has also come to represent blight and disarray to the current community, which describes the site as unsafe and as an eyesore. There is a tension between how various groups view the site's image and future. In April of 2022, a local court ordered the demolition of the Packard auto plant, citing that it had become a public nuisance. The city claims that it will not demolish a portion of the site; instead, it will be marketed for redevelopment. In May of 2024, the city along with Detroit Economic Growth Corp. issued an open request for proposals for the future redevelopment of the site, hoping to find a developer who will preserve and reuse the plant, citing its meaningful history.

Considering the plant's history of production turned to decay, *Wasteland Spolia* proposes an alternative path, one that prioritizes design-by-reuse and preservation, rather than accepting that such a historically significant site will become mostly demolished or redeveloped into something disingenuous to the site's complex historical narratives. I advocate for a design approach where found material becomes reused on-site as needed, with any excess material being exported for community-based rebuilding projects. This transformation represents an opportunity for reclaimed beauty and value for the city, its occupants, and future visitors to the site.

The Packard Plant was once the largest factory in the world.
Its concrete is still intact, even 100 years later.
It is strong, yet fragile.
It is old, but it is also ready for reinvention.
As time chipped away, breakage occurred.
Standardization was always a fantasy.
There is beauty to be rediscovered in this strange and disarrayed landscape.

Material remnants indicate a rich history.
The materials can never be what they once were.
They break apart and crumble, moving away from old wholes into new pieces.
These must be preserved to remember the history of manufacturing.
Production has an afterlife, one that is scattered, and misaligned.
It crumbles away and slowly returns to the earth.
Can we intercept one last moment before it slips out of our control?
The canvas already exists.
We can remake the world with the leftovers of our past production.

Packard Automotive Plant, Detroit, MI (2015)

DETAIL OF END
SECTION
SASH
HEAD & CORNICE
NOTE
SCALE FOR
DETAIL OF
CESSPOOL
END ELEVATION
PLAN
SEP-20-1915

CATALOG the found materials, spolia, and site conditions.

DISASSEMBLE the existing structures as a careful alternative to demolition that allows for the spolia to be preserved or reused.

TEST and **EVALUATE** the strength, capacity, function, use, and appearance of assemblies through drawings, collages, and physical mock-ups.

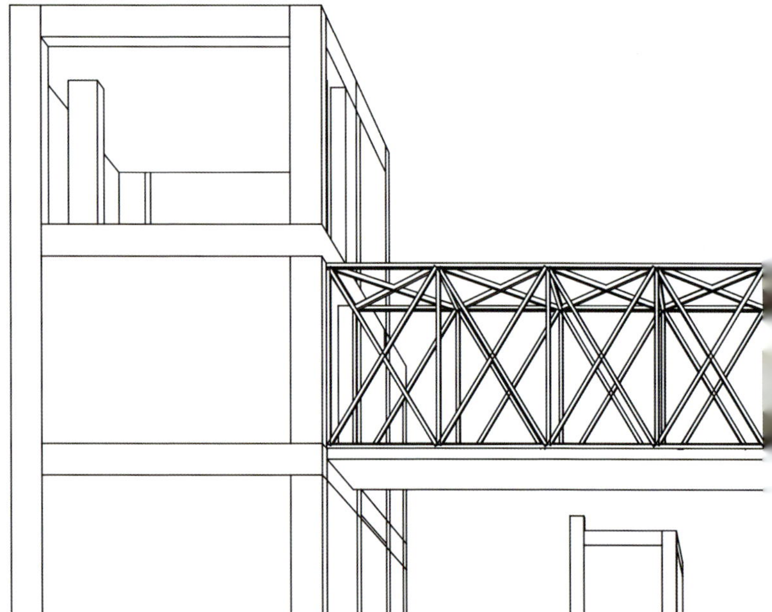

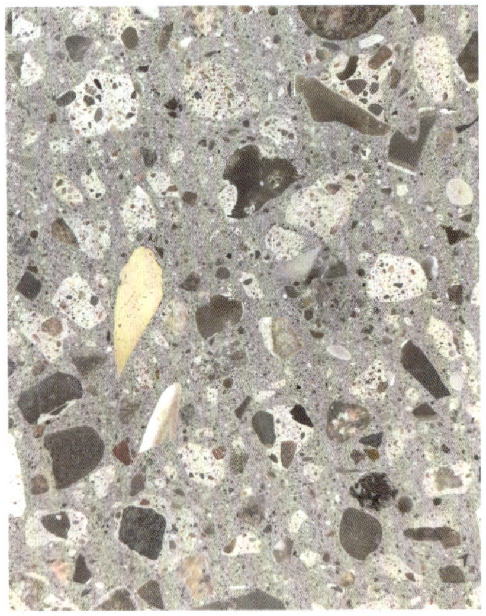

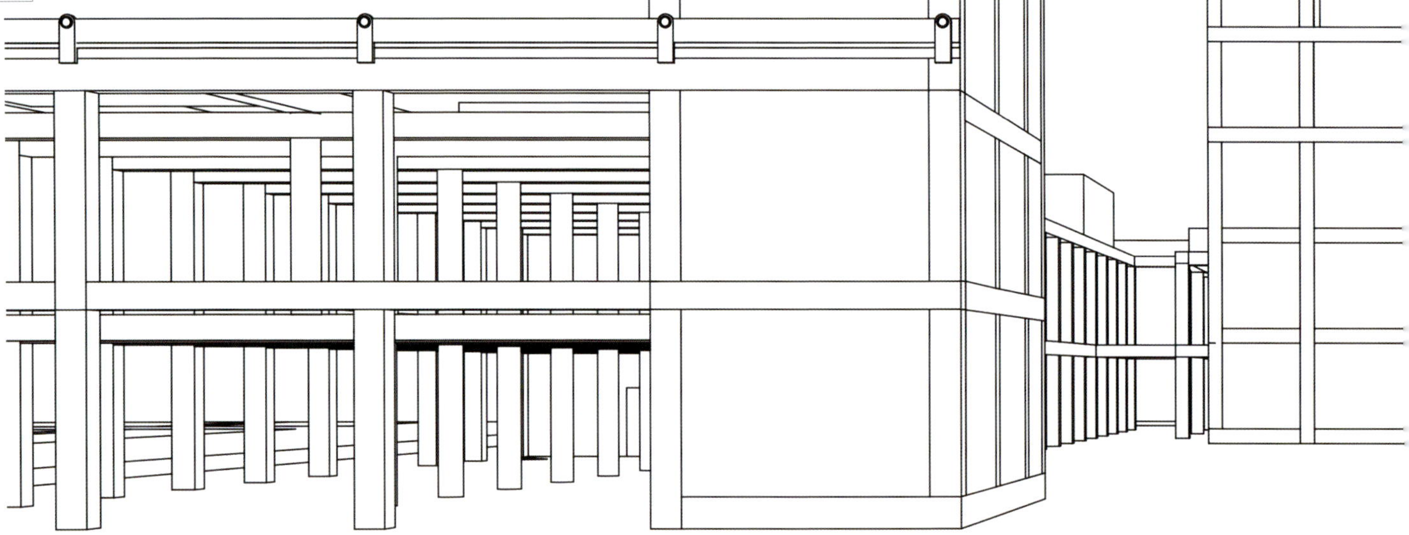

RECONSTRUCT with the site's spolia to make new structures and assemblies.

DESIGN with the catalog, sketches, and testing results in mind, using dump, disperse, rebuild, and revitalize as methods of material reuse.

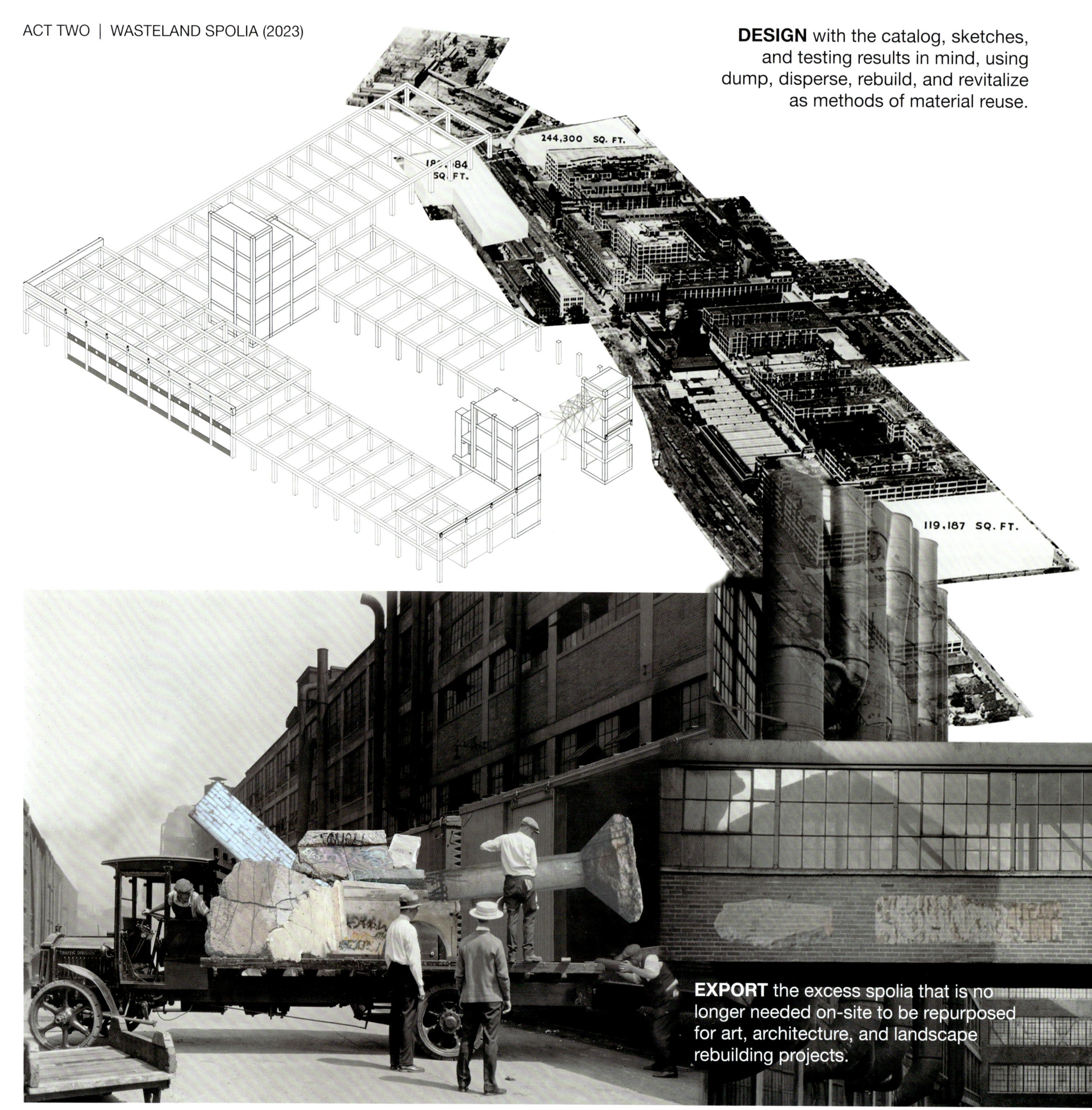

EXPORT the excess spolia that is no longer needed on-site to be repurposed for art, architecture, and landscape rebuilding projects.

SORT all spolia according to size, performance, and type.

POSTHUMAN ARCHITECTURES (2023)
PATRICK SARDO

Posthuman Architectures is a speculative and critical project working in a specific interpretation of posthumanism, where production, efficiency, and consumerism are prioritized over human life in the architectural design of a structure. Buildings for nonhumans emerge as a reification of current values: technological advancement, efficiency, and increase in shareholder value. The following four building typologies are the present and imminent future of architectural design guided not by the desires of human occupants, but by capitalist desires for expansion, efficiency, and profit. Future economic, political, technological, and environmental conditions will force architects and designers to reconsider best practices, building codes, and existing design constraints. Buildings will be vastly larger, denser, and more efficient while operating under unique internal climatic conditions to increase production. The location of these buildings will be driven by access to natural resources, energy availability, existing and new logistics networks, and changing population data. Each building typology has unique requirements and constraints, but all of them may eventually operate without humans to further augment a posthuman society.

Currently, humans design, create, and train complex machines[9] to manage processes and complete tasks for us, but these digital minds must have a physical presence, housed in a human-designed building. Eventually, the intelligent machines of the future will become the surveyors, designers, and constructors of supermassive structures that serve human and machine. Fulfillment centers will automatically and rapidly deliver goods, automated greenhouses will provide consistent food sources, semiconductor chip fabs will develop and build the brains of the complex machines inside computers, and data centers will store humans' digital footprints and house the minds of the complex machines on delicate silicon.

The project intentionally avoids ideas of posthumanism that decenter humans and focus on other living organisms like plants and animals, as our society is ultimately more focused on developing synthetic life through digital means. Instead, the project views humans as unimportant to the function of certain building typologies while they exist to serve humans and provide us with goods and services. The role of humans is a central idea in the philosophy behind this project, whether we view ourselves as rulers of the world because of the tools we've created, or as merely a small part of the vast world. Buildings without humans in this example are a contradiction, as the four typologies explicitly serve humans while excluding them from the processes of production, maintenance, and distribution.

Posthuman Architectures is not an Edenic or dystopic reading of the possible future but instead is interested in highlighting the bizarre potential realities of a near future. An optimistic perspective might hope that future technologies enable a post-work society for humans while advanced robotics perform the tasks we previously did. However, the more pessimistic viewpoint seems to be more likely, where a select few corporations and people control the highly automated systems of production and use them to exert control over the rest of humanity.

As we approach the post-Anthropocene, "a new age of nonhuman actors where it is technology and artificial intelligence that now compute, condition, and construct our world,"[10] we must also consider what will happen to all these new posthuman buildings in the future. The steel and concrete might be melted down and crushed to bits or they could be left to decay and be reclaimed by ecological forces. Will the robotic occupants go to sleep forever or make an attempt at self-preservation? Future anthropologists might study these posthuman buildings and never truly understand what their function was. If our digital footprint disappeared overnight, the physical buildings that enabled every aspect of our globalized world would be the only surviving remnants, decaying into chunks of spolia, concrete, and rusted steel.

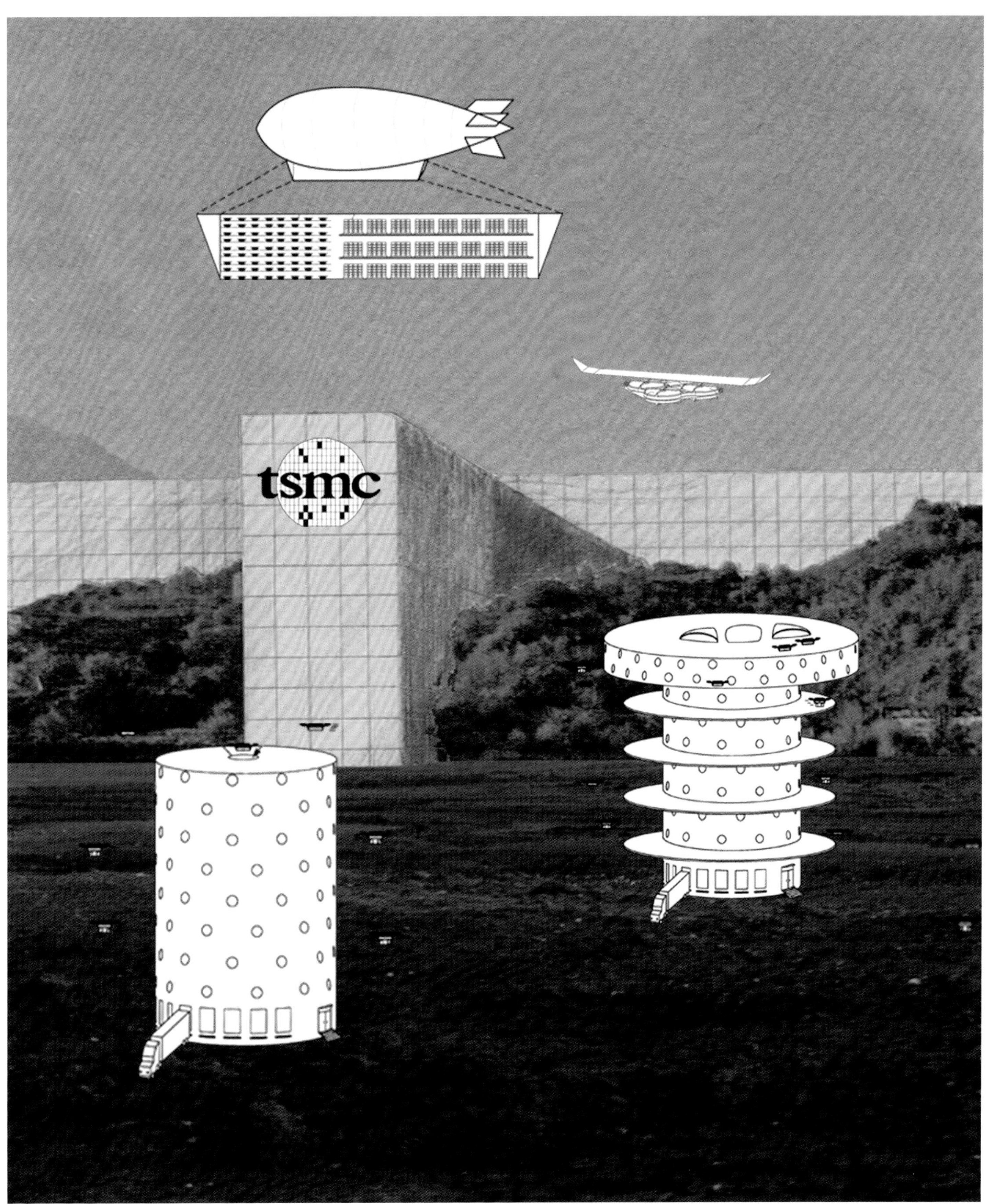

Posthuman Architectures: Buildings without Humans (2023)

AUTOMATED FULFILLMENT CENTER

The Automated Fulfillment Center is a vital component of our globalized, consumerist society that must adapt to changing needs, growing populations, and new technology. Human laborers will soon be fully replaced by intelligent machines for safety, efficiency, and cost reasons. Currently, humans and robots work together, separated by fences to limit injury. Robots perform the most menial and intensive tasks, while humans perform the most complex and challenging tasks. In the most advanced facilities, storage is no longer static racks of goods, as they are picked up and moved as drive robots bring them to workers when an order is placed. Racking is arranged according to demand, creating gradients of desire driven by efficiency. Soon, the tasks previously performed by humans will be fully automated, allowing for drastic changes to building scale, layout, and density.

The proposed fulfillment center is driven by the grid. The building grows as regional demand for goods increases. A 50' column grid informs interior layout and allows for future development of more modules to be added, increasing capacity and introducing newer technologies.[11] Automated racking systems and delivery drone stations may be added onto the sides or top of the existing structure to optimize the buildings' operations based on logistics and business algorithms. The proposed fulfillment center territorializes the landscape using physical and digital logistics networks to connect people and goods. While the singular fulfillment center grows as local demand increases, the larger network of delivery centers and air freight hubs will also grow to support domestic and international demand for goods.

On the ground floor, inbound and outbound processes bring goods in to be stowed, and when orders are placed, the goods are brought down from the upper floors to be packed and shipped. A maze of conveyance systems, robotic drive units, and robot arms operate towards the goal of peak efficiency in bringing in goods and sending them out. On the upper floors of the fulfillment center, the entire floorplate is occupied by robotic drive units which pick up pods filled with goods to be picked and sent down to packing. The floor layout is constantly buzzing around and changing, determined by item demand and purchasing frequency.[12] In areas where growing horizontally isn't an option, the building can grow vertically. The typical multistory fulfillment center is about 100 feet tall but could become much taller, with more storage space, to act as a regional distribution center. Without humans, clear heights can also be lowered for increased density and floorplates can be interrupted more often for easier vertical movement of goods.

The prototypical designs of each multinational corporation will continue to appear in the exurban outskirts of cities, but also in both highly urban and remote areas.[13] New facilities will be built as phased construction as demand grows and changes across the country, but when construction is finished on each new section, humans will never step foot inside the buildings again. No one will witness the machines moving through the highly efficient and complex logistics system in pitch-black darkness, guided by radar or other non-visible light spectrum sensors. As long as we continue to purchase goods online, there will be a need for the advancement and proliferation of highly advanced logistics and the construction of more warehouses.

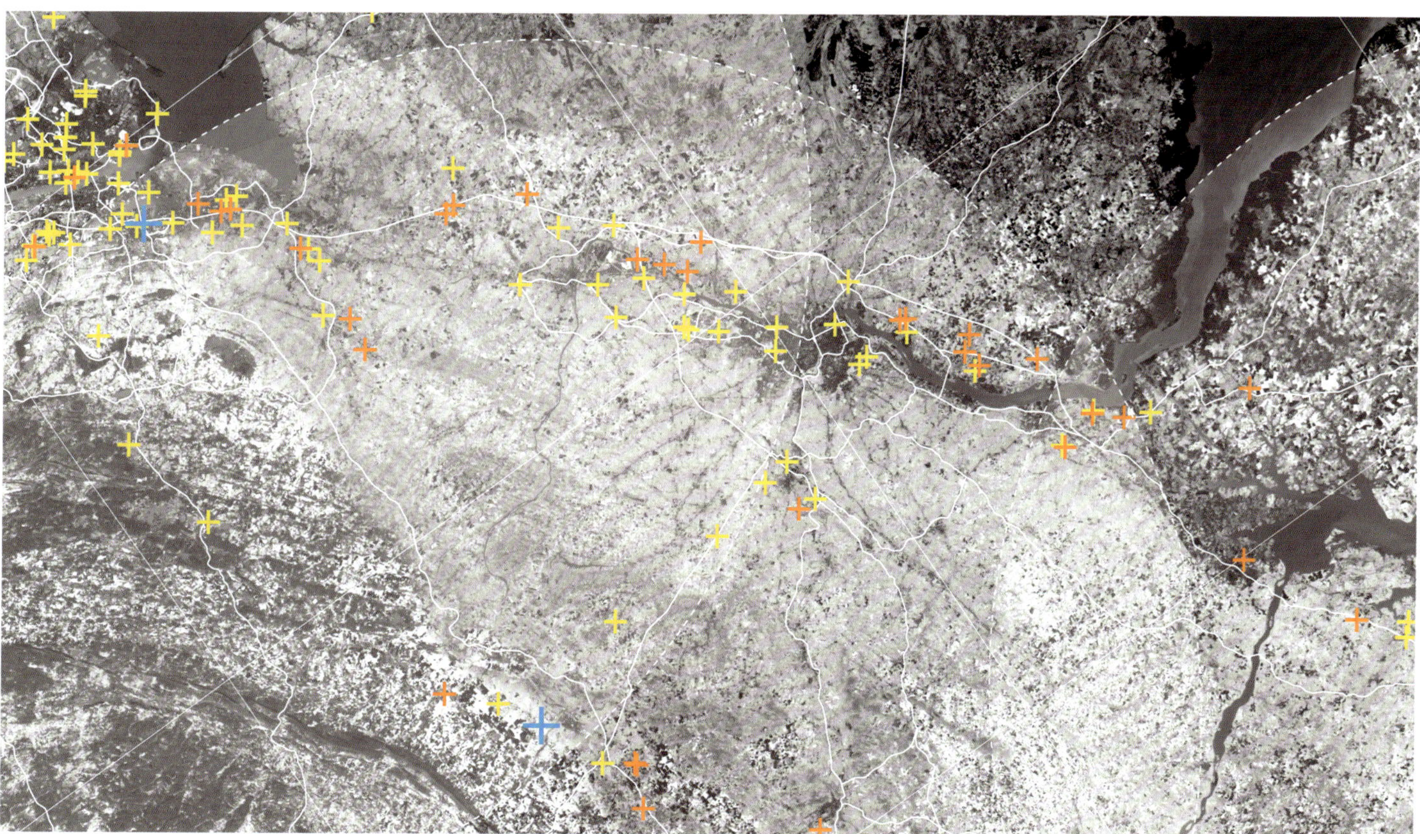

Fulfillment Center animation still and regional logistics plan (2023)

DATA CENTER

The Data Center is the only physical manifestation of the Internet and the vast "clouds" of data. But while a few select employees roam the data halls, billions of people are digitally connected to the buildings' humming server racks. The Internet is not a shapeless digital thing; it has a physicality in dense server racks housed in beige, faceless buildings. Without the digital networks we have built up over the last 70 years, the world as we know it will cease to exist. The unseen cloud continues to grow rapidly, demanding more physical space as we continue to fill hard drives and servers with emails, videos, photos, and streams of text. Advancements in digital minds and intelligent machines will only demand more bandwidth, more servers, and more data centers.

The proposed data center is a continuous physical and digital network. Such massive demand for digital storage and interconnectivity will drive companies to increase their footprint and move to new areas around the world, chasing increased access to water, cheap electricity, and more customers. The data center is an unbroken grid of servers moving across the landscape both above and below ground. The previously unseen digital infrastructure network will demand more visibility in the built environment as internet use and demand continue to grow exponentially in between and within our cities, suburbs, and rural areas.

The infrastructure scale project of constructing a continuous underground building is only matched by the massive scale of the digital world we have created for ourselves. Artificial intelligence, satellite surveillance tools, and ground-penetrating radar define the path the building follows to avoid obstacles above and below ground and optimize the layout of the overall structure based on the water and energy network nearby. The structures are built below ground for increased cooling efficiency but would occasionally emerge from the ground as a monolithic reminder of the immense infrastructure needed to sustain our modern world. Vast solar arrays providing energy for cooling follow the building adjacent to the heat exchangers that dot the landscape above the building. Raised flooring and drop ceilings allow for cooling water and power infrastructure to run above and below the server racks that are maintained and expanded by small robots.[14] The few human employees that once serviced data centers will no longer be necessary as intelligent machines roam the data halls 24 hours a day, swapping in new hard drives and installing new servers.

New data centers are being constructed to keep up with exponential growth in computing and storage demand in every part of the world, but there is a constant uproar from those who live and work nearby. The already skyrocketing energy use will only continue to grow, straining the energy grid and delaying the necessary change to renewable energy.[15] The cloud network of websites, data storage, and artificial intelligence will transform itself into a physical network of structures connecting us all without allowing us inside. We will continue to become alienated from the production, storage, and transmission of our data until our digital world becomes so vast that we must face the physical ramifications of its exponential growth.

Data Center perspective collage and site plan (2023)

AUTONOMOUS GREENHOUSE

The Autonomous Greenhouse could save our civilization from collapse if the delicate agricultural ecosystems were to fail due to climate change. Vertical farming techniques are still in their infancy, but research and development into different techniques of growing food could help alleviate scarcity issues and replace traditional agricultural methods. Farming at these scales is becoming more automated and influenced by artificial intelligence but could continue to scale up to match current production levels or more. If typical farming practices are threatened by rising temperatures, changing rainfall patterns, or soil degradation, thousands of massive greenhouses might be necessary for humanity's survival.

Thomas Jefferson's desire to create a nation of "yeoman farmers"[16] led to the establishment of the Public Land Survey System. American industrial farming practices are shaped by Jefferson's Cartesian grid. One-mile square sections can be split into smaller plots for individual farmers and their families. If climate patterns drastically change and current farming practices are no longer viable, major corporations may purchase entire one-mile sections that can no longer support traditional farming techniques and build massive interconnected agricultural production and logistics centers.

The proposed autonomous greenhouse operates under highly regulated conditions for temperature, humidity, light, and air composition. A perfect interior environment helps eliminate many of the variables that may threaten crop yields in traditional agricultural practices. This type of highly controlled food production may be enhanced by extremely precise and powerful machine learning and automation technologies. Intelligent machines control the crop management systems for each greenhouse, monitoring each with sensors and cameras to ensure the crop yields are near perfect. Plants can be watered and lit with grow lights individually based on need rather than larger scale irrigation techniques of the past. Pests and other contaminants from air, water, and humans are filtered out before they can touch the plants inside. The typical footprint of the greenhouse is split in half, with the smaller middle portion used for shipping and planting bays on each side. Some will be flat, single-story buildings while others may be tall, multistory facilities depending on the type of crop grown inside.

The Autonomous Greenhouse is not just a singular building, but a large-scale agricultural network that shares resources between buildings growing different crops. It may be one of the few solutions to ensure a consistent food supply for humans when climate change affects the current agricultural systems. Humanity may need to hand over control of agricultural production to limit unwanted contaminants and inefficiencies that come with human workers and human-designed systems and structures. Humans may oversee the operations more broadly, but algorithm-driven machines would control all aspects of actual production, where fast-moving roof-mounted robotic arms swing between bays of plants, meticulously monitoring and cultivating food that they can't consume. Humankind's discovery of organized agriculture practices facilitated our civilization's rapid growth and development, yet the fragility of our massive, interconnected world demands more regulation and control than the traditional practices that have sustained us for thousands of years.

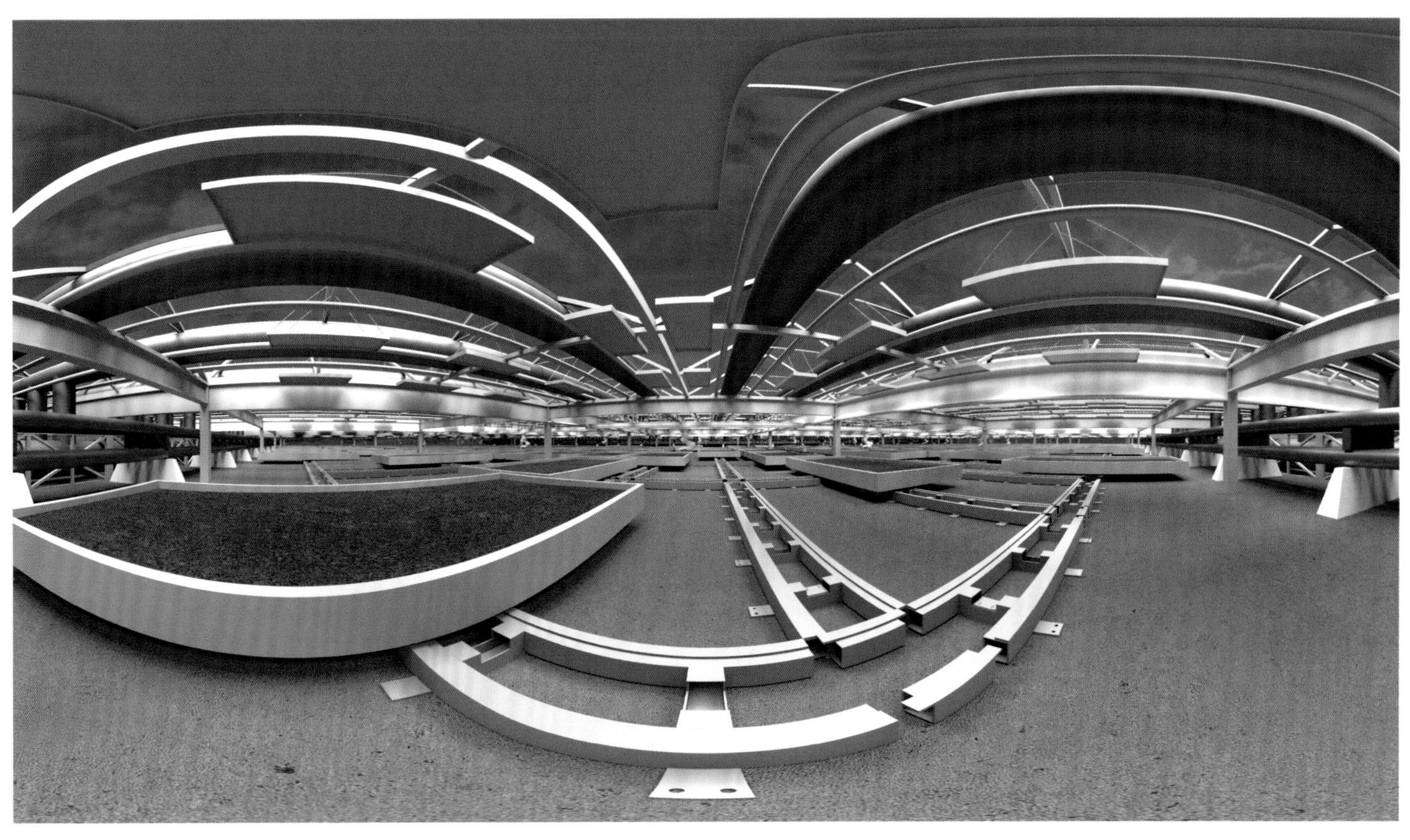

Autonomous Greenhouse robotic 3D camera screen-capture and aerial collage (2023)

SEMICONDUCTOR CHIP FAB

The Semiconductor Chip Fab is the most complex and bizarre of the four typologies. These buildings are dense, multilayered structures filled with precise machinery used to engrave and lithograph tiny silicon computer chips with billions of transistors. Rather than a single building, fabs are massive complexes with dozens of structures covered in extensive piping, ductwork, and interconnecting pathways. The purest air and water flow between each piece of the complex to aid the process of building a digital mind out of silica and metal. The ultraclean interior environment and highly efficient design makes the semiconductor chip fab an example of what a hypermodern building could be, as imagined by modernist architects 100 years ago.[17]

A complex series of logistical processes is required to make semiconductor chips. Silica quartz is mined, refined, and then cast into large ingots to be sliced into thin wafers that are sent to fabs to be engraved, lithographed, and cut down before being installed into phones, cars, computers, or manufacturing robotics. This logistics network could be either a large international operation or increasingly localized as political and economic factors increasingly impact the industry. Currently, many chip fabs and important parts of the logistics network are in regions of the world that often experience political instability, so many leading nations are looking to localize chip manufacturing for national and economic security purposes.[18] If the supply chain of material and manufacturing falls apart, the limited supply of microchips would cripple our digital world.

Semiconductor chip fabs are filled with complex mechanical systems to support the processes of chipmaking and maintain a clean environment. The highly regulated interior environment requires ultraclean air and ultrapure water for all the manufacturing processes, attended by human workers in bunny suits. The cleanrooms of semiconductor fabs are filled with lithography and engraving machines, tracks for moving wafers and chips, and a maze of pipes and ducts to move water, air, and chemicals needed for manufacturing. Each section of the fab is connected by overhead tracks for small pods that carry bundles of chip wafers around and between buildings. As new generations of chips are developed, new proprietary facilities and machines are needed to build them. Old portions of the fab might be gutted and renovated, or new structures added on and connected to the existing infrastructure.

The proposed semiconductor chip fab of the future is a constantly growing series of structures connected by the vast infrastructure of water, air, chemicals, and robots. Humans supervise the operations remotely, as the interior environment would be inhospitable for human occupancy. The main source of contamination to the delicate wafers and chips is humans themselves, and without them, some parts of fabs may operate under a vacuum to prevent contamination from any airborne contaminants. The hyper-digital world of the future will only continue to demand more chips to power artificial minds and intelligent machines as they become more powerful and more prevalent in society. These highly intelligent machines might learn how to make new forms of chip technology on their own, replicating themselves and evolving over time. Like the constantly growing buildings, machines powered by microchips will learn easier and more efficient ways to make more powerful chips, thus creating a cycle of exponential technological development.

Semiconductor Chip Fab exterior and interior collages (2023)

Posthuman construction non-sites are vacant, terrain vague, metered by the pervasive slab and the logic of The Engineer's Aesthetic,[19] structural trusses off the shelf. There is no need for the light of day nor surrogate luminous resources by night.

Peter Waldman

Posthuman buildings are infrastructure temporarily posing as architecture until the moment that all humans can be removed from the premises. From then on, intelligent, sensor-driven machines are the new subject and focus of the architecture.

Patrick Sardo

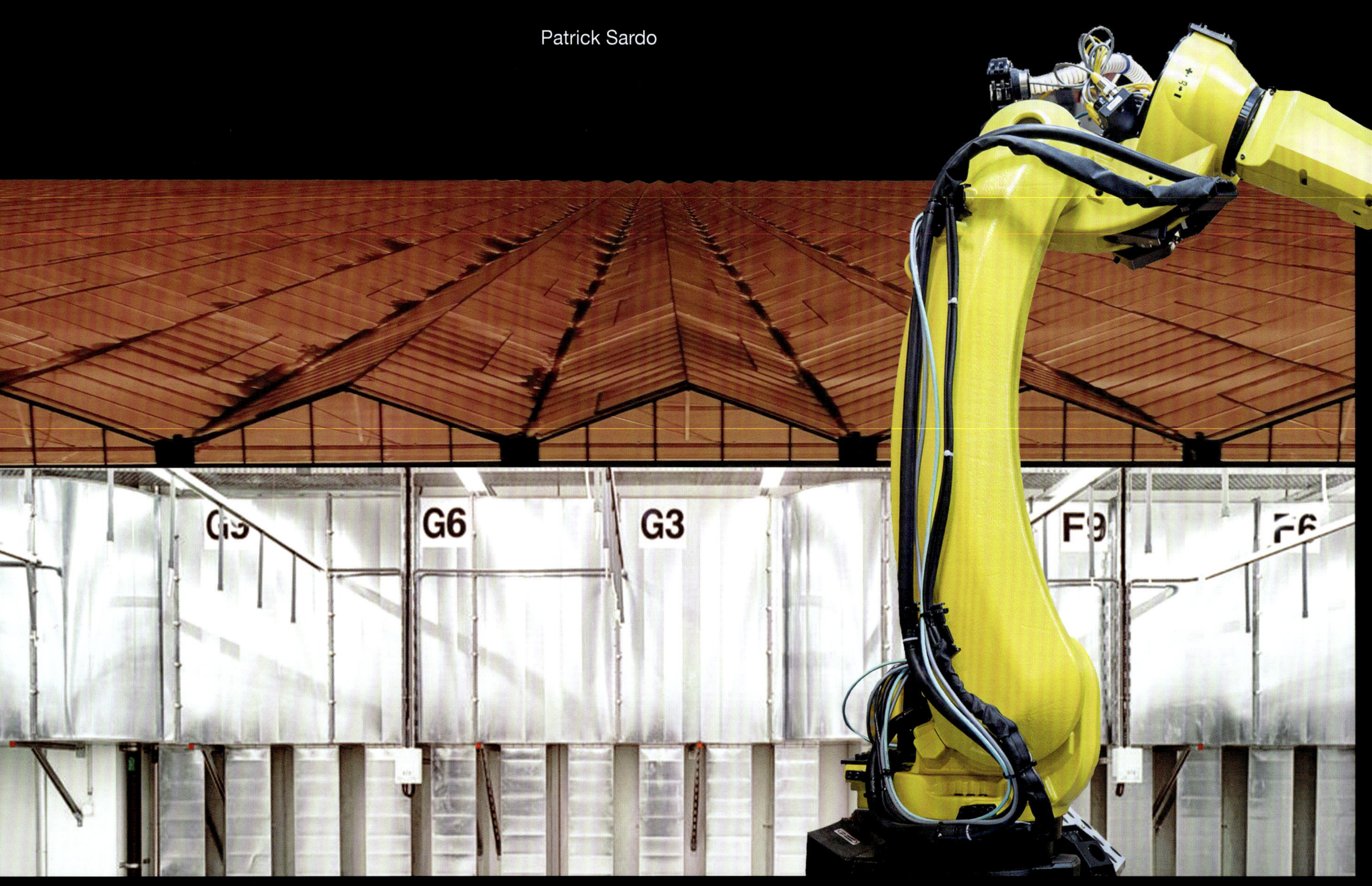

FANUC Robot
M-20iD25
LEONI

The issue of nonhuman architecture as predetermined by off-the-shelf products, systems within systems of the industrial, and engineering evidenced-based design as BIM was an economic decision by *inventories in cahoots with ethics*.

Peter Waldman

CAUTION

DAVID IRELAND'S HOUSE AS MUSEUM
GHOSTS AND ECHOES OF THE ABOVE

David Ireland's house at 500 Capp Street in the Mission District of San Francisco was the site he dwelled in, revealing both the spolia of the past and the immensity of domestic multitudes, of vast schools of sardine cans, painted blue to put them at ease, of an Armada of abandoned brooms left behind by the previous hoarder owner, bound together and placed by a south-facing bay window he entitled "Brooms with a View", now part of the MoMA permanent collection on loan to the house when I toured July 15th, 2023, a month after the solstice. Ireland's work and workplace are inseparable, as mirrors for the moon with golden reflections all day long and where welding/blow torches are ignited as suspended chandeliers at night.

We entered the museum not by the Front Door but through a side street door to the former Tuba Repair shop, a gold leaf sign still retained on the front window next to the Front Door.

This room was dark, dominated by a fireplace littered with what seemed construction debris, but soon the ancient ochre of plaster yielded a golden-toned halo due to a lacquer sheen. As we moved through the house, we noticed the cracks in the plaster, as Gordon Matta Clark's saw-cut transformations, results of several severe earthquakes since constructed in 1892.

Ireland, from Bainbridge Island, Washington, and a long-term leader of African safaris and great game hunter, had an obsession with long horned Antelope skulls, which stare down on the many guests of his long refectory table in the dining room as well as to bear witness to the everyday endurance of wildlife.

I left this amazing, "amusing" house as museum realizing it was full of Spolia, as John Soane's House and that of its contemporary Jefferson's Monticello, who also authored the vast construction site of the Academical Village, intentionally framing his Immense Continental Imagination witnessed by Lewis and Clark and realized by the Louisiana Purchase of Thomas Jefferson as the third US President, all of which brings me back to Sofia and Patrick's theses and the potential power of this *Five Finger Exercise*.

Peter Waldman

500 Capp Street—David Ireland House (2024)

On July 15th, 2023, I arrived out of anxiety an hour early at the corner of Capp and 20th Street in the Mission District of San Francisco for a 2 p.m. guided tour of what was to be David Ireland's house as museum. I arrived at the front door on Capp Street just to confirm the appointment as it appeared locked and closed, and was eventually reprimanded to come back at 2 p.m. and use the side door on 20th facing Alioto Mini Park. I knew little of David Ireland, except for the Marin Peninsula Headlands Restroom Installation, which was amusing indeed, and very little of the conceptual art movement emerging from the SFAI, the San Francisco Art Institute, except it was housed in the Bernard Maybeck masterpiece.

The front of the 1890s Victorian two-story house, with a to-be-revealed secret basement grotto cum quarry, was facing west on Capp and North on 20th clearly and urban flank, and had been built as the home and repair shop of an Accordion Specialist whose golden-lettered sign remained as an instrumental echo/agency of two hands and ten digits. It made me smile to recall simultaneously the two flanking colonnades of the Academical Village and my early Princeton provocation to my students that even modern abstraction demands the specification of at least 10 centimeters of gold leaf to make magic, especially in the 20th century.

Peter Waldman

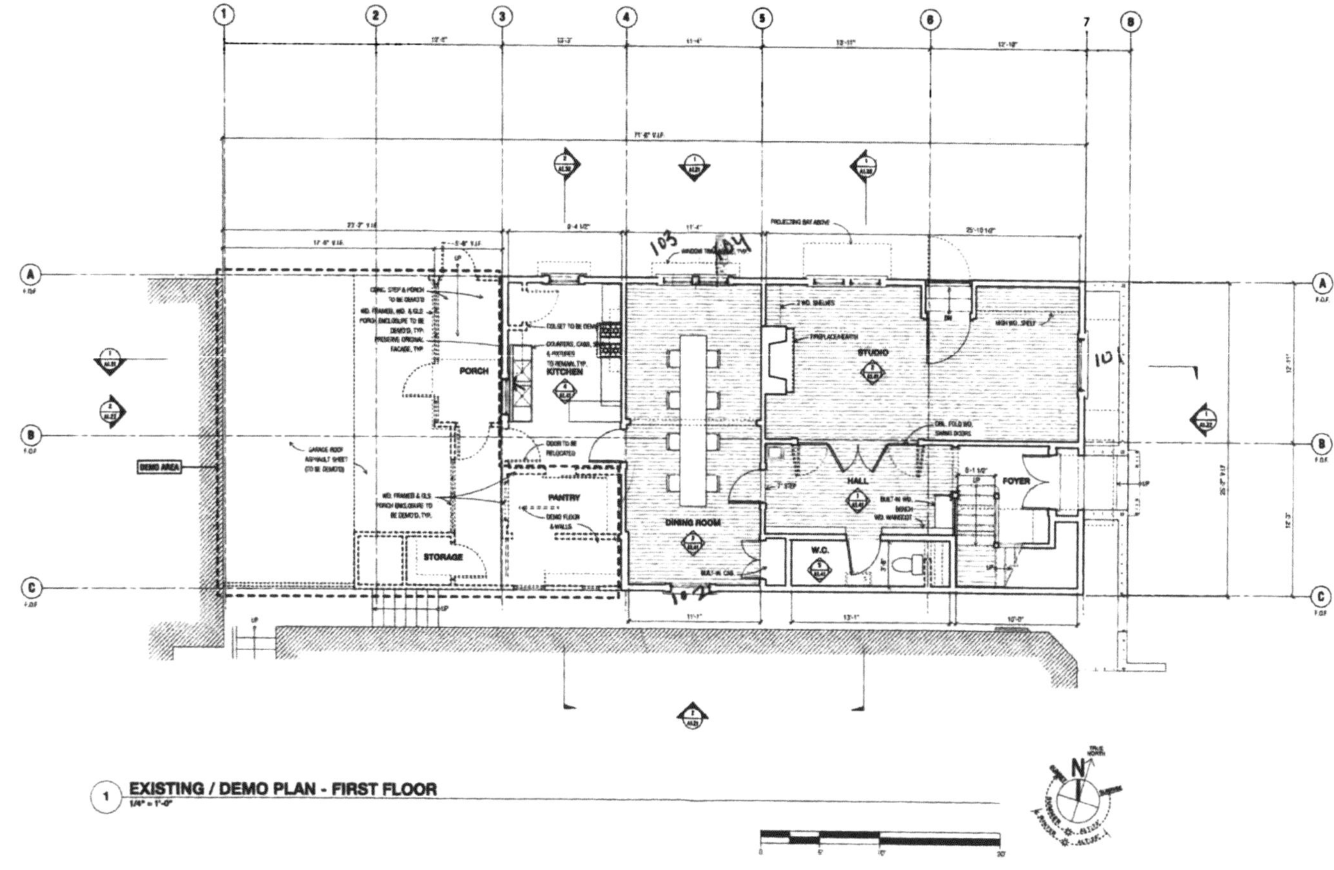

First Floor Plan, 500 Capp Street—David Ireland House (2016)

On May 17th, 2023, after taking a sharp turn off the state road onto an unpaved gravel path, we drove slowly into a seemingly pristine Arcadian landscape, framed by greenery-draped mountains, where turkeys, deer, and bears roam freely, snakes bask in the sun, and birds sing sweet melodies. Traveling down the dusty road, the Parcel X Encampment emerges from the trees, serving as a curious beacon to the wide array of characters who have visited over the past 30 years. The steep driveway is framed by rocky outcroppings and the vast forest, opening up to reveal the expansive steel-framed windows on the western facade and a modest front door. Dappled light shone through the dense late-spring tree canopy onto the weathered copper, steel, and concrete, dancing across the facade. Peter and Nancy's greeting welcomed us into the dark yet warm kitchen, where one side was lined with open shelves of dishware illuminated by a row of bare lightbulbs, and the other featured a curved concrete block wall interrupted by a simple double-hung residential window at its apex.

Although the visit initially intended to provide guidance on watering houseplants during their several-week absence, it evolved into an informal tour of the house, featuring sparse stories about architectural details, gilded-framed drawings, and eclectic furniture. Each object and design decision had a detailed story behind it, usually with friends, colleagues, and collaborators referenced. A theme that emerges in Waldman's work is humble collaboration, where every collaborator is credited and even the short version of the story must acknowledge them. To see Parcel X is to witness decades of history, dozens of collaborators, and the common themes that form connective tissues between people and projects alike.

During our following visits to Parcel X on May 24th and 25th, we documented the approaching summer light through our eyes and lenses, armed with several cameras. This exercise would serve as the second catalyst for this project, following Ben Small's 2021 photography, and would introduce two new characters to the play in the making.

Sofia Kuspan and Patrick Sardo

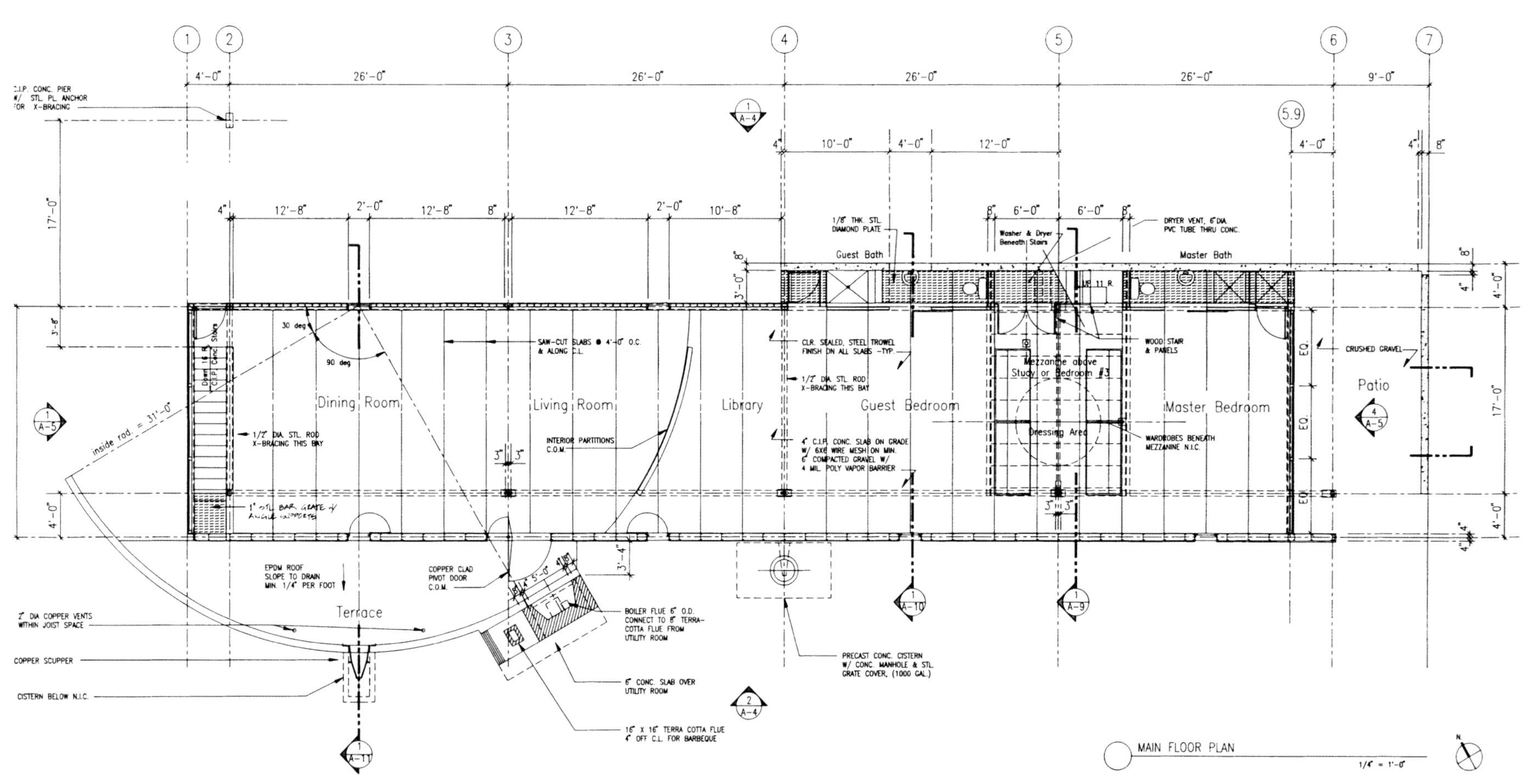

Main Floor Plan, Parcel X (1994)

SPACES FOR MAKING, TEACHING, EATING, LIVING

500 Capp Street and Parcel X serve as homes, living studios, and places of education. David taught courses at several Bay Area universities and brought students and his peers to the house to share his unique way of seeing art, architecture, and labor. Peter invites students, professors, visiting faculty, critics, artists, and welcome strangers to Parcel X in North Garden, where he shares homemade meals and the detailed stories behind each artifact, sculpture, and painting on display. These characters have all entered the encampment by passing through the low kitchen and up the concrete stairs, adjacent to large expansive windows offering a glimpse into the surrounding woodlands. The welcoming scene unfolds in the dimly lit industrial box, revealing a tall, open dining area with a black monolithic table set with wine glasses reflecting glowing candles and neatly arranged cutlery. The table is a permanent fixture in the encampment, having hosted generations of visitors from its first gathering to the present day. Parcel X and the Goodwin Memorial are joined in the company of 500 Capp Street, providing meeting places oriented around a table as a stage set within itself, guided by their respective stage managers to reveal ongoing spatial scripts.

The Eric Goodwin Memorial Pavilion on the North Porch of the University of Virginia School of Architecture has served as a memorial, teaching tool, and meeting space for the past 20 years. A wood-slat table built into the pipe framing of the east-facing concrete panel gives faculty, students, and strangers a place to meet, share meals, and learn from one another. The project originated from a design-build studio led by Peter, where classmates of the deceased student collaborated to construct a pavilion celebrating his life and curiosities. Situated next to Campbell Hall's North Porch, the pavilion embodies an architecture of generosity and generational resilience, serving as both a theater for civic engagement where Citizens and Strangers gather, and a commitment to the memory of an exceptional student. It is an ongoing construction site that reflects its past site context, its present state as a gathering space, and a future defined by processes of weathering.

Dining Room, Parcel X (2023)

Meeting Table, Eric Goodwin Memorial (2024)

The dining room of 500 Capp Street hosted countless meetings of friends, strangers, and students during and after David's life in the house. As he transformed his house and exhibited work around the Bay Area, David made connections with other artists, students, and patrons who would inform, learn from, and support David's work. He was part of a tight-knit group of newly emerging Bay Area artists who often shared materials and opportunities as they supported and influenced each other's projects. This group, along with David, taught art courses at local universities as they used 500 Capp Street as a classroom, office, dining space, and an example of what an alternative art practice could be. David was a social animal and enjoyed having guests over for meals and tea at the rough wood table surrounded by his curated artifacts.[20] Under David's ownership, one of the first gatherings at 500 Capp Street celebrated the 95th birthday of the former owner, commemorated by a photograph and a sealed jar containing a remnant of the birthday cake, an artifact of human action.[21] David viewed the house as more than a living space; it was a place to unveil the history of others and create his own mythology, encompassing his past, present, and future as an artist and individual. Through Greub, Gordon, and Ireland, he preserved and altered the history of the Victorian home.

A simple double-hung window casts a warm glow on Parcel X's kitchen table inside the dark cave, evoking the *chiaroscuro* of a Caravaggio painting. The small dining table in the lower-level kitchen provides a more intimate space away from the main floor's vast open floor plan, one that is reminiscent of a dining area a visitor may find at home. Sofia and Patrick shared a meal at this humble table with Peter and Nancy as they discussed this intergenerational collaboration.

Over the decades, thousands of people have sat at the four tables to share food, stories, and knowledge back and forth between generations of artists and architects, students and teachers, friends and strangers. Collaboration and the inclusion of references are essential drivers in Peter's pedagogy. The sourcebook continues to grow with each conversation, and each one yet to come. Gathering around a common table, whether lit by the sun, fire, or even swinging blue blowtorches, is an ancient ritual that continues to be practiced today, enhanced by the creation of intentional and materially fruitful spaces.

Sofia Kuspan and Patrick Sardo

Dining Room Table, 500 Capp Street (2023)

Kitchen Table, Parcel X (2023)

ARTIFACTS OF BYGONE ERAS

Parcel X and 500 Capp Street are both filled with objects, fragments, and artworks that reflect the values and experiences of David and Peter's lives. Each home is a vessel filled with a collection of memories that shape each space through the positioning of artifacts.

Two blowtorches loosely suspended by wire greet visitors on their way in. An old chair settles into its new role as spolia on the entry wall, providing a seat for the fallen dust. The wall corners extend into jagged edges seemingly bitten off by time, surrounded by jars of forgotten debris and leftover rubber bands. The surfaces bear battle scars, dripping off a perfect candle-holder containing no flames. The cracks are exposed in the glossy walls as they reflect a brighter day outside. Mounds of concrete fit into crevices, holding up books and past stories never told. Animal skulls adorn the dining area. Wires and cracks are seen throughout, revealing something incomplete that can never be what it once was. This assemblage of artifacts reveals the value that David found in the mundane and often overlooked everyday objects. He reimagines their display with both an appreciation for their humbleness and a sense of humor in doing the unexpected.

David's work was aligned with other contemporary artists from the Fluxus and Italian Arte Povera movements,[22] who emphasized the artistic process as performance and explored the connection between everyday objects and materials and the act of making. He believed that the process of creating his artwork was equally, if not more, important than the final piece itself, as he sought to embrace objects that held the traces of history, the presence of others, and were shaped by entropy. He used human behavior and actions to create art performance pieces that highlight the process of making as integral to the work of art. These performances often considered the experiences of daily life, with David stating, "you can't make art by making art."[23] In his pieces called *Dumbball*, David formed concrete balls by passing wet cement back and forth for up to 24 hours, being careful not to impose any vision onto the material. The process of movement itself shaped the concrete. The distinctions between art and life were blurred, as these acts of making became interwoven with his lived experiences.

David was a builder who explored architecture as a vehicle for his artistic practice. While he had close connections to the discipline, he observed that he is more removed from architecture than any other art discipline. He viewed architects as problem solvers, while he "preferred to explore without any purpose or end in sight."[24] He regarded architecture as a subcategory of the art discipline, yet the very factors that distinguish architecture from art are the constraints that would limit David's vision and freedom. The economy of restrictions, including code, life safety, structure, and budget were antithetical barriers to his spatial explorations that often led to something out of scale, incomplete, deconstructed, or even dangerous. These are evident across his home and expanded art practice, as seen in the excavated dirt from the foundations of his basement to the spilled concrete down a stair to nowhere for his 1987 exhibit at the San Francisco Art Institute. While working with David at Phillips Academy, Henry Moss told him to focus on executing his vision, and he would ensure that the code requirements were followed. Even David's original intentions to renovate 500 Capp Street became part of a larger artistic intervention, as a collection of sculptural fragments.

Artifacts of 500 Capp Street—David Ireland House (2023)

In Parcel X, shattered fragments of colorful porcelain embellish the patio, scattered among found aggregate and growing moss. Ceramic tiles from an old theater in Princeton lay themselves down sacredly across the concrete, with diffused sunlight casting shimmer on the surface cracks and faded glaze. Radiators are dispersed inside, reminiscent of the cattle figures grazing in an empty field from a past life across the gravel road. Treasures from Peru brighten the dim metal box, offering fabrics draped with vibrant colors and patterns. Over the years, Parcel X has accumulated souvenirs of Peter's travels and life, including artifacts and relics. Similar to 500 Capp Street, the space is filled with his past work and collaborations: sketches, drawings, and models. His Princeton thesis map of Houston has been transformed into a table, and a large wooden wheel, titled *Three Transformations or Totem to Tomb*, previously submitted for an exhibition at the American Craft Museum in 1988, now serves as a spatial framer and divider for the open floor plan. The relics spill outside onto the porch and the forested landscape beyond. Four distinct concrete piers with steel angles identify and point to the cardinal directions. They are topped with spoliated runway lights that were a gift from a friend, now reclaimed as an outdoor sculpture. Architectural elements and details have as much of an impact on shaping the space as the knickknacks and tchotchkes accumulated from generations past and present, including gifts from former students turned colleagues, past mentors, and guides who have accompanied Peter along the path from New York to the present Piedmont.

Sofia Kuspan and Patrick Sardo

Artifacts of Parcel X (2023–2024)

THE HOUSE AS AN EVOLVING AND EXPERIMENTAL SPACE

"I was after the real bone of this abode and with it I was finding the marks of old architectural styles. I was finding the evidence of old doorways that went to rooms that no longer existed. I was seeing the effects of earthquakes that ripped long, wide fissures in the white chalky cliff-like walls. And then there was a stain. It was mostly stained. Yellow stain that I saw as signatures of a tempest that had come through weaker parts of the roof.

I was after something more and while I thought I knew what that was, I was not completely sure. I would have to take the chance that might not be repairable if it failed. While I was carving at the bone, I felt that I wanted to separate this containment from the comfortable recess that makes a home.

I wanted the space to speak of its history. I wanted the marks and scars to be like the trails of civilizations that had passed through. I wanted you to see this and not search out traces of architectural completeness or restoration. To achieve this I stripped away the window trim that was named for a queen that we never knew. I ripped up the baseboard and let the walls float free from the floor and now they were frescoes with a new presence and different from the intentions of the maker. And there were relics. Relics everywhere. They were there always waiting to be uncovered by the gentle whisk of a soft broom."

David Ireland in a letter to his sister, 1980.[25]

Parcel X and 500 Capp Street are subjects of memory, subject to the forces of entropy and the shifting processes of decay and weathering. With a rich history in the urban context as a Victorian structure, 500 Capp Street underwent a transformation in the 1970s when David stripped its surfaces down to their most honest expression by removing window moldings and wallpapers, sanding down surfaces, and coating everything—walls, ceiling, and floors—with a glossy polyurethane to highlight his delaminated interventions. The boundaries between life and art became blurred as the acts of labor became as integral to the art as the resulting curation of everyday objects and materials. David's home is no longer an active endeavor, as his markings have become fossilized, and his rituals preserved. His artifacts are curated room by room, offering strangers a glimpse into his unconventional practice of making. His artistic endeavors were shaped by his past lives and expansive fascinations. He was once an aspiring stage designer, an architectural illustrator and draftsman, an adventurer and nomad, and a seller of African safari souvenirs. The dining room is filled with ghosts from a foreign land, evoked by his dealings with skulls and bones, while his early interest in stage sets is evident in the careful placement of art and remnants that frame each room with haunting memories.

For David, the project was never complete. The last brushstroke of polyurethane didn't represent a completed work but rather marked the beginning of his homebound explorations. His artwork and Capp Street were intended to be experienced in the present and the future through the accumulation of weathering. In his transformation, he deliberately chose to acknowledge the past owners and occupants, using leftover brooms, a jar of rubber bands, and a heavy safe that gouged the walls on its way out to emphasize their existence. These displays rendered the space an archaeological exploration of a person's home and their behavior. Art and architecture were not seen as a single image of the finished project in its most perfect and pristine state, but instead were seen as processes of evolution.

Sofia Kuspan and Patrick Sardo

005

David Ireland's House
A maintenance activity

Parcel X is a volume of stripped-down surfaces that were intentionally constructed to reveal their essential state, as seen in the exposed cement board topped with foil-faced insulation board, the two strips of aggregate on the floor, and the ceiling lined with open-web joists and exposed plumbing and electrical conduit. Over time, the basic material expressions have remained, glowing with a slight patina of age. The past 30 years have witnessed a series of small-scale interventions, repairs, and rearrangements suggesting that the home is an incomplete act of construction. In 2004, Peter and his students Brian Tabolt, Barrett Eastwood, and Justin Walton removed a wall of glass block to create a rotating steel door, glowing through a perforated metal screen, which now pivots onto the patio towards the remains of the removed glass block.

When the unbearable heat and humidity of Virginia summers became too much, air-conditioning was installed. Shiny ducts intrude into the ceiling-scape, at home with the exposed copper pipes and steel electrical conduit. While this addition aimed for human comfort, the duct became a notable fixture in the house. When the sun hits the end of the duct, it reflects a figure onto the window glass that resembles the moon, while bright yellow caution tape drapes down from the duct, serving as a reminder that the home continues to be an evolving construction site.

Peter's colleagues have proposed possibilities for further transformations. Mario di Valmarana suggested that a courtyard was needed in Parcel X, from the skylight down to the manhole. During this collaborative project, we explored the concept's possible evolution by sketching and studying plans of figural gardens in French hotels, as well as Giulio Romano's circular courtyards of a Palazzo in Mantua.

The inevitability of entropy continues to shape the next acts of Parcel X. The cleared-away forest has reclaimed its stakes, slowly creeping up to the walls. The weathered volcano is now surrounded by a roof garden of vibrant moss. Murals of efflorescence stain the walls, to Peter's delight. The house is fuller in a multitude of ways: new displays, collections, and a gallery that grows with each new painting, drawing, and sculpture. Both David and Peter explore the home as a site of evolving experimentation. These spaces developed a novel character with the addition of new objects that adorned the wall or floor surfaces, and each fragment of another time or place found new life in their homes. The 25' × 50' modest Victorian from 1886 and the 26' × 117' "*shipping container perched on Mt. Ararat*" differ in their surroundings and intentions, with one responding to an existing historical structure and the other to an unscathed landscape condition. The common thread between the two stage managers decades apart is evident in their spatial arrangements that embrace creative expression as an agent of learning and collaboration.

Sofia Kuspan and Patrick Sardo

SCENE 1

ON MEETING DAVID IRELAND'S HAUNTED HOUSE: THE SECRET LIVES OF BUILDINGS

Peter Waldman alone, a perfect stranger, enters stage right through the flanking shop door on 20th Street. David Ireland emerges stage left from the kitchen, hands grasping a dish towel and greets me with a moist glistening handshake, which reflects off the polyurethane-glazed ocher-stained all-paper glue-centuries-old plaster. It is 2 p.m. and he was just finishing up lunch at the back-of-the-house dining room. He gestures immediately to the front, facing Capp Street and to a window ablaze with Gold Stenciled letters, Accordions, P. Greub proprietor.

DAVID IRELAND

That's the previous owner and I am the most recent artisan, dwelling since 1975.

David turns Peter 180 degrees again and hands him concrete balls quarried from the massive seismic foundation walls in his basement grotto below, to steady him.

DAVID IRELAND

I know there is a Minotaur down there, and I am working to retrieve it to mount on my dining room feasting hall with other worldwide trophies.

David quickly turns Peter 90 degrees now toward the interior stair hall and points to a light well which rises to a rooftop skylight, which does not leak too much.

DAVID IRELAND

These watermarks started long before I got here, but I delight they expanded as I tore away previous coatings and added my territorial markings, leaving fingerprints in the act of making. Hey, that's how you learn to play the accordion, an iterative five finger exercise on each side.

They go up the stairs, coming full circle, and from there we look down to the light well below and see it disappear into the watery shadows of the Grotto below. David drops a coin in homage to the Minotaur and to make it stir as he directs Peter to make another 180-degree turn. Disoriented, Peter enters a room with a bay window on the 20th Street side facing a pocket park across the street. Ireland is tall and puts a hand on Peter's shoulder to stabilize him before he crashes into a six-foot-high collection of silver sardine tins left by the previous owner.

DAVID IRELAND

Did you know what I did when I first saw them and was about to toss them out? Well, I thought old man Greub would be fond of them as they glistened like accordion keys and piled them up to see what the resultant angle of repose was. When I encountered them, I decided to leave them and splashed blue paint on them to refresh them and also to keep them glued together, a version of the refreshing action of the polyurethane coat.

David forces Peter to make another 90-degree turn into the front second-floor parlor facing Capp Street. There, 16 battered brooms are entwined as a teepee in front of the South-facing bay window.

DAVID IRELAND

Broom Collection with Boom, on loan from the SFMOMA permanent collection.

They go down the stair and onto the back dining room, rather reading as a feasting hall, the largest room of the house with wildlife trophy heads from African Safaris and a small window slot to the light well back in the center of the house bouncing late-afternoon light into this Sistine Chapel proportioned hall. Still with dish towel, now on his shoulder, David shakes Peter's hand again, now dry and calloused and ice cold, as Ireland departs below to quarry future watermarks in his self-reflective labyrinth of enduring myths, seeking the gritty blisters and requisite scars which secures/promises one is still alive here and now. Peter wakes up at 2 a.m. from this nightmare in Parcel X in the light of a Red Moon and smiles, "the smile of the Macauley people which said yes to all things."[26]

ACCORDIONS
P. GREUB

SCENE 2
DAVID IRELAND'S GHOSTLY PRESENCE HAUNTS THE PACKARD PLANT

The Packard Plant will soon be transformed through visions of spolia. The initial assessment of the site's present state is ongoing. Sofia is carefully cataloging the various buildings, materials, and remnants, making note of what should be preserved and spoliated.

David Ireland enters the scene, intrigued by the Packard Plant's rich quarry of dilapidated material.

David glances over the catalog and insists on preserving the plant's decayed state.

DAVID IRELAND

The piles of crumbling remnants should remain. Their presence is important to the site's history. They are integral witnesses to past production and the processes of weathering.

Sofia writes down NOTE TO LEAVE ROOM FOR PILES in her notebook. She nods in agreement, recognizing the importance that any design intervention must honor decay as a significant moment in the site's story. We do not want to obliterate this history.

The next phase of disassembly begins. David enters the scene as a witness to the exposure of the concrete structure, the skeleton of the factory.

John, draped in Visqueen plastic, is saw-cutting the floor plates in between the existing structural grid. The chunks of concrete are brought down with a large crane, forming a pile of remnants. David looks toward the sun.

DAVID IRELAND

The light will be wonderful, the shadows of the grid beaming against the crushed concrete pathway.

His gaze is directed towards the growing pile of concrete floor plates. David walks over to the pile, inspecting his palette for making. Reaching for his toolbelt, he swings his hammer, as the concrete slowly shatters to form a pile of dust that dances around the simple sweep of a broom. These piles form a loosely curated assemblage of debris. He collects the pieces, placing them in glass jars to transport back home to the honey-glazed walls of Capp Street. The chunks of concrete, decaying wood, and shards of spray paint-stained glass will find comfort in the presence of his growing collection of everyday artifacts.

The plant's disassembly is complete and the on-site inventory is ready for viewing.

David inspects the sorted material inventory, as he is asked to create a site-specific installation. He continues his spontaneous explorations of space, light, and material. He wishes to highlight the history, the decay, and the weathering in the leftover artifacts of this archeological ruin of past production.

DAVID IRELAND

I'm eager to continue exploring these stripped-away surfaces. The leftover automobile parts are stained with a lovely patina and rust, a mural of discoloration and age. They are a testament to a past life and represent a new artistic endeavor.

He continues to strip away the surfaces of the Packard Plant, carving away the chunks of degraded concrete with its bits of rusted rebar sticking out like a dagger. He is animated by the working palette of degrading CMU blocks, throwaway tires, and crumbling bricks: the materials have slowly peeled away to reveal their most vulnerable state.

SCENE 3

CONSPIRACIES OF THE NEW AND OLD: HUMAN AND NONHUMAN SPACES THROUGH DAVID IRELAND

The ghost of David Ireland arrives into a posthuman future, leaving behind the world he once knew. Once idyllic farmland, these exurban and suburban sites of former production and digital storage are now rusting and eroding into ruins no different from their 20th-century counterparts. Patrick, former designer of posthuman buildings, and Sofia, explorer and spoliator of postindustrial ruins of America meet the ghost of David Ireland at a former automated fulfillment center.

DAVID IRELAND

What are these buildings? Who worked here before these were abandoned?

PATRICK SARDO

These were warehouses for shipping manufactured goods. At one point, they were filled with only human laborers, but they eventually transitioned to fully automated robot workers. They changed the design of the buildings as a result, so the first time humans occupied these buildings was after they were abandoned.

SOFIA KUSPAN

Like previous generations of industrial ruins, scavengers raided these buildings for any valuable materials, but a lot of useful materials were left behind for others. Architectural materials, chunks of concrete and steel, beams and joists, shells of robots, and circuit boards.

Patrick, Sofia, and David squeeze through a small gap between two concrete walls eroded by time and by human intruders. The space expands into an immense, cavernous hall, lit only by sunlight bursting through cracks and openings in the roof. Densely packed mezzanines, platforms, overhead tracks, and machines collide with one another in a web of entangled spolia around the characters. Some rust and crumble away while some have become host to vines and moss that continue to creep in wherever the light allows.

PATRICK SARDO

Scavenging through these buildings is notoriously hard; they weren't designed to allow humans inside so you might have to crawl through shafts and jump between different floor levels.

SOFIA KUSPAN

Would you be interested in taking artifacts from here back to Capp Street? Or would you prefer doing a site-specific project here? Maybe something akin to the project at Boott Mill in Lowell?

DAVID IRELAND

Maybe. My work at Capp Street was both anthropological and archeological, but a building like this is very different from anything I have done before. How can I expose a person's life or their behavior and actions when humans never occupied the building?

David begins scrubbing off dust and grime from a dilapidated machine near his feet. He pulls a small rag out of his back pocket and starts to polish the painted metal surface when the robot starts rolling away across the pitted concrete floor. Decades have passed since these complex machines moved under their own power, now re-energized by a ghostly human hand.

0249
20253
20150
20253

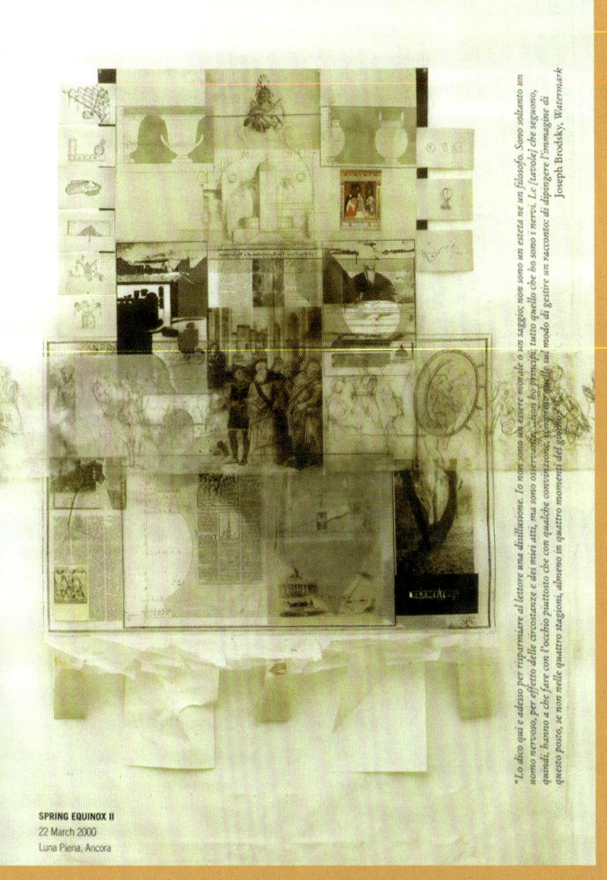

Winter Solstice and Spring Equinox Collages from Peter Waldman's *Deep Frieze: Speculations on Villa Aurelia as Construction Site* (2000) for American Academy of Rome Fellowship.

ACT THREE:
IMPROVISATIONAL SCRIPTS

STAGE SETS

The intention of this incremental collage process is to commence with the accountability of a plan and/or section, the documented facts evidenced by a **Surveyor** as a Field Condition, to which is added the enigmatic figure of the **Nomad** who exudes fictional baggage, referencing the juxtaposition of the combination of the Accountable Pyramid and the Enigmatic Sphinx in the fluid context of shifting sands and recurrent floods. To this assemblage of frictional dualities (Figure and Field) is added the magical qualities offered by the **Lunatic** who uses mica to reflect Mirrors for the Moon. This recipe, to be repeated many times over for evoking kaleidoscopic space, becomes stage sets as well as scrims for improvisational scripts as stories to be recounted by the collective voices of the Cast of Characters, and the meandering haunting figure of David Ireland through 28 (XXVIII) PLATES in growing complexity, ending in six annotated dense vellums.

SURVEYOR

A surveyor comes from the south to remark with instrumental baggage the two solstices. A surveyor encounters a site and renders it accountable. A surveyor with the use of a compass first finds true north. A surveyor then determines the cornerstone locations by rod and compass. A surveyor determines precise perimeter boundaries and calculates the total gross area. At times, the surveyor transcribes zoning code regulations such as set-back lines onto the survey as a map with pre-conditions for construction. Both a site plan and a site section are mutually interdependent and often indicate both the paths of the sun and the moon bracketing a leap-year condition. It is rumored that some urbane surveyors include the location of both existing infrastructure as well as the markings of previous occupations of the site in question. Peter Jefferson, father of Thomas, was a surveyor, and willed his instruments to his son.

A surveyor enumerates a field condition as précis.

NOMAD

A nomad comes from the north under a new Moon to reconfirm the location of secret oases at least once a calendar year. A nomad arrives at sunset and has time to build a substantial fire for kit and kin. A nomad takes note of lofty palms and deep wells, of burning bushes and recent footprints and understands he is never alone. A nomad will weave a story of other strange oases that trace a meander of hierophanies in the homogeneous culture of 21st-century landscapes of familiarity. A nomad never reveals the whole truth, nothing but the truth, but rather keeps the place strange to himself, his tribe, and others who are nourished by secrets, oracles, and sustained enigmas.

A nomad articulates expanded arguments of labyrinthine trace and circumstantial pause.

LUNATIC

A lunatic operates in the darkness of night and is not concerned with the systems referenced by the surveyor or the scattered self-evident truths of the nomad. A lunatic works with the precise permutations of the Moon adjusting once in four years for the leap of faith where these sensitivities appear to witness a blue Moon paired with a solar eclipse. Sectional calculations are imperative to the lunatic as one who controls the tides and human fecundity. A lunatic is often mistaken for a magician, which we all know too well that the swiftest magician is an encyclopedic scientist who moves more swiftly than those with little faith in the power of spatial tales of origin and connective tissues.

A lunatic reflects on the mythic power of heuristic narratives serving the modern & the archaic.

PLATE I

Foundation plans of Megarons[1] provide both linear footings and Cartesian piers and emerge in the first stages following excavation as garden walls and potential apertures for framed apertures.

The first progress payment to a General Contractor is made when the foundation is constructed to receive subsequent framing. I have learned over the years that though these foundation walls and piers might seem irrelevant as they are often out of sight and thus out of mind; they are indeed of great diagrammatic clarity as already a garden anticipating an eventual dialogue with the reciprocal spatial apertures reframing the Sky.

Peter Waldman

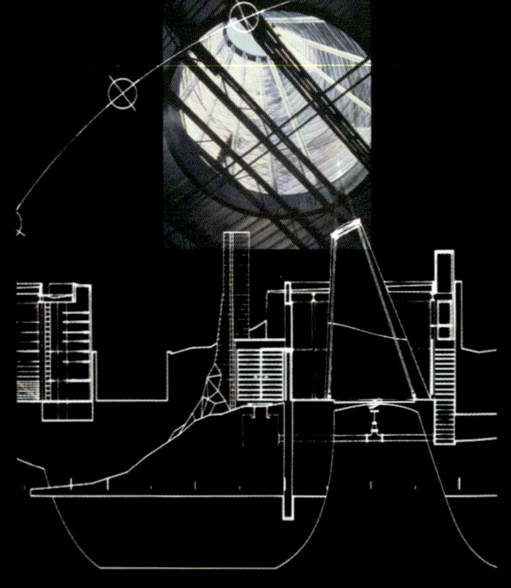

Parcel X transverse section and “Volcano”

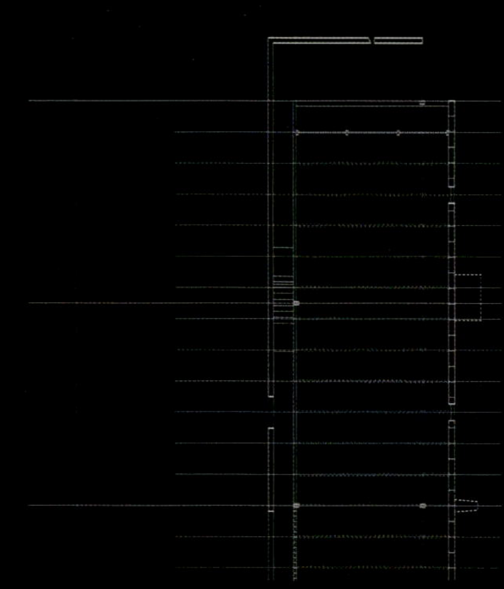

Parcel X Plan of the Ruler

Foundation walls being poured at Parcel X.

Concrete footings, walls, and foundations in progress at Parcel X.

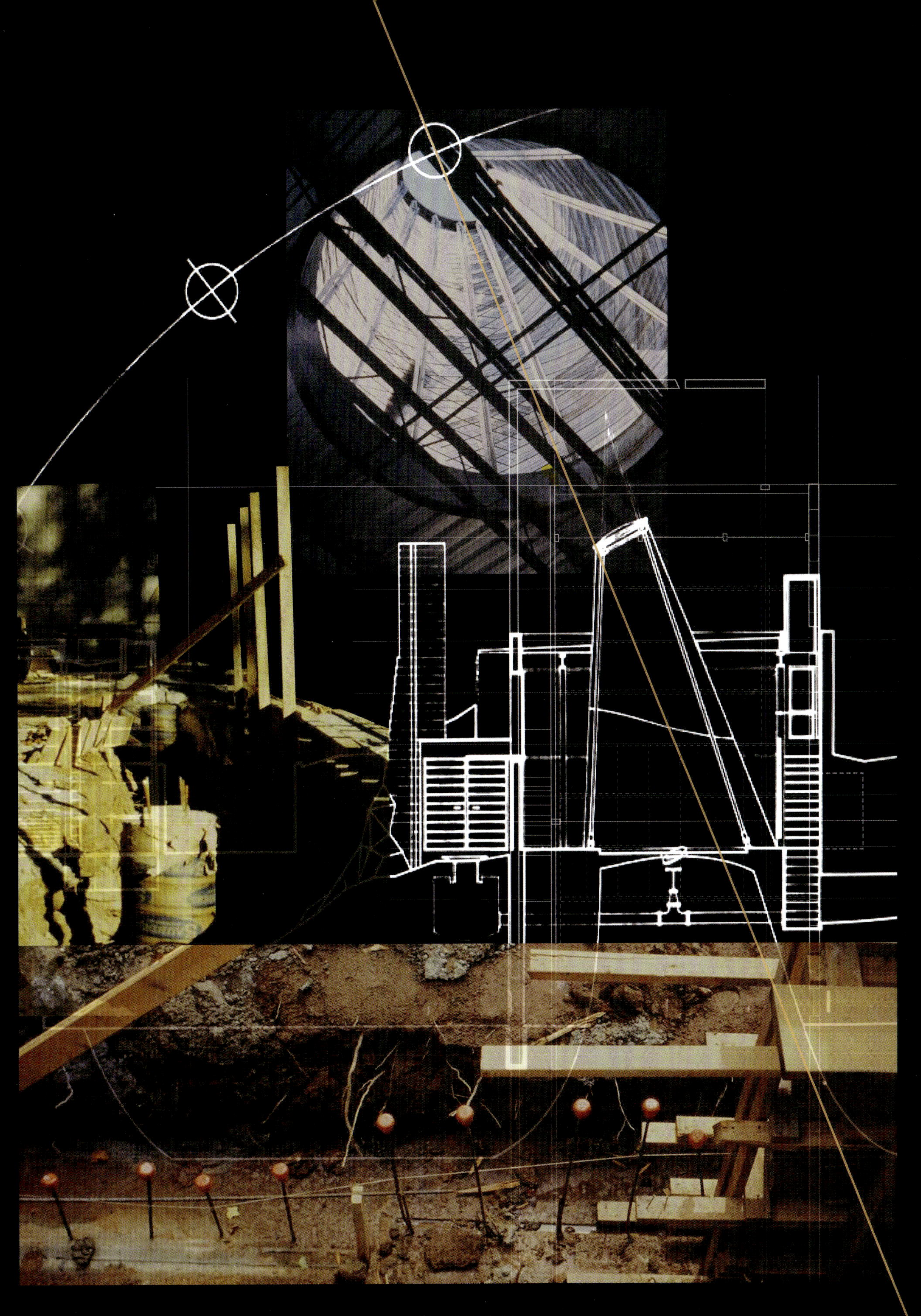

PLATE II

It made me recall the role of preconditions of this geologically fraught remnant of the last Ice Age and the subsequent vast hardwood forest, the lowlands of which were cleared in vast tracks as farmland in aptly named North Garden and subdivided over centuries into Parcels ranging from vast precincts of hundreds of acres down to the smallest, steepest, most wildly difficult for neither landscape nor constructed artifice, and thus termed site remnants or parcels, good primarily for periodic timbering, so dense as to preclude the sky.

Peter Waldman

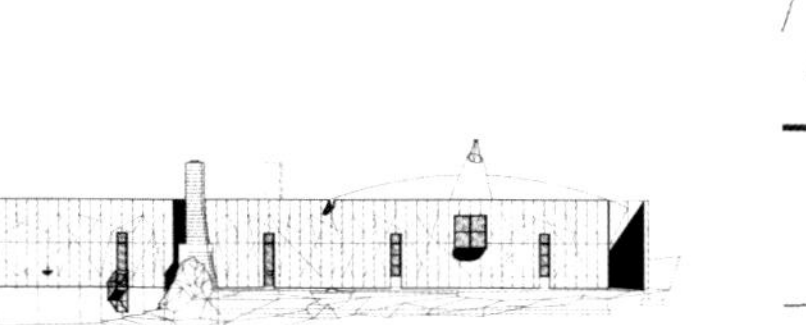

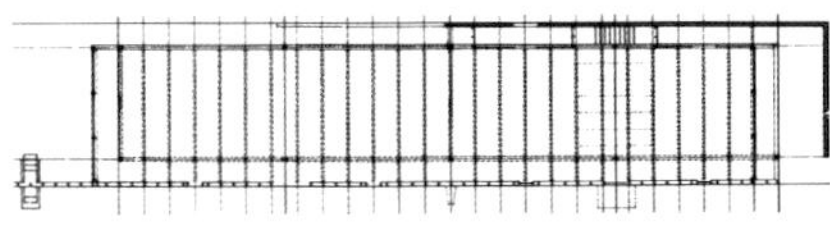

South Elevation and Plan of the Ruler of Parcel X.

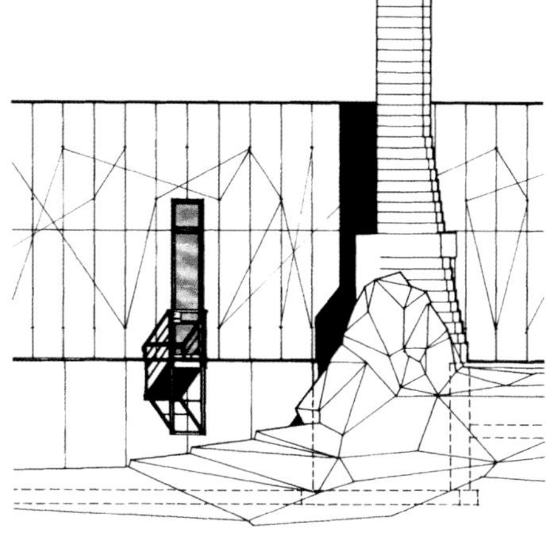

Close-up elevation detail of Parcel X.

Parcel X study model

South facade of Parcel X with compass pier enlarged in foreground.

PLATE III

Parcel X is an Oasis where both the preconditions of the site are totally in dialogue, a sign language of the meters and consequences of construction, with a long history of no waste, and materials on hand for the next move in this Game of Chess.

Peter Waldman

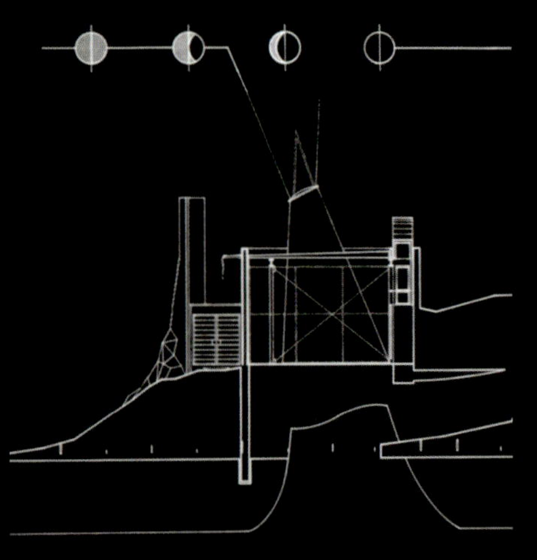

Transverse section of Parcel X

Scrims of Parcel X

John in Visqueen saw-cutting concrete control joints in Parcel X.

Ceiling of Parcel X and theater linesets

PLATE IV

Rock, Paper, Scissors: Excavate two Parterres and one Singular Cleave; Cut Reinforcing Rods to make two Playing Fields; then Invite David Ireland to join in this Chess Game with Sam and Justin to pour slabs, repeat again and again; lift with success and then failure, and finally stabilize this kaleidoscopic buttressing frame.

Peter Waldman

Eric Goodwin Memorial Pavilion with section and site strategy plan.

Construction photographs of the Eric Goodwin Memorial Pavilion.

David Ireland repairing the sidewalk outside 500 Capp Street in 1976.

Eric Goodwin Memorial Pavilion

F
11'-0"
E
6'-8"
D
2'-8"
C
- 0'-3"
B
- 2'-0"
A
- 3'-6"
3
2
4
13' x 13' slab
concrete footings
and knee walls
17' x 17" slab
grass
brick
grass
brick
4'-0"
24'-8"
brick removed
1

PLATE V

A volcano rose from the Piedmont, illuminating the sleeping loft as a teepee below. The plan of the compass aligns with the plan of the ruler to bring cardinal axes to the regimented grid.

A decade later, a pleasant shade tree for remembering exceptional faculty is met with a new memorial for an exceptional student, completing an axial relationship to the porch and the school.

Patrick Sardo

Parcel X "Volcano" and floor plan.

Eric Goodwin Memorial Pavilion with section.

Parcel X under construction in 1994.

Study model for the Eric Goodwin Memorial Pavilion.

PLATE VI

David Ireland joins the workforce on projects somewhere between San Francisco, Detroit, and North Garden at the scale of the humble human step on an ascending path from here to there.

Peter Waldman

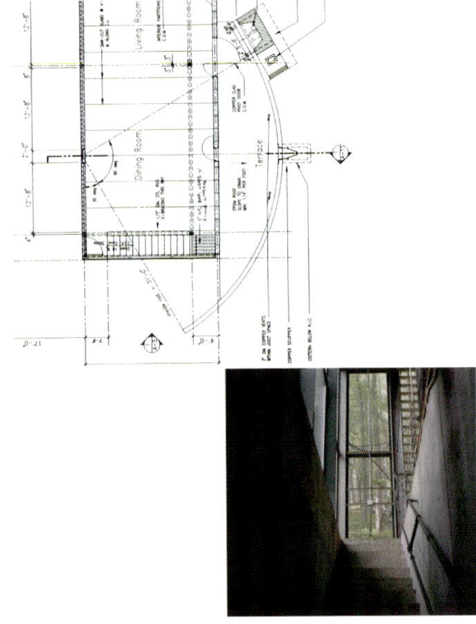

Parcel X stairs and floor plan construction document.

David Ireland repairing the sidewalk outside 500 Capp Street in 1976 (top) and Parcel X floor slab pour preparation (bottom).

500 Capp Street basement in 1987 (top) and *Smithsonian Falls, Descending a Staircase for P. K.* (1987) by David Ireland (bottom).

Parcel X stair and railing detail.

Living Room
Dining Room
Terrace
INTERIOR PARTITIONS C.O.M.
COPPER CLAD PIVOT DOOR C.O.M.
EPDM ROOF SLOPE TO DRAIN MIN. 1/4" PER FOOT
1/2" DIA. STL. ROD X-BRACING THIS BAY
2" DIA COPPER VENTS WITHIN JOIST SPACE
COPPER SCUPPER
CISTERN BELOW N.I.C.
inside rad. = 31'-0"
90 deg
30 deg
12'-8"
8"
12'-8"
2'-0"
12'-8"
4"
17'-0"
4'-0"

PLATE VII

Both Sides Now:
Two Models of Specifications for Construction

Cast-in-Place:
Packard's Mushroom Columns & Frame and Parcel X's Retaining Walls

Tilt Slab Construction:
Fulfillment Centers, Data Centers, and Goodwin Memorial

Peter Waldman

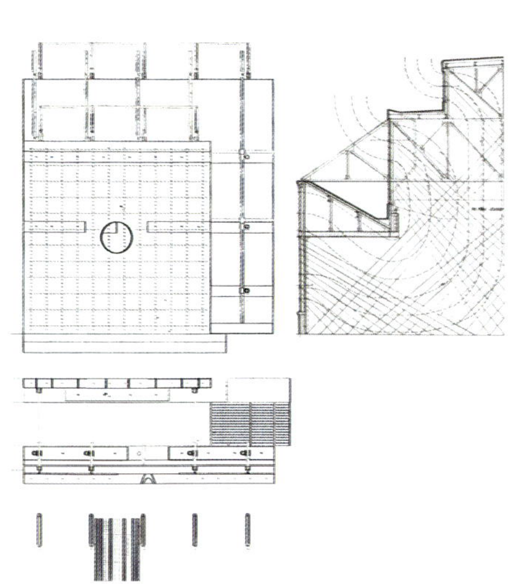

Eric Goodwin Memorial Pavilion plan and elevation (left) and Packard Automotive Plant ventilation section (right).

Packard Automotive Plant ruins (top) and speculative warehouse under construction (bottom).

Close-up detail of concrete column from 1920s factory.

Parcel X patio

PLATE VIII

David Ireland with concrete mixer and John Smith with saw-cutting blade join up to resurrect Packard's framed Spolia into a Contemporary Fulfillment Center.

Peter Waldman

David Ireland repairing the sidewalk outside 500 Capp Street in 1976 and *Concrete Study* (1993) by David Ireland.

Concrete frame saw-cutting collage from *Wasteland Spolia* (2023)

Close-up detail of concrete column from 1920s factory and *Concrete Acorns in Wire Basket* (1993) by David Ireland.

Parcel X concrete patio wall and John in Visqueen saw-cutting concrete control joints in Parcel X.

PLATE IX

Artifacts reveal the rich inner lives of each home. In San Francisco, a pair of deep-blue blowtorches dangle above the visitors, suspended in reason, as an ornate candleholder supports a fragile assortment of wire. In the Piedmont, the cast-iron radiator grazes against the exposed cement board, sheltered from the patio where shattered ceramic cups spill over. They are loose fragments bound by the logic of linear plans and regulating lines.

Sofia Kuspan

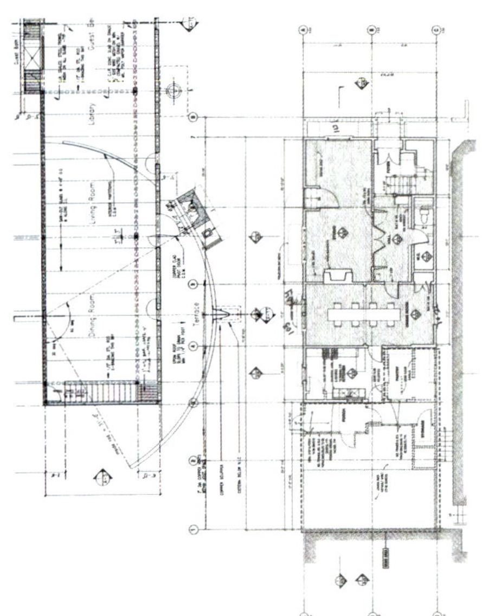

Parcel X construction plan drawing (left) and 500 Capp Street demolition plan (right).

A reclaimed radiator in Parcel X and suspended blowtorches in 500 Capp Street by David Ireland.

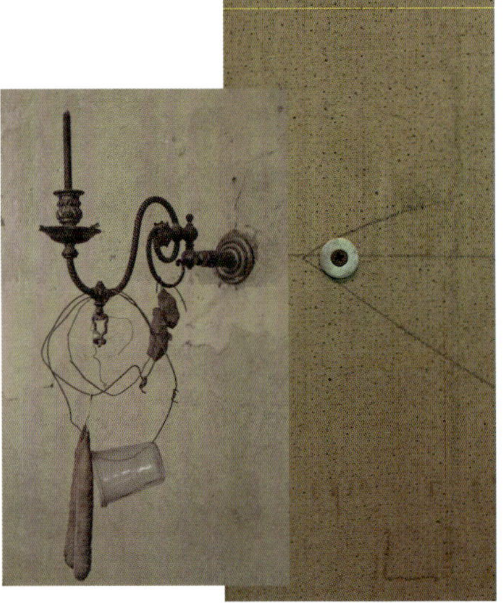

Light fixture with wire sculpture in 500 Capp Street by David Ireland and Parcel X cement board wall panel close-up.

Eric Goodwin Memorial Pavilion and broken ceramics and gravel on the patio of Parcel X.

Guest Bath
Library
Living Room
Dining Room
Terrace
COPPER SCUPPER
CISTERN BELOW N.I.C.

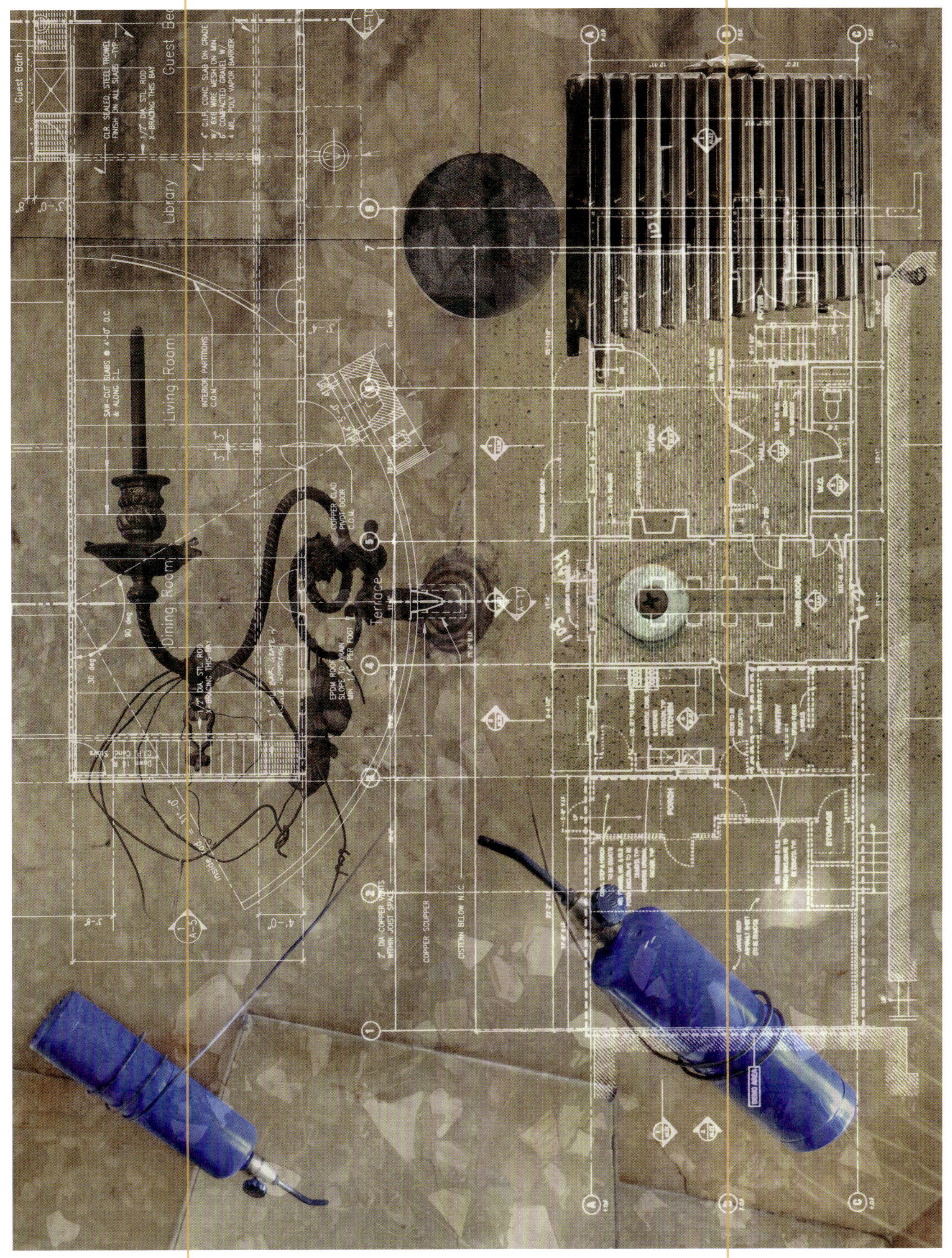

PLATE X

Floor Plan of Automated Fulfillment Center

The Eric Goodwin Memorial Pavilion and the basement of the David Ireland House at 500 Capp Street.

Close-up detail of concrete column from 1920s factory and ruins of the Packard Automotive Plant.

Fulfillment Center under construction—exterior and interior.

PLATE XI

The disparate pieces of the Packard Plant and Academical Village site plans come together as unified spaces for making, learning, and collaborating. Parcel X echoes the repetitive metering of windows, allowing sunlight to reflect off the smooth concrete surfaces. A crystalline curtain sweeps in to divide the heavy metal box.

Sofia Kuspan

The site plans of Parcel X and the Goodwin Memorial also contain responses to Packard and the Academical Village in that they contain reciprocal walled-in Courts & Figural Gardens, Communal Domains and Private Retreats.

Peter Waldman

Parcel X study model

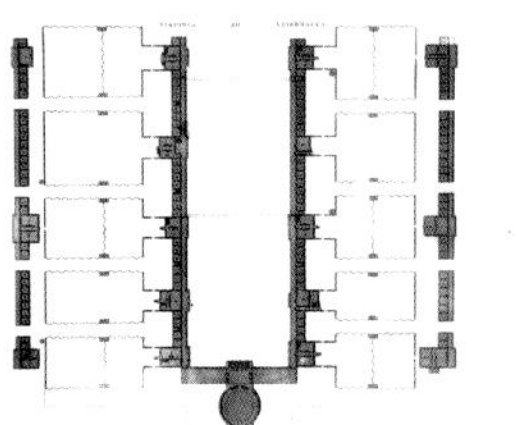

Thomas Jefferson's Rotunda and plan for the Academical Village at the University of Virginia.

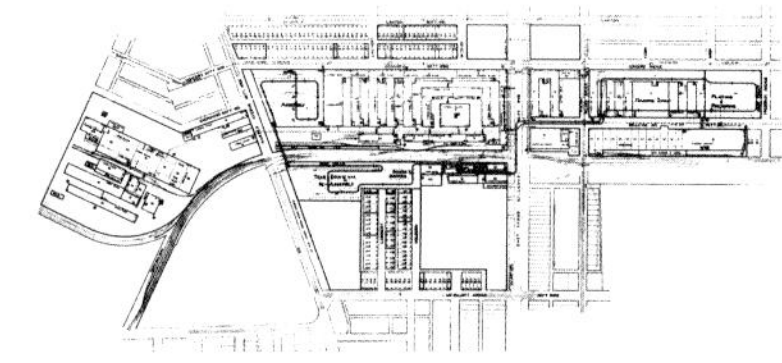

Packard Automotive Plant site plan and pedestrian bridge.

Parcel X interior

PLATE XII

Choreography of agents and the infectious subversive qualities of tire tracks. Fingerprints/footpaths in the act of making. Jurassic Park and the Modern Cohort of construction equipment and the Trojan Horse or the Vast Spanish Armada reconstructed in Bilbao's Guggenheim: Backhoes, Concrete Trucks, and Cranes.

Peter Waldman

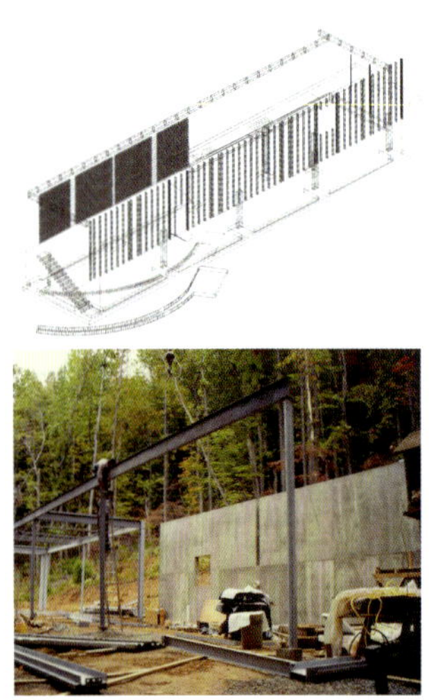

Assembly drawing and construction photograph of Parcel X.

Parcel X under construction and a speculative warehouse under construction.

Construction site in Arequipa, Peru

Construction crane at Arcosanti, AZ

PLATE XIII

500 Capp Street front door and Parcel X East Elevation drawing.

Eric Goodwin Memorial Pavilion steel plate detail.

2024 photograph of the kitchen of Parcel X (left) and light fixture in 500 Capp Street (right).

Close-up photograph of *Three Transformations or Totem to Tomb* (1988) by Peter Waldman, Christopher Genik, and Edward Wilson.

PLATE XIV

The Roof plan with Volcano is a neglected set of geometries to be developed as the First Garden of the New Millennium to be cultivated above, since it is unfulfilled except for the island of moss-covered leaves and a scupper repair, which leaves a great catalytic stain on the midsection of the library below.[2] The Archival library is a Compost site of sorts, containing a Model of Houston with raised Bayous and depressed Highways, gifted by Rice students on our departure (1992), a Wheel/Museum Installation demonstrating a diptych of Architecture and Craft (1988), a black scrim/veil framing a manhole to a cistern below, and a Peruvian steerhide portending a reciprocal Garden of sorts, emerging within this evolving Memory Palace.

The counterpart in the Capp Street house is the emergence of the swarms of now separate light fixtures that infest the skylight, a bit of *Fantasia* cinema of dancing brooms reminiscent of Pinocchio, swarms of sardine cans, and Safari Taxidermy Souvenirs all assembled for a celebratory feast, resembling the Limbourg brothers' *Les Très Riches Heures du Duc de Berry*.

Peter Waldman

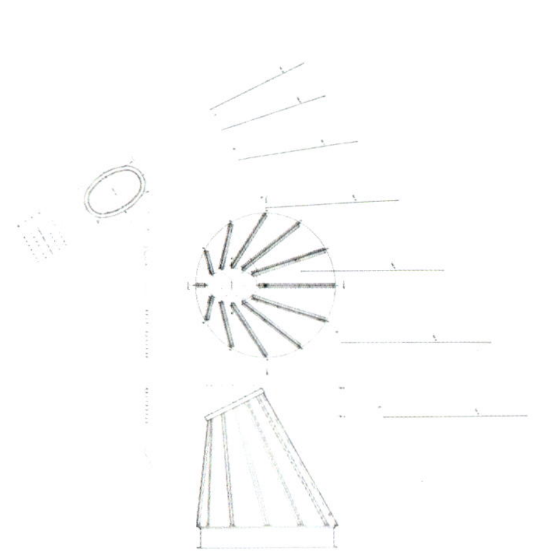

Parcel X "Volcano" skylight drawing

Parcel X study model "teepee" and Parcel X roof and "Volcano."

500 Capp Street solarium and skylight

Parcel X "Volcano"

PLATE XV

Spatial Tales of Origin haunt the Spolia thesis from the start, while *Specifications for Construction* is a Template, a written code of (con)-sequences assembled by an Army of AI programs.

Peter Waldman

Excavations of the Lunatic lead to new beginnings, where spolia is resurrected and fulfillment centers are agents for posthuman surrogates.

Sofia Kuspan

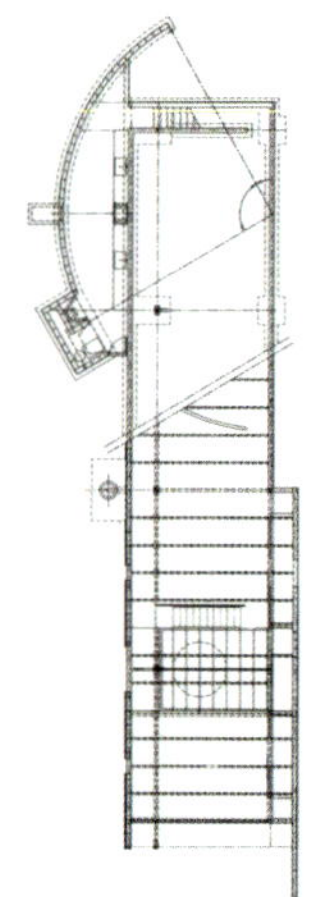

Parcel X lower-level floor plan

Posthuman building agents at a fulfillment center under construction and the ruins of the Packard Plant.

David Ireland creating a concrete wall painting for the 1976 *18 Bay Area Artists* exhibition and the basement of 500 Capp Street.

Parcel X exterior and interior under construction.

PLATE XVI

The artist's hand brings imperfection and texture to objects, surfaces, and spaces. *Fingerprints in the act of making* are only left by the hand; perfection is not intended or desired. The natural impulse of a human maker is to leave their mark to let another human know they were there. To introduce the complex machine to artistic production is to remove the flawed humanity in constructed environments.

Patrick Sardo

"Torpedoes" and other concrete mixed media sculptures by David Ireland.

David Ireland creating a concrete wall painting for the 1976 *18 Bay Area Artists* exhibition at the Los Angeles Institute of Contemporary Art.

Posthuman agents: a robotic arm and robot pod tracks.

Untitled (Scheme #2 M.O.C.A. L.A.) collage (1988) by David Ireland for a proposed installation at the Los Angeles Museum of Contemporary Art.

PLATE XVII

The empire has run its course. Site fragments transform into a garden filled with spolia. Future courts and gardens of the Lunatic will soon emerge. The Pastoral State features shattered windows and eroding columns, surrounded by the greetings of all-encompassing plants that welcome a new life.

Sofia Kuspan

The Course of Empire: The Arcadian or Pastoral State (1836) by Thomas Cole.

Drawing from Peter Waldman and Chris Genik's Times Square Competition (1983) and tree and planting sketches from *Wasteland Spolia* (2023).

Parcel X from northern hillside

Packard Automotive Plant, Detroit, MI

PLATE XVIII

Weathered surfaces on both the outside and inside of Parcel X and 500 Capp Street reveal an *Architecture of Time*,[3] the subject of a recent symposium at the University of Pennsylvania (2024) by long-term soulmates David Leatherbarrow and Michael Benedikt, and are evidenced by Waldman's generously-scaled Skylight, recalling both a Volcano and a Teepee, as well as a Myriad of electrical fixtures, bare light bulbs, blowtorches and a light well illuminating a Grotto in Ireland's Oasis.

Peter Waldman

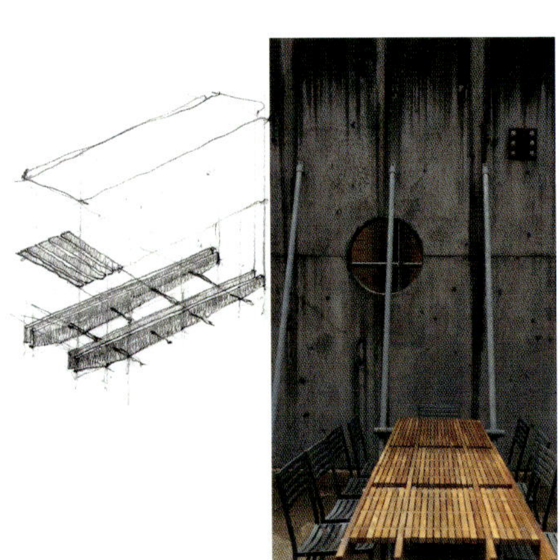

Design sketch of Eric Goodwin Memorial Table and built version, updated in 2024 with wood from UVA Grounds.

Light Fixture with Wire Sculpture in 500 Capp Street by David Ireland and rusted steel artifact outside Parcel X kitchen.

Ductwork and shower plumbing in Parcel X

Weathered surfaces of Parcel X: efflorescence and tarnish on interior wall and rusted steel at the base of the "volcano."

PLATE XIX

Dining tables turned stage sets have hosted hundreds of characters, flanked by golden sunset-lit glass block, aged fabric scrims, glowing amber polyurethane varnished plaster, and relics of decades past turned props. Stories of art and architecture, friends and colleagues, strangers and ghosts are shared over plates of food and ancient artifacts.

Patrick Sardo

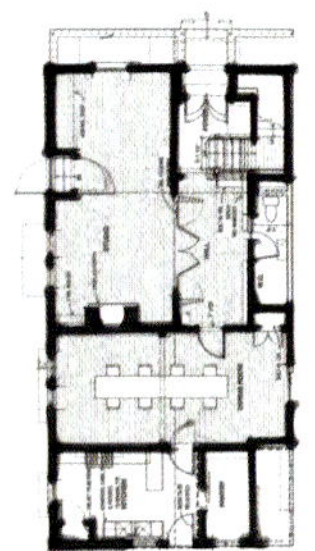

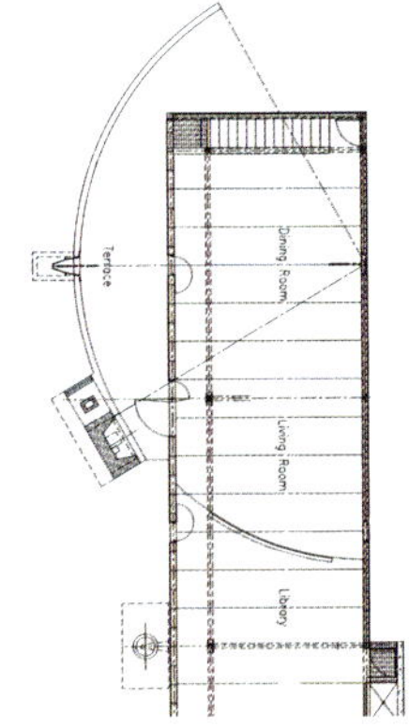

Ground Floor Plans of 500 Capp Street and Parcel X.

Dining table at 500 Capp Street covered with artifacts and artwork by David Ireland.

Dining Room of 500 Capp Street

Dining space of Parcel X

PLATE XX

Planes and Frames, walls and hearths, bear witness to Spatial Scripts both in the incipient sequences of construction sites, as well as in the *Spolia* of fragmentary ruins.[4]

These two scripted sites are now newly encountered by Surveyors, Nomads, and Lunatics under a New Moon understood as the Beginning and the End, the stories recalled in Genesis and Exodus, of Fire and Water, and the fecundities of the Volcano and the Well as the project of Nomadic Encampments making possible the cultivation of a second Eden for the Next Millennium.

Peter Waldman

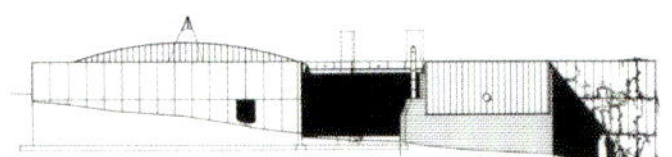

North Elevation of Parcel X and "Volcano" above the sleeping loft in Parcel X.

Table of safari spoils and shrine in David Ireland's house at 500 Capp Street.

Chimneys of Parcel X

West-facing concrete tilt-up panel of the Eric Goodwin Memorial Pavilion and the ruins of the Packard Automotive Plant.

PLATE XXI

The built worlds of Peter and David are assembled by a rich palette of distinct textures. Markings of time's fingerprints leave behind a reminder of each passing day. Some are shiny, reflecting the promise of new days to come, while others are bruised and battered by moments from the past. The surfaces are varied, smooth, cracked, continuous, rough, unified. They work together as a canvas to create collages and compositions.

Sofia Kuspan

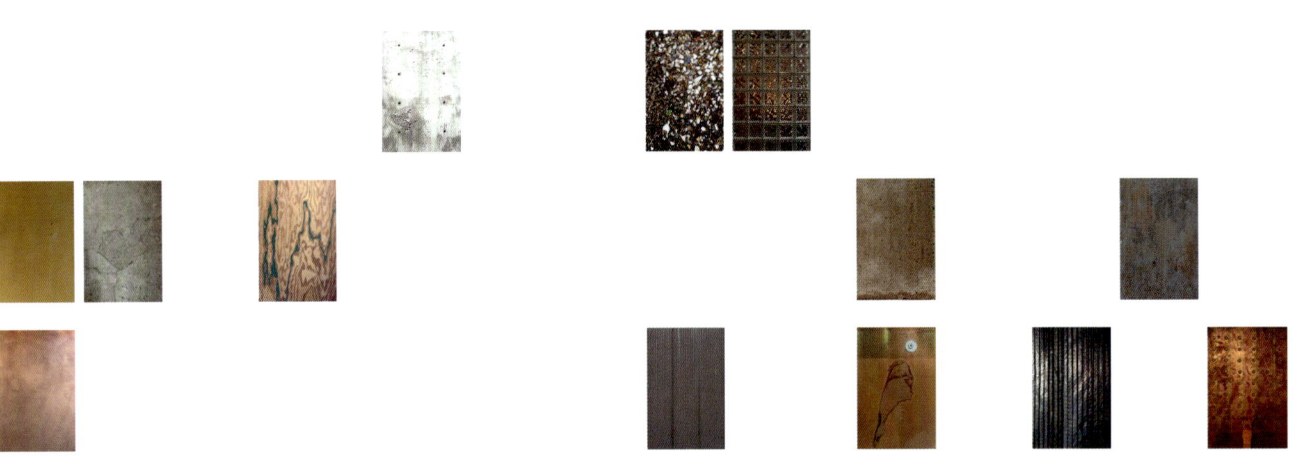

Textures of the David Ireland House at 500 Capp Street

Textures of the Parcel X exterior

Textures of Parcel X interior

Textures of the Eric Goodwin Memorial Pavilion

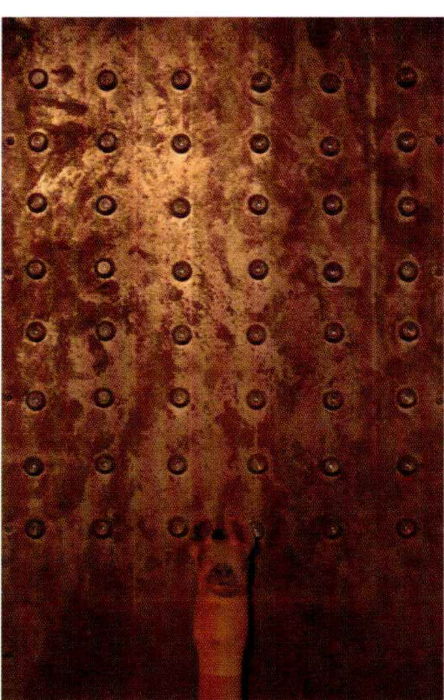

PLATE XXII

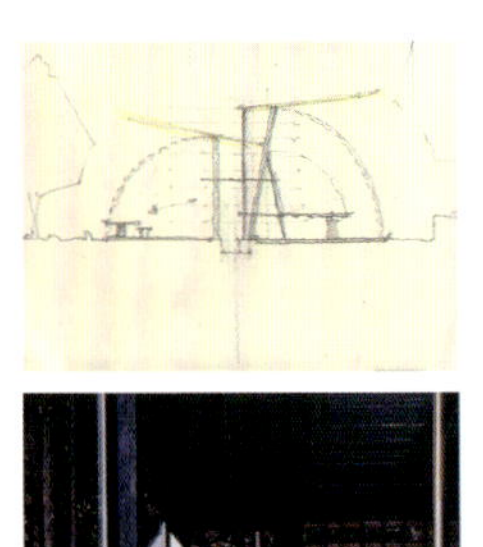

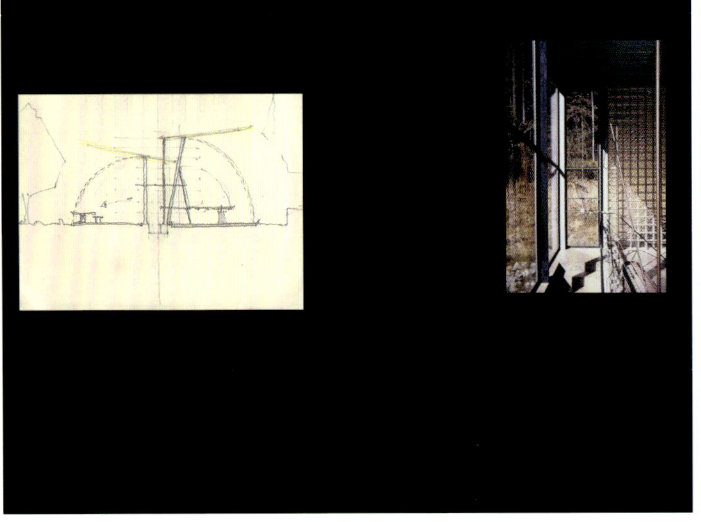

Preconditions:

Our Site, the North Face of Carr's Hill, is not easily described as Level Ground.

A review of the archive of maps of Carr's Hill since Jefferson's inception reveals numerous fictions as to the location of True North.

Thus, to date, we Citizens of Campbell Hall are not certain where North is precisely located.

We need to use the strategies of construction to orient ourselves.

This summer we propose to construct one by one with each new moon five concrete slabs determined by the meter of the structure of Campbell Hall.

The first slab is the formwork for the next as one proceeds from east to west.

With each sequential pour, the previous one is tilted to the sky.

Each totem is braced.

Shadows dance around and imply a village of teepees.

We will first use both enduring concrete markers as well as ephemeral strings to give measure to this difficult topographic condition.

We will second use the same fixed points as concrete benchmarks, tables in the broadcast sense, together with a sense of dynamic approximations to help Citizens & Strangers alike to find true North as the one requirement of Anticipated Graduation.

The ethical responsibility of Architecture as Orientation is the first and only Lesson of the North Porch

We are to project experimental theaters and landscapes for a Tent, a Table or two, and a myriad of commemorative and transformative Tablets at the scales of both bricks as well as civic mirages.

The spatial setting of the North Porch will be nothing less than the construction site of the intersecting lessons of civic literacy commencing with the ABCs of the Acropolis, onto Bilbao, then the Campidoglio, with the Ise Shrine as pivotal, and ending, no doubt, in Zurich at the threshold of a tent perched between the mountain and the Zee.

Surveyors will construct concrete Markers to measure the Horizon first from Ground to Mountain Ridge.

Upon these slabs additional Horizontal Slabs of varying lengths will give measure to the Hill to be then tilted Vertically to Frame a Window to the Sky.

The tilt slab panels will be incised with the names of departed students and faculty, generous donors, and legendary caretakers alike as a pre-requisite of citizenship.

Upon these Window plinths a swarm of spiders will insert telescoping poles and cables as stanchions for the eventful tent reliably erected by a band of Nomads in the midst of May.

It is rumored that a lunatic in the ruins of an ancient fraternity site will supervise a Deep Casting Pit that is quarried as formwork for incubating Groundhogs to sustain the stress of tent-induced wind loads.

A Forest of Pylons and Correspondent water runnels syncopate the Hill.

Fires Burn

Columns begin to Dance.

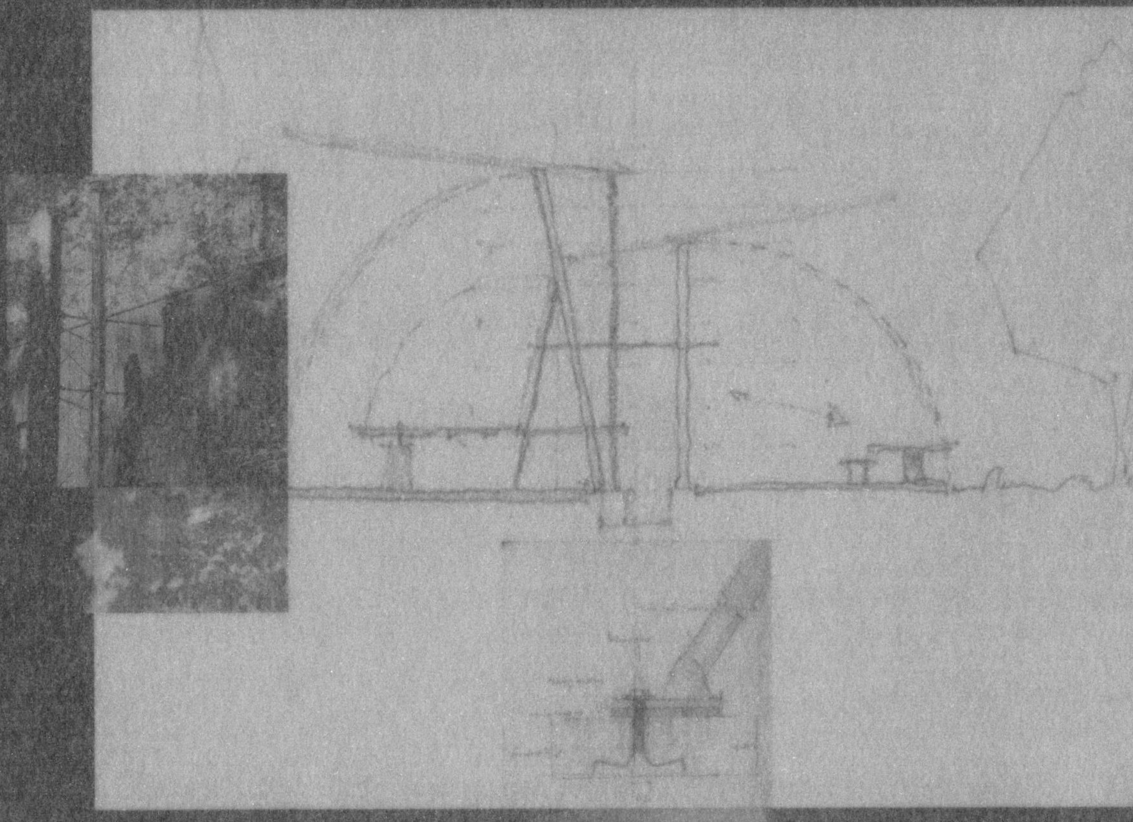

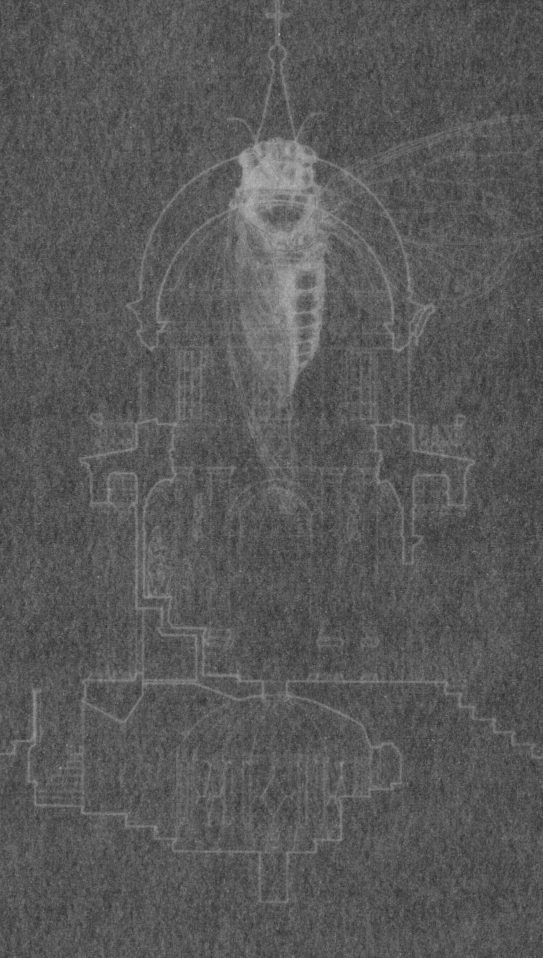

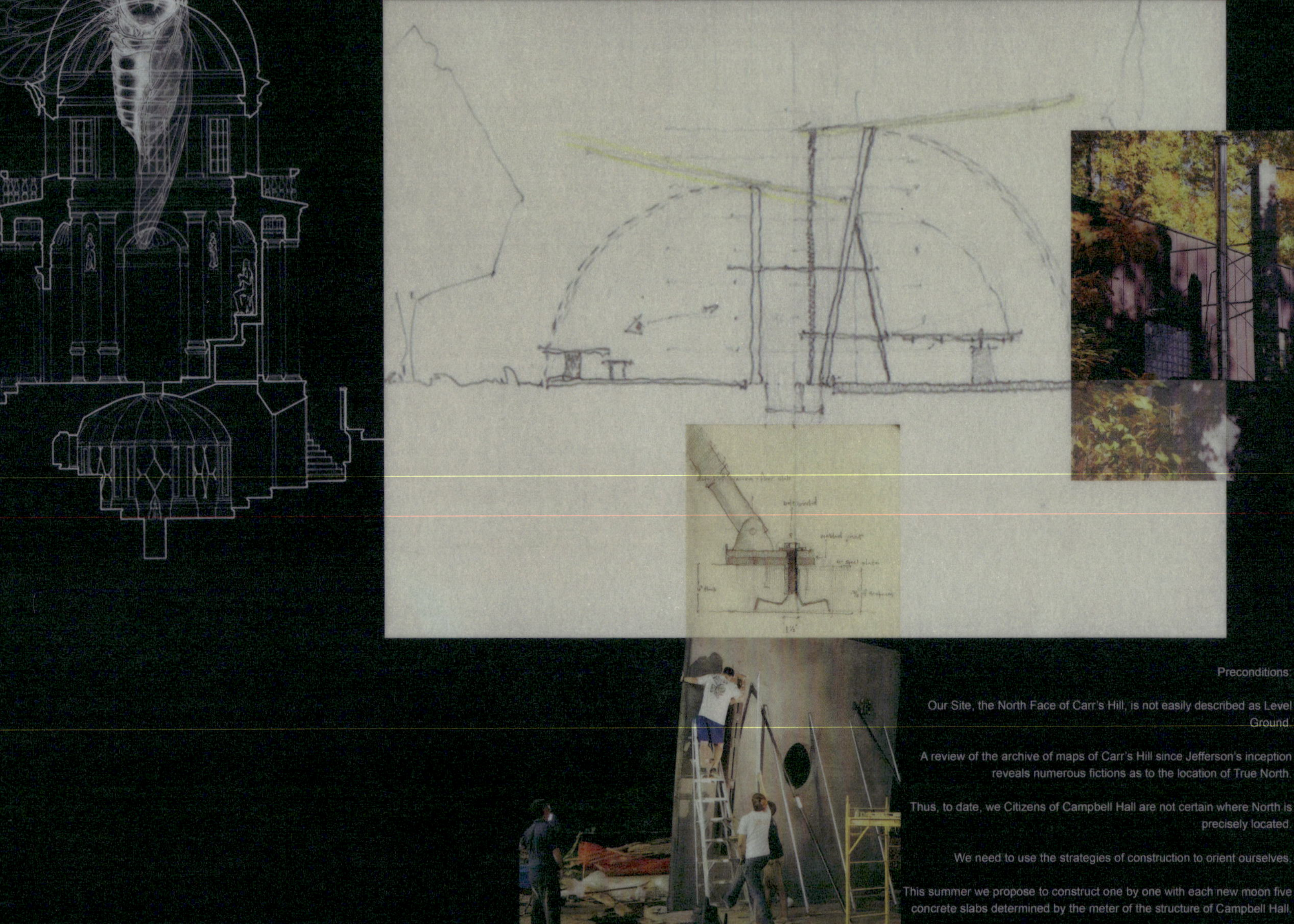
Preconditions:
Our Site, the North Face of Carr's Hill, is not easily described as Level Ground.
A review of the archive of maps of Carr's Hill since Jefferson's inception reveals numerous fictions as to the location of True North.
Thus, to date, we Citizens of Campbell Hall are not certain where North is precisely located.
We need to use the strategies of construction to orient ourselves.
This summer we propose to construct one by one with each new moon five concrete slabs determined by the meter of the structure of Campbell Hall.

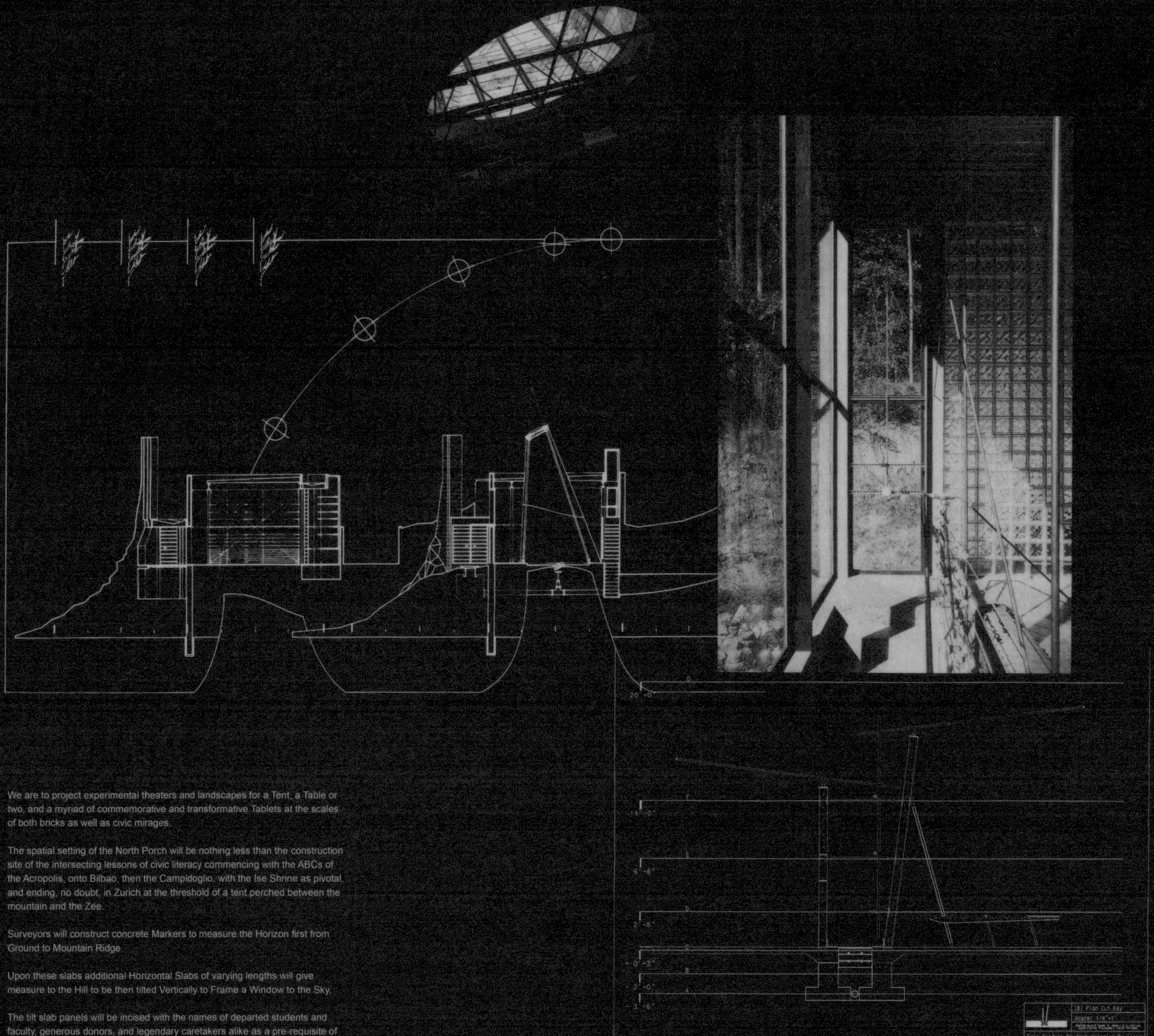

We are to project experimental theaters and landscapes for a Tent, a Table or two, and a myriad of commemorative and transformative Tablets at the scales of both bricks as well as civic mirages.

The spatial setting of the North Porch will be nothing less than the construction site of the intersecting lessons of civic literacy commencing with the ABCs of the Acropolis, onto Bilbao, then the Campidoglio, with the Ise Shrine as pivotal, and ending, no doubt, in Zurich at the threshold of a tent perched between the mountain and the Zee.

Surveyors will construct concrete Markers to measure the Horizon first from Ground to Mountain Ridge.

Upon these slabs additional Horizontal Slabs of varying lengths will give measure to the Hill to be then tilted Vertically to Frame a Window to the Sky.

The tilt slab panels will be incised with the names of departed students and faculty, generous donors, and legendary caretakers alike as a pre-requisite of citizenship.

Upon these Window plinths a swarm of spiders will insert telescoping poles and cables as stanchions for the eventful tent reliably erected by a band of Nomads in the midst of May.

It is rumored that a lunatic in the ruins of an ancient fraternity site will supervise a Deep Casting Pit that is quarried as formwork for incubating Groundhogs to sustain the stress of tent-induced wind loads.

A Forest of Pylons and Correspondent water runnels syncopate the Hill.

Fires Burn

Columns begin to Dance.

PLATE XXIII

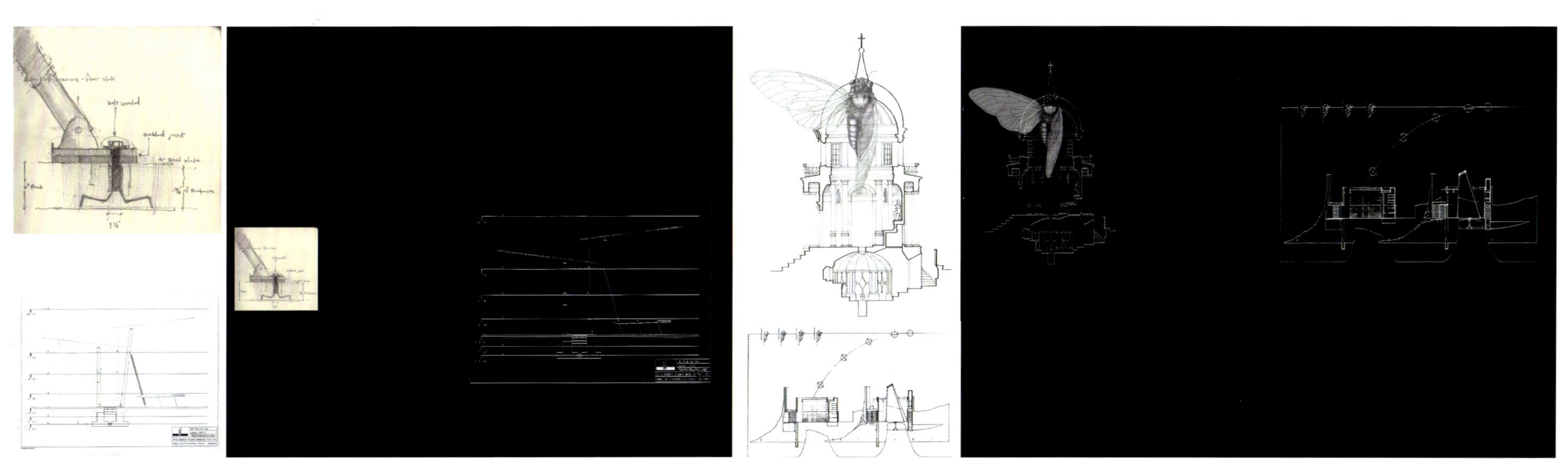

SEQUENCE OF COMPONENT ELEMENTS OF PLATE XXIII

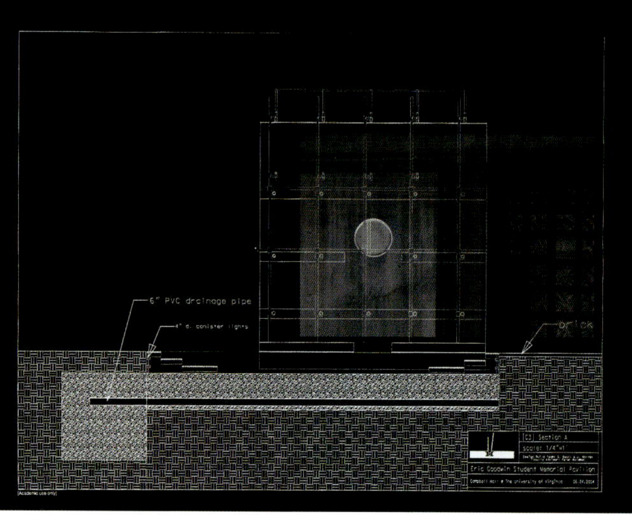
6" PVC drainage pipe
4" d. canister lights
brick
[C3] Section A
scale: 1/4"=1'
Eric Goodwin Student Memorial Pavilion
Campbell Hall @ The University of Virginia 06.24.2004
[Academic use only]

Alkaid
Alcor
Mizar
Alioth
Megrez
Dubhe
Phecda
Merak

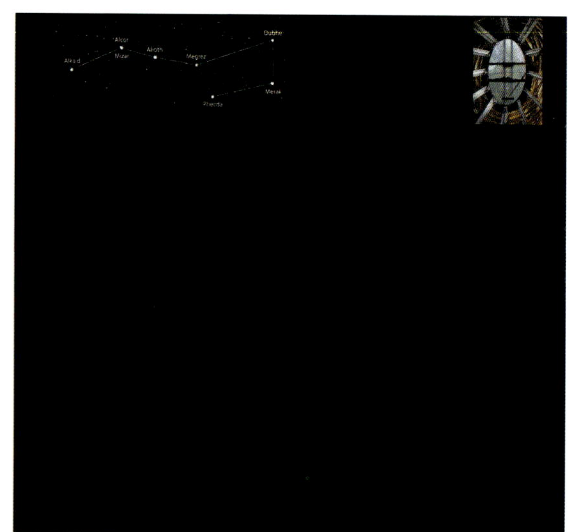
Alkaid
Alcor
Mizar
Alioth
Megrez
Dubhe
Phecda
Merak

Alioth
Mizar
Alkaid
Megrez
Merak
Phecda
G
0'-0"
F
1'-0"
E
6'-8"
D
2'-8"
C
0'-3"
B
2'-0"
A
3'-6"
6" PVC drainage pi
4" ⌀ conister ligh

PLATE XXIV

Faculty Advisor: Peter Waldman
Eric Goodwin Student Memorial Pavilion
Campbell Hall @ The University of Virginia 06.24.2004

Goodwin Student Memorial Pavilion

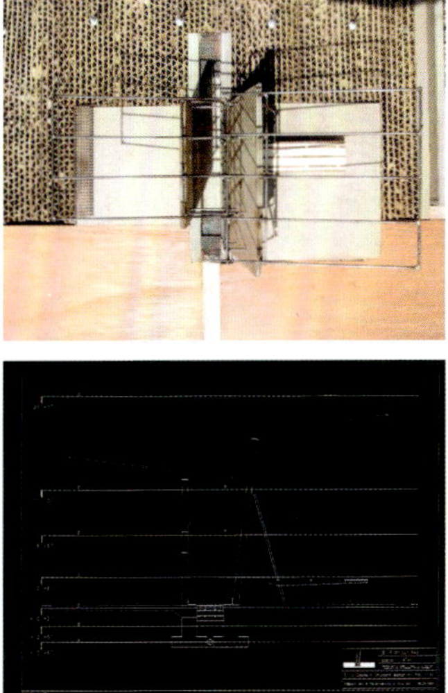

SEQUENCE OF COMPONENT ELEMENTS OF PLATE XXIV

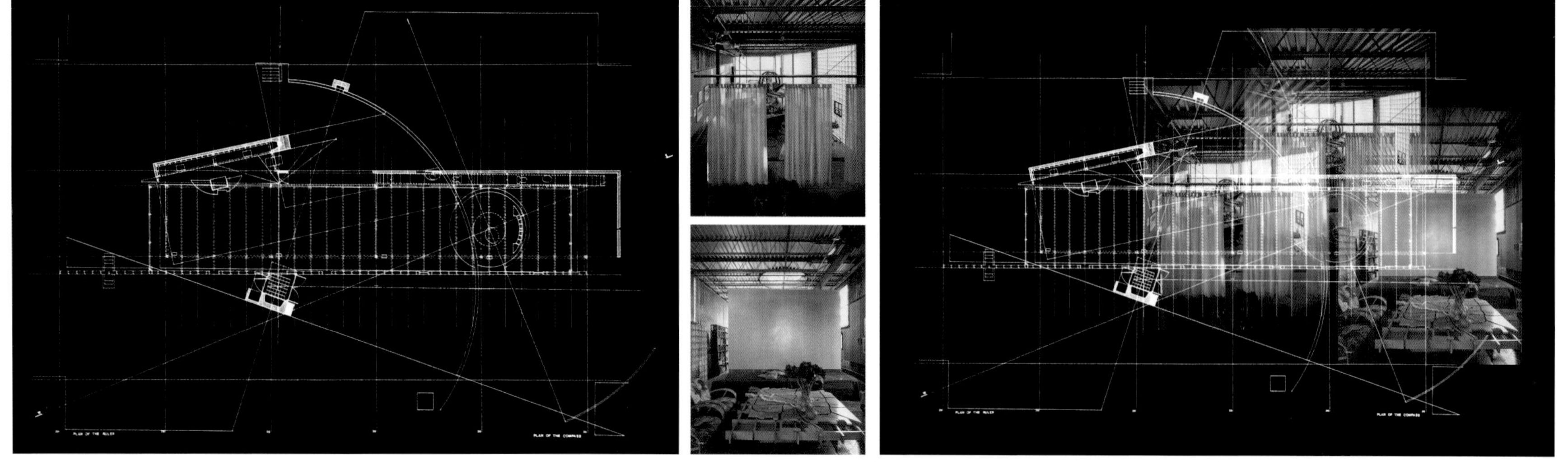

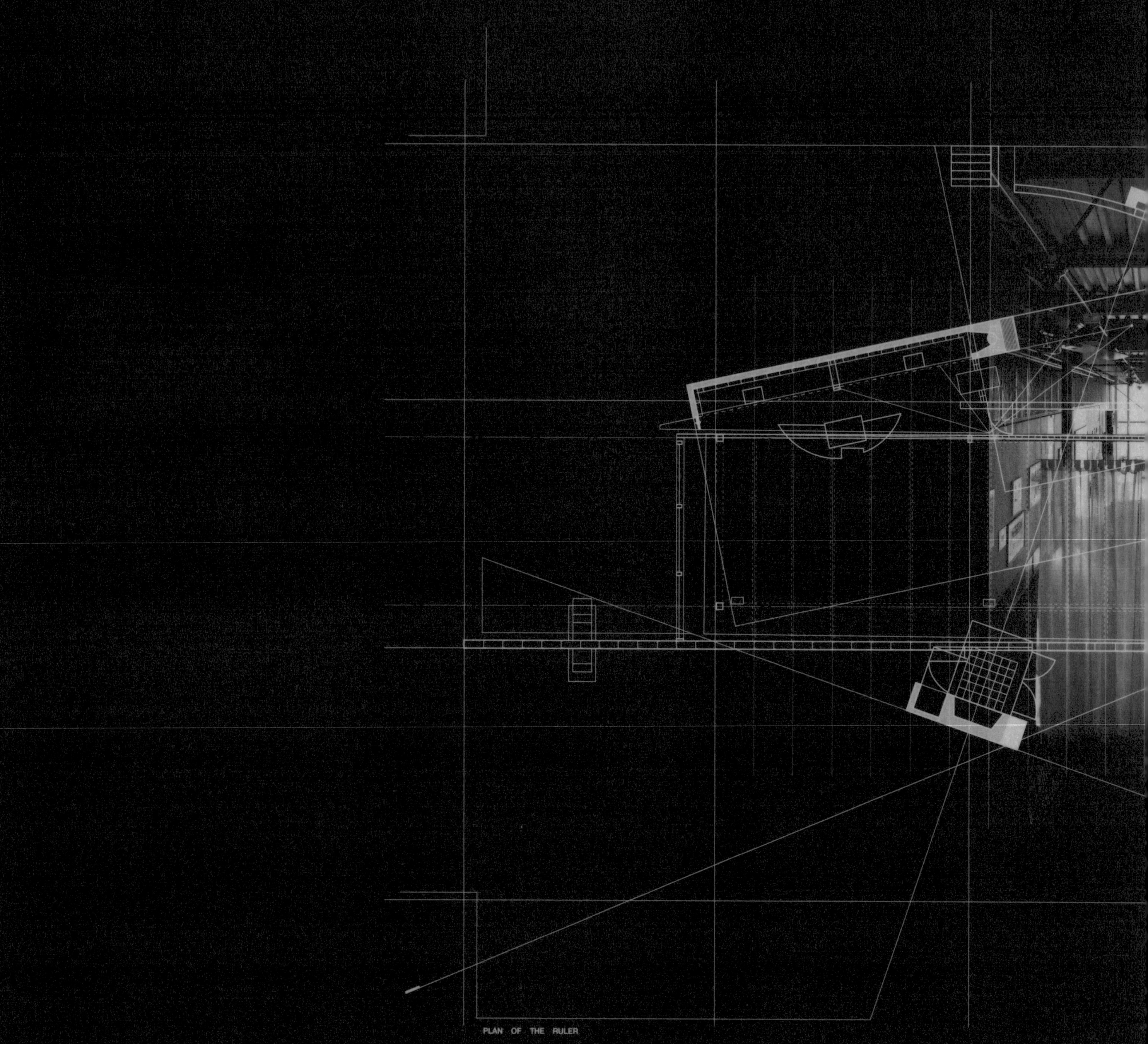

PLAN OF THE RULER

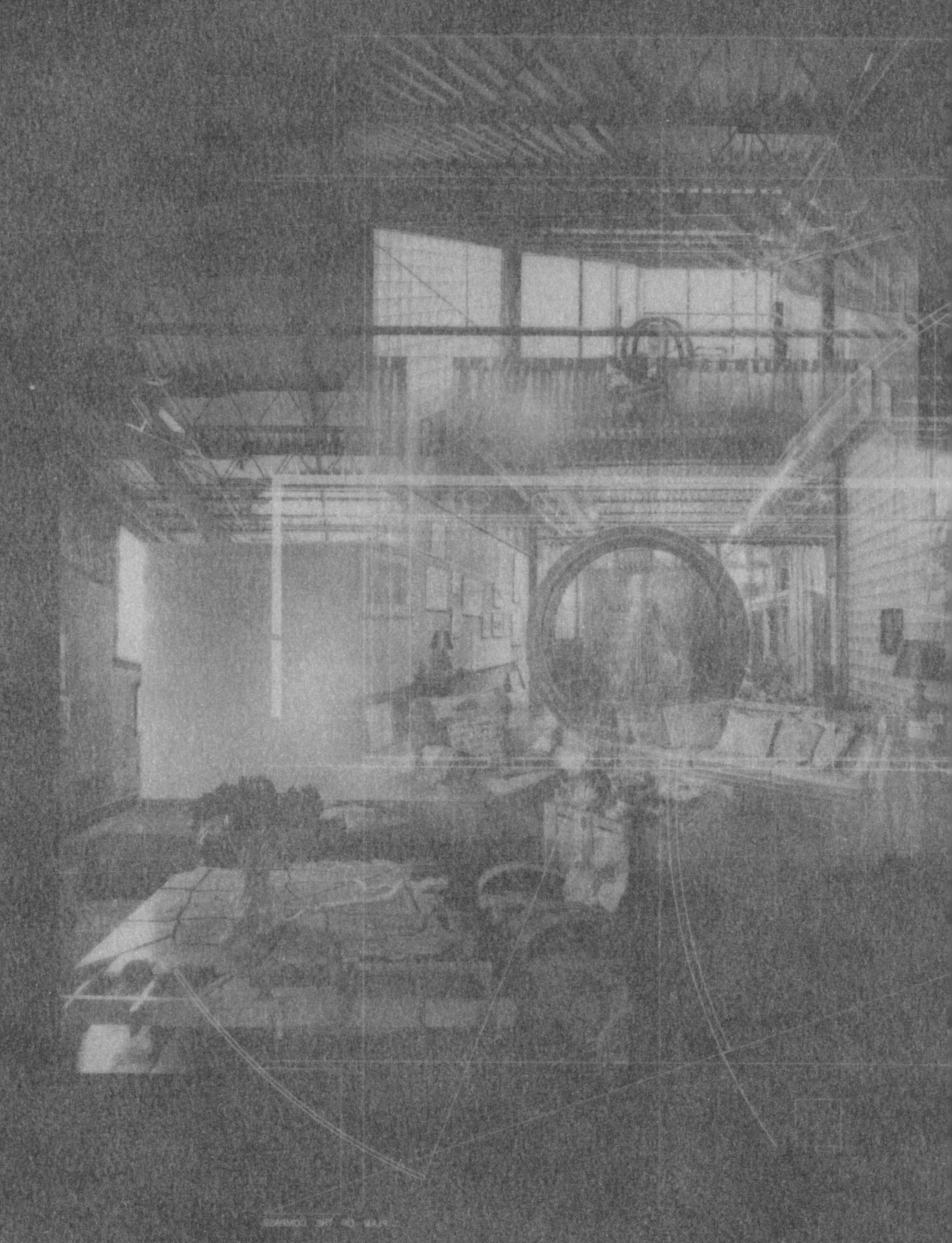

SEQUENCE OF COMPONENT ELEMENTS OF PLATE XXV

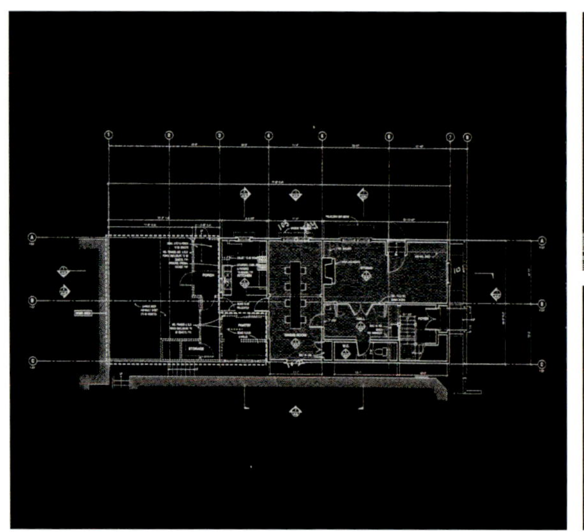
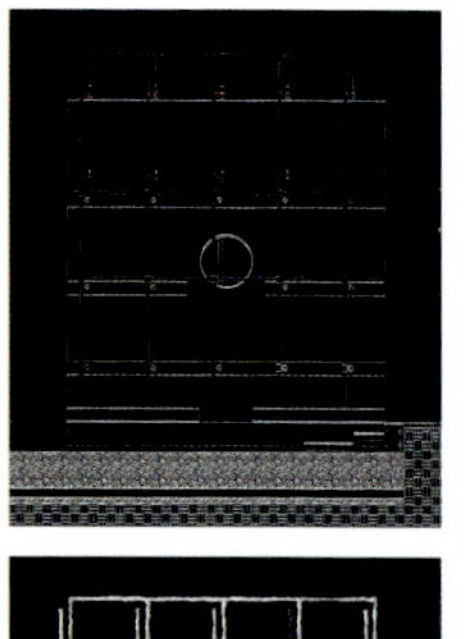

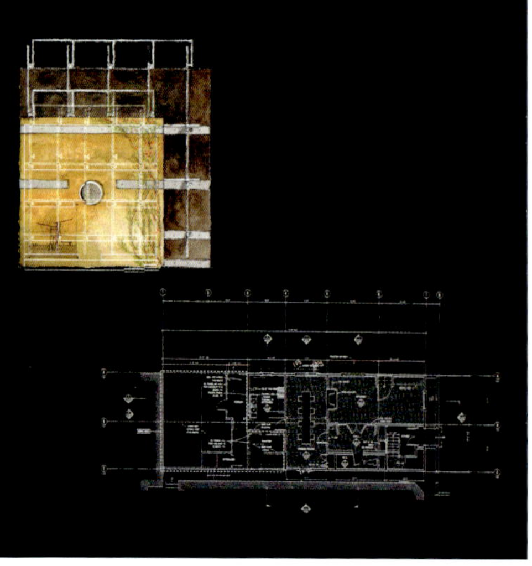

PLATE XXVI

SEQUENCE OF COMPONENT ELEMENTS OF PLATE XXVI

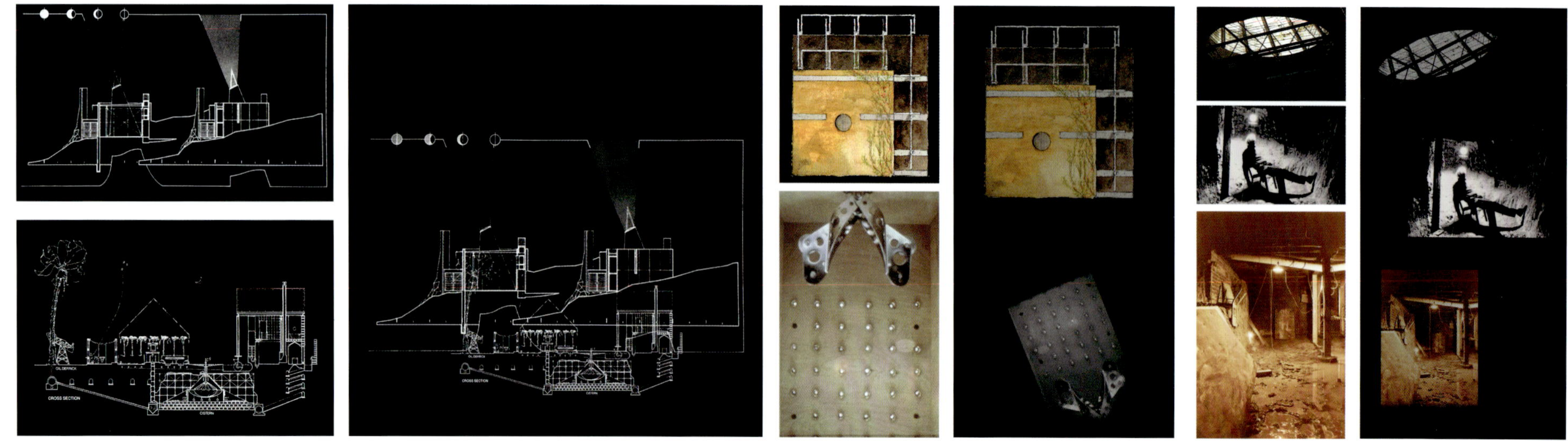

PLATE XXVII

DEMO AREA
PORCH
KITCHEN
PANTRY
STORAGE
DINING ROOM
STUDIO
HALL
W.C.
FOYER
103
101

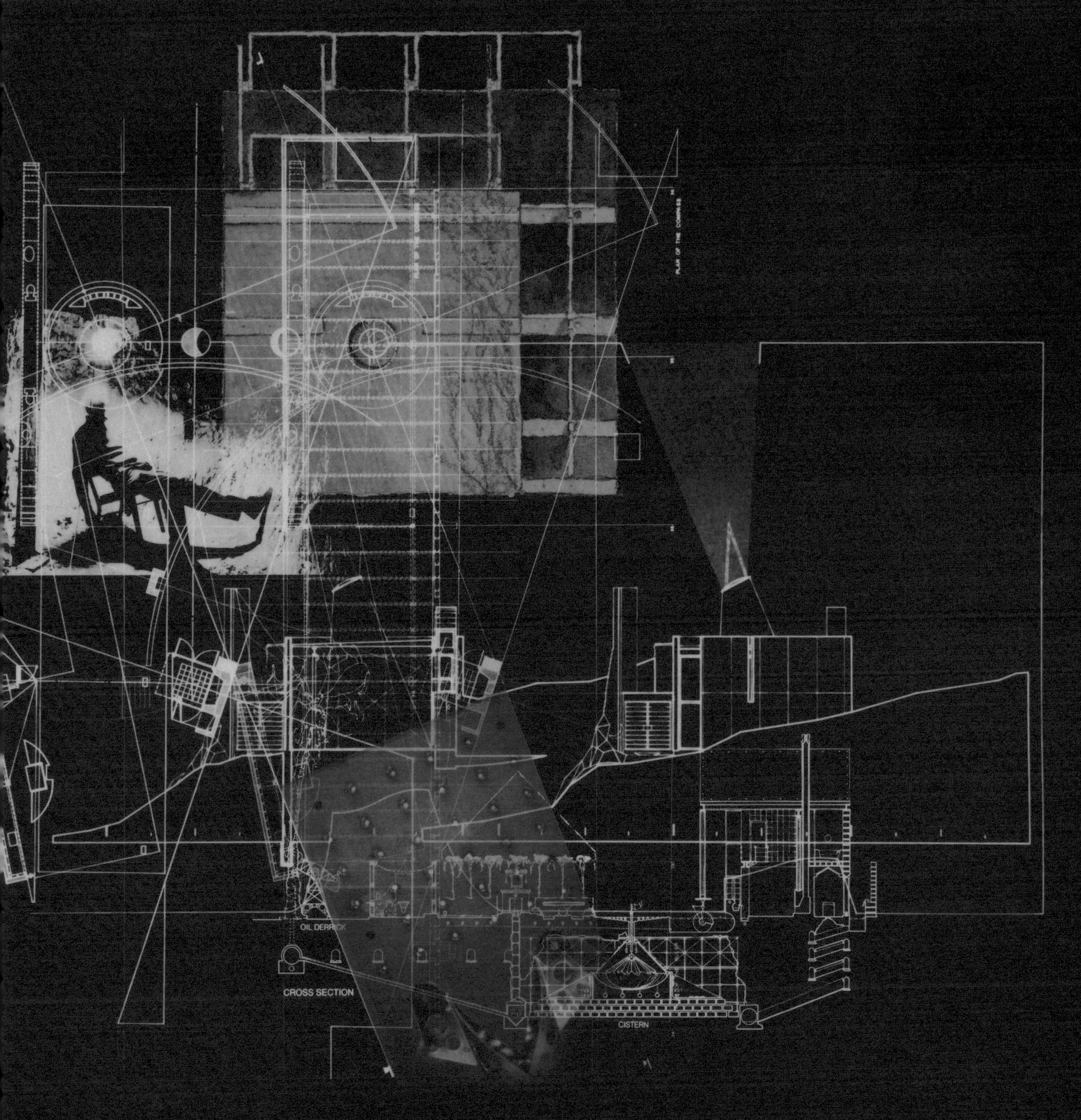

PLAN OF THE COMPASS
OIL DERRICK
CROSS SECTION
CISTERN

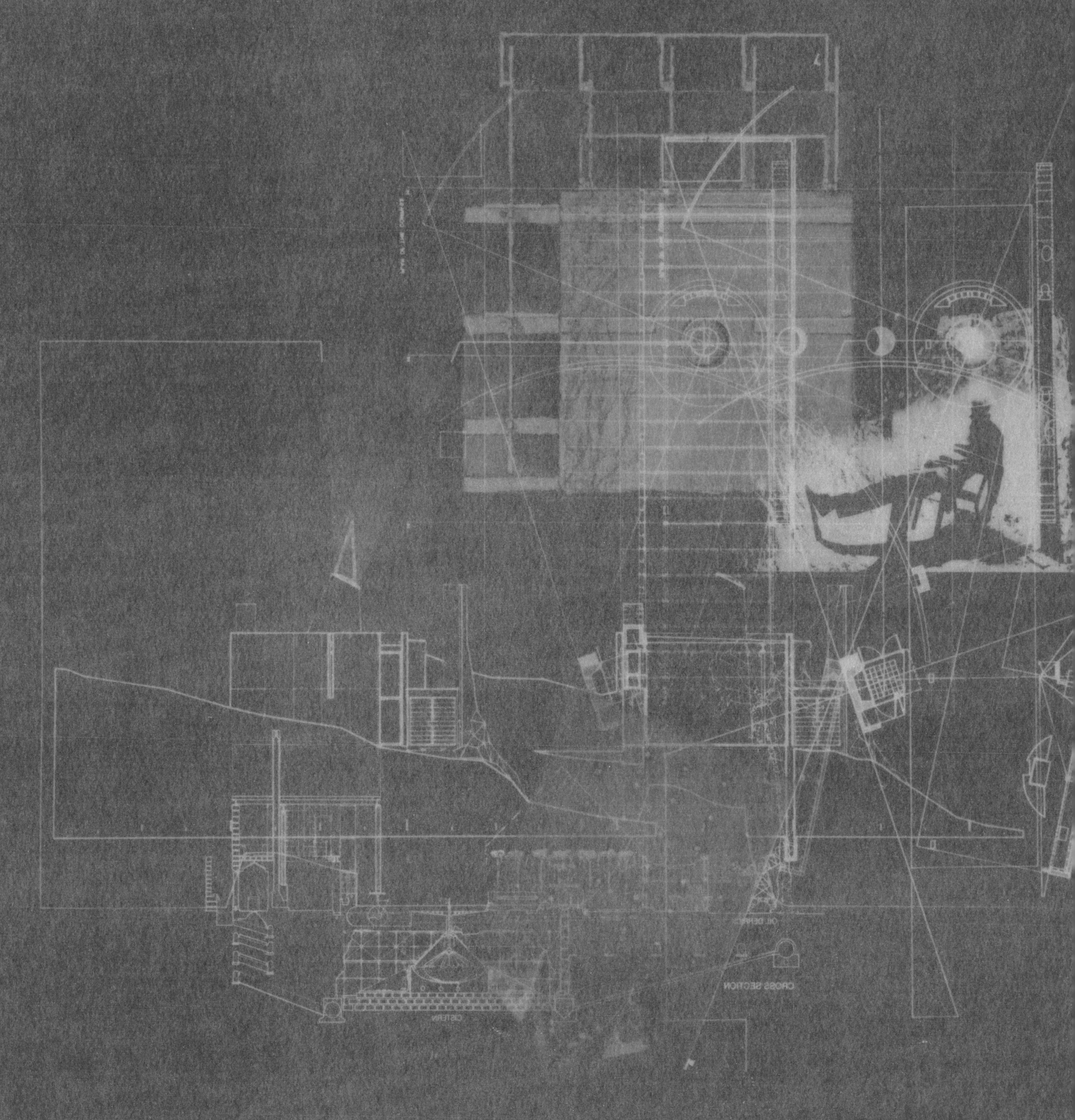

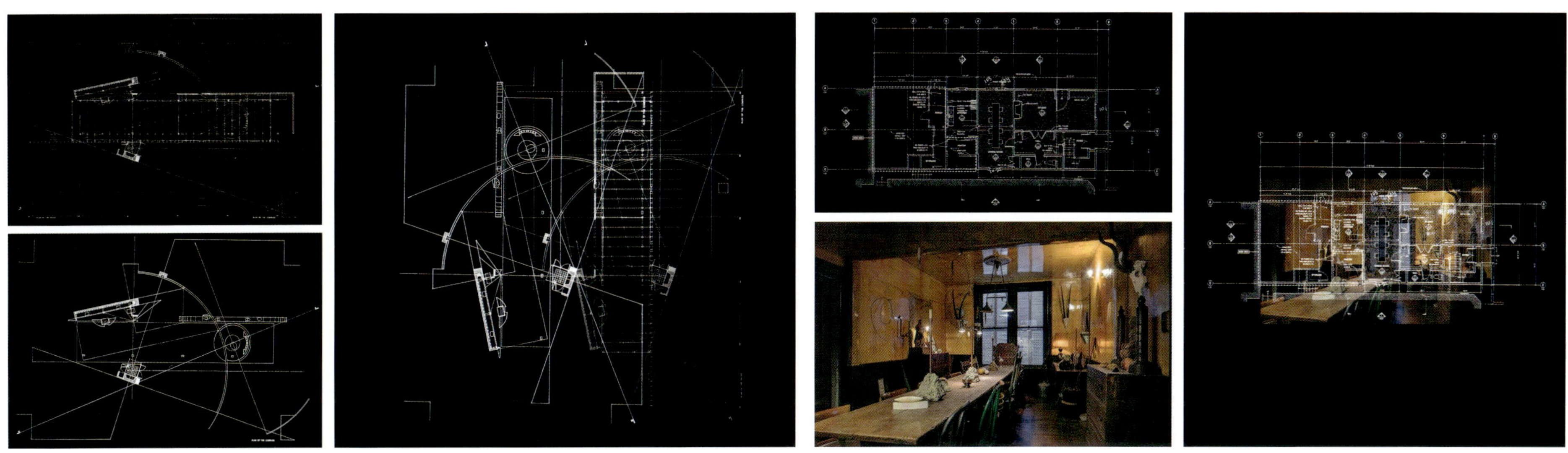

SEQUENCE OF COMPONENT ELEMENTS OF PLATE XXVII

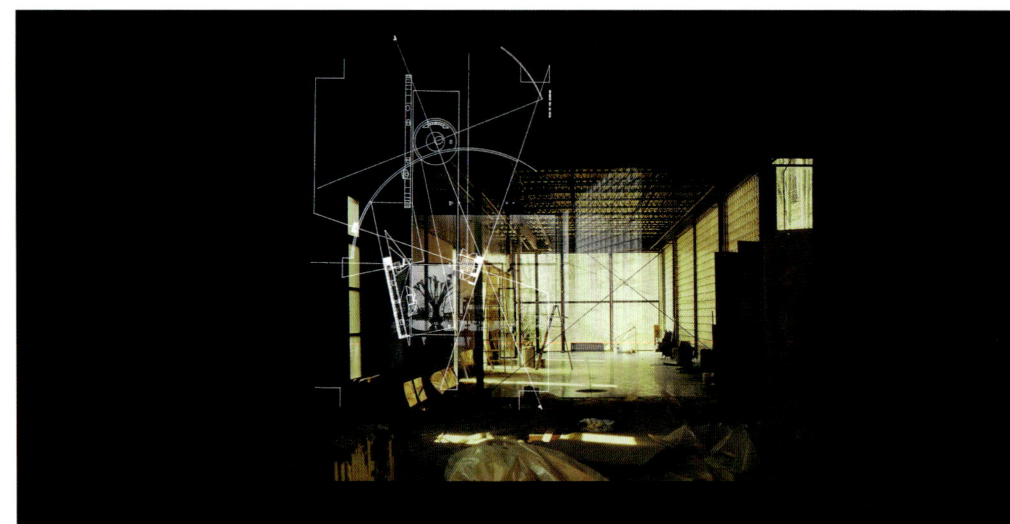

PLATE XXVIII

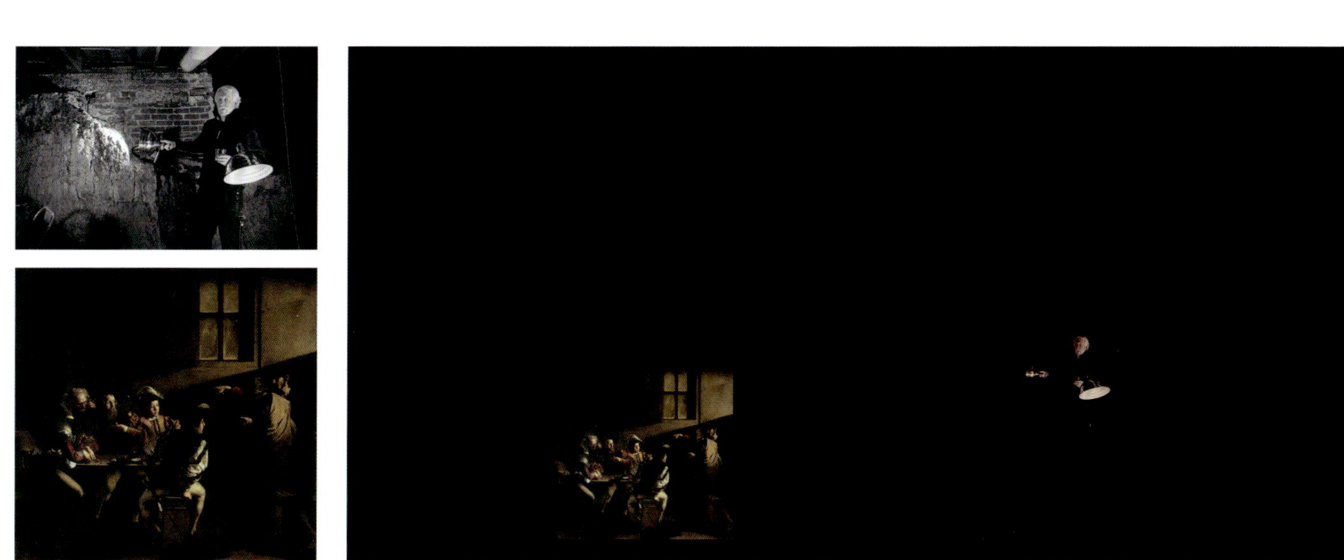

SEQUENCE OF COMPONENT ELEMENTS OF PLATE XXVIII

David Turnbull, an educator and architect, and I met when he served as an early collaborator with James Stirling who designed, in 1981, the Additions to Anderson Hall, the School of Architecture at Rice University. He has been a witness to my teaching and practice through his blogs on the Internet for more than four decades and has collaborated with me on thesis reviews at the University of Virginia for three decades now. David was very much a part of my evolution on *Lessons From the Lawn* and *Connective Tissues* as we would meet over the past 10 years in the Mudhouse Café in Crozet, VA, on intermittent early mornings. He advised me to write A Note to the Readers and to structure my stream of consciousness tendencies with a chronological frame commencing with my collages at the American Academy in Rome and ending with an essay on the 8/11 White Nationalist Invasion in Charlottesville revealing Landscapes of Aggression. When I commenced with this project with Sofia and Patrick and their photo revisions, I realized Ben Small had helped me see these projects anew two years earlier and that David Turnbull had been helping me see my work over many, many decades of blogs when I gifted him my archive of the Hurricane House drawings developed with yet another then student collaborator Christopher Genik.

David Turnbull is the President & CEO of the Cosanti Foundation, based in Paradise Valley, Arizona. He is also a senior advisor at GROW Oyster Reefs LLC in Los Angeles, California, working on aquatic ecosystem restoration and Blue Carbon, and a Senior Research Fellow of the Urban Futures Lab (UFL) in Las Vegas, at UNLV, working as a member of the "Desert Cities Research Group." From 2003–2018, he was a Director of ATOPIA Innovation and Design Director of ATOPIA Research Inc./PITCHAfrica from 2004–2018, an award-winning 501(c)3 tax exempt organization with a specific focus on the construction of building types that address global ecological and social challenges.

His academic career started in 1989 at the Architectural Association in London while he was working in the office of James Stirling, Michael Wilford and Associates, leading major projects in Spain, Japan, and Singapore. He has held academic appointments at Cooper Union, Columbia University, University of Bath, University of Pennsylvania, University of Toronto, Yale University, Cornell University, and African University of Science and Technology.

EPILOGUE

OBSERVATIONS
DAVID TURNBULL

We dreamt the same dreams—American dreams about Europe—European dreams about America. We talked about cities, about the wilderness, about deserts, mountains, lakes, rivers, the coast. We talked about the plains and prairies. We talked about freedom, about heaven and hell. We talked about the past. We talked about the future… and then we stopped.

April 13th, 2018

Looking through the structure, of steel and shadows… 04/13/2018 at 11:35 EDT.

I met Peter Waldman in 1988, in Texas, and have seen him almost every year since, somewhere on a line that links Rice University to Princeton to the Cooper Union via the University of Virginia. In 1989, we wandered around his construction sites in oil-rich Houston, where dinosaurs dance with drilling rigs. We have spent hours discussing drawings.

In 1994, we walked purposefully on a wonderful wooded slope in North Garden, VA, inspecting the footings for a kitchen and the retaining wall that would establish one edge of a large "loft." I watched, periodically, as in-situ concrete work was completed, precast elements installed, and the steel frame erected. We met again when the building volume was weathertight—the long-standing seam copper wall and roof, glass-block north wall, glazed end-walls, exposed ductwork, pipework and conduit, were in place. The completed kitchen, with masonry walls, two doors, a massive stove and cooktop, large refrigerator, well-stocked steel shelves, and a timber table next to a window had already become the locus of his new life in the woods, 25 minutes from the University, by car.

In 1996, the house was photographed for *GA*[1] and *Japan Architect*, but was far from finished. A permanent "construction site," the house evolves—acquiring additional layers, devices, patina and gifts, as it responds to the weather, to changing circumstances, and gathers together friends on the numerous special occasions that punctuate each year. I check in from time to time—every visit a great pleasure.

December 29th, 2017

Parcel X—seen on December 29th, 2017, at 15:30 EST, from Sutherland Road, in North Garden, VA.

As the eastern retaining wall caught the end of the afternoon sun, I understood the relationship of the dark steel structure, the glass, and concrete with the hill and the woodland—the open-sided court receives the morning sun to wake the private quarters of the house. Guests at endless extraordinary dinners look west through the trees to the valley, in the setting sun or moonlight.

Since passing WG Clark's house in Charlottesville and discussing his beautiful short essay "Replacement" (2000)[2] with friends, who love it, I have been reading Thoreau, and thinking about his insistence that life should be lived deliberately… which makes sense, profoundly, in a place like this, where deliberation can be abundantly rewarding.

December 30th, 2017

Parcel X—seen on December 29th, 2017 at 15:45 EST in North Garden, VA.

House warming: when Thoreau was ready to build his fireplace and chimney, he studied masonry, and collected secondhand bricks that had been used for the same purpose—robust, encrusted, hardened by heat and time. Fired. While he worked, he dreamt about villages in ancient Mesopotamia built using "second-hand bricks of a very good quality, obtained from the ruins of Babylon"—Babel, on the banks of the Euphrates, the dominion of Nebuchadnezzar, the resting place of Alexander, founded by Nimrod, Noah's great-grandson, who built a tower of burnt brick in defiance of God. You know what happens next—you have experienced the babble of incomprehension.

While Thoreau builds, he thinks deeply about "the accidental discovery of the warmth of fire."

Vitruvius tells a story about this accident that is worth retelling: "The men of old were born like the wild beasts, in woods, caves, and groves, and lived on savage fare. As time went on, the thickly crowded trees in a certain place, tossed by storms and winds, and rubbing their branches against one another, caught fire, and so the inhabitants of the place were put to flight, being terrified by the furious flame. After it subsided, they drew near, and observing that they were very comfortable standing before the warm fire, they put on logs and, while thus keeping it alive, brought up other people to it, showing them by signs how much comfort they got from it. In that gathering of men, at a time when utterance of sound was purely individual, from daily habits they fixed upon articulate words just as these had happened to come; then, from indicating by name things in common use, the result was that in this chance way they began to talk, and thus originated conversation with one another." In this story, the accidental discovery of warmth anticipates the gathering, 'the deliberative assembly," "social intercourse," and language—comprehension before architecture.

In Vitruvius' *De architectura* book II, chapter I—the house is built around the fire, with other houses, together, a collective act; heat first—houses later. Thoreau, in 1845, in silence, builds a hearth into his house near Walden Pond; house first, heat later… alone.

February 7th, 2018

The "hearth"—furnace enclosure and kitchen—of Parcel X, built as a ruin anticipating a house on Sutherland Road, in North Garden, VA—seen on February 7th, 2018

Tomorrow afternoon, I will join Peter Waldman and Sanda Iliescu in a conversation with students at the University of Virginia. I am sure that this will be as enjoyable as the many other conversations that I have had with Peter since meeting at Rice University in 1988. In late December, I took a photograph in his house that I have been waiting to use—I think that this is the right time, for many reasons. It shows a staff, with a carved head, supported by a ring that is part of a large wheel made from steel and timber. A staff is not a rod. It could be a wand, a sceptre, but never a stick. Despite their differences—in this place, this staff must have miraculous power. The wheel, like the staff, carries many possible associations, as “Chakra”, the primordial, cosmic energy of Shakti, the home of the serpent-goddess, Kundali, a ring, the Moon and her sister the Sun, Sól in old Norse, the Vitruvian circle, eternal love, bliss.

Moses uses his staff to part the Red Sea, and to bring water from a stone. He has a beautiful brother, Aaron—as described in the Qur’an, and in the Book of Numbers of the Torah—whose staff, the staff of Levi, when placed in the “Tent of Meeting,” with others, one from each of the leaders of the 12 tribes, sprouts and blossoms overnight, bearing almonds. The same staff is transformed into a serpent when the Pharaoh asks for evidence of a miracle. This story does not have a happy ending. In the Book of Psalms, 23:4, the staff is a crook, an instrument of compassion. The rod represents authority. Shepherds use both. In pre-Christian Scandinavia, the “volva” seer, carried a magical staff, a wand. She could interpret omens, intervene in a battle, change the course of a river, fill a Fjord with fish in a period of famine. She could be extraordinarily seductive. Her wand was an instrument of magical transformation. Prophets, shamans, tribal and religious leaders in many cultures carried a staff—some still do.

This staff has the face of a sheep and the ears of a wolf—it is held upright on the vertical axis of the wheel… Tomorrow, I will have a question. Given the chance, I shall ask it…

February 8th, 2018

The staff, seen at Parcel X on February 8th, 2018 in North Garden, VA.

I spent the afternoon with Peter Waldman, talking about drawing. Inevitably some time was spent discussing measurement, and the “measured drawings” that were once obligatory, like drawing the “orders” or roman lettering, exercises in accuracy—profile, contour, and inflection—in relation to line making, and line-weight. I have always liked the technical implications of the conjunction of line and weight—the complexity of hardness, softness, the pressure that is applied, and the angle at which the drawing instrument, a pen or a pencil, is held and how. I also like the conventions of skiagraphy.

For more than a decade, I have passed a small didactic structure that Peter built with students.[3] It extends a pair of lines from inside the school of architecture into the middle distance, establishing a spatial and temporal connection with a tree that had been planted “in memoriam,” and the sun. Oriented north-south, apertures in the east and west walls, and shadow-making scaffolding columns, beams, props and ties, make fleeting, transient marks, points and lines, gradients, shadows, projected shapes, on the concrete walls and on the floor—drawings, which cannot be rolled up or put away. The drawings describe forms that should be predictable, could be measured, but however memorable they are when present, are unreliable. Affected by atmospheric fluctuation, seasonal norms or climatic anomalies, they can be absent for days. The structure is incomplete without them, lost, unloved. One day they will return, once inevitably, now, no longer. When they do, the drawings will be extraordinary.

April 14th, 2018

Eric Goodwin Memorial Passage, seen on 04/13/2018 at 19:30 EDT.

Peter Waldman was a Fellow at the American Academy in Rome.[4] He has many stories. We didn't talk about the Academy yesterday, but I have become aware of the impact the experience of living and studying there had for him, and for others. I have been thinking about my dear friend Diane Lewis. She talked about it a lot. She loved Rome, it changed her, provided focus, and supplemented a body of knowledge with embodied learning, history, lived in the present. A year ago she was very ill and would die soon. In her last classes at the Cooper Union she drew plans, of Rome.

It was possible, some time ago, to assume a shared ability to recall the ambience, specific qualities, plans and sections of buildings, places, even entire cities—to communicate in shorthand, with a quick drawing accompanied by a sound, but not a word…

April 14th, 2018

Eric Goodwin Memorial Passage, looking toward the memorial tree. The channel should be full of water, a canal that cannot be crossed...
4/13/2018 at 11:30 EDT.

In the morning, as the projection of the eastern oculus touched the floor…
04/13/2018 at 11:15 EDT, as I arrived.

In the evening, the projection of the western oculus approaches the horizon…
04/13/2018 at 19:25 EDT, before sunset.

ENDNOTES

PROLOGUE

A Note to Readers

1. Luigi Pirandello, *Six Characters in Search of An Author* (Milan, Italy, 1921).

2. Lars Lerup, *Building the Unfinished: Architecture and Human Action* (Sage, 1977).

3. **Architecture Between Memory and Amnesia** is an essay by Diana Agrest on the La Villette Competition, 1976.

4. With **Ben Small**.

5. With **Sofia Kuspan** and **Patrick Sardo**.

6. Posthuman, in the context of the project in Act Two of this book, is rooted in posthuman/transhuman ideology, focused on technological advancements as enhancing human society and its capabilities.

7. Alice Walker, *In Search of Our Mothers' Gardens* (Harcourt Brace Jovanovich, 1983).

page vii

8. **Lessons of the Lawn** is the title of the course "ARCH1010: Lessons of the Lawn," commenced 2000 to the present.

page ix

9. 2021 was the year for the emergence of Brood X cicadas across the Eastern United States, specifically much of Northern Virginia.

10. This text, titled **Didactic Intentions**, is borrowed and edited from A Note to Readers from *Lessons From the Lawn: The Word Made Flesh: Dialogues between Citizens and Strangers* (ORO Editions, 2019).

ACT ONE

page 1

1. **Surveyors, Nomads, & Lunatics:**
Peter Rowe, in *Design Thinking* (MIT Press, 1985), identified Peter Waldman's pedagogy and practice as examples of self-generated narratives requisite of the heuristic process. At the time, the author was not aware of that self-conscious posture, let alone its spelling, but had persistently delighted in connecting science, phenomenology, and psychotherapy through "spatial tales of origin" as "specifications for construction," some call epistemology in academic circles. Heuristic thinking presents facts, some now call evidenced-based design, which require the engagement of fictions to reveal universal truths generated from unique if not singular discoveries. Rebecca Solnit's *A Field Guide to Getting Lost*, is then offered as a mapping exercise for work-as-life in the guise of our school's foundation course, "Lessons of the Lawn," as well as his studio curriculum.

Ever since the sandbox and the oceanfront sandcastle, we have all been Good Architects. "Lessons of the Lawn," the course, reveals for all of us as global citizens an appreciation of the synthetic capacities of surveyors, nomads, and lunatics creating the Academical Village in collaboration and not in isolation.

The Surveyor arrives at noon to mark solstice/equinox with instrumental baggage.

The Nomad arrives at sunset in time to build a substantial fire for kit and kin while taking note of lofty palms, deep wells, others' ashes, and recent footprints, sensing one is never alone while keeping places strange to oneself, and sustaining enigma.

The Lunatic operates in the ethereal light of the Moon and is ambivalent to the systems referenced by the Surveyor or the scattered self-evident truths of the Nomad. The Lunatic is often mistaken as a magician, who knows all too well that the swiftest magician is an encyclopedic scientist and who moves more swiftly than those with little faith in the power of spatial tales of origin. Rowe, three decades later, might conclude that Waldman is still invested heuristically in the beginning and the end, and is now here radically grounded in this Piedmont condition.

2. Saigyo (1118–1190), *Mirror for the Moon: A Selection of Poems*, trans. William R. LaFleur (New Directions, 1978).

3. **Citizens and Strangers:**
The author is the self-conscious son of orphans: his mother, motherless at birth, migrated as a child to America from Vienna in 1920, voicing all her life recollections emerging from "the other side" (of the Atlantic); his father, son of immigrant parents from Prague and Budapest, was orphaned at five and sent to Pittsburgh's Home for Hebrew Children. Early years in postwar New York City made the author pathologically optimistic and inclusive that one could be a citizen and stranger simultaneously. When friends and family played "cowboys and indians," the author always elected to be an Indian tool-maker of bows and arrows, tomahawks, and amazed his classmates in elementary school that he could predict time by the sun with remarkable accuracy, because he fictionalized even then that he grew up on a Comanche reservation. His father called this son *Smoh-hawk*, a Jewish Indian. Citizens and strangers is a spatial demographic the author uses in his urban studios as the nomadic condition of past and future cities, and it resonates in all his narratives of inclusion and possible dialogues.

page 3

4. **Spatial Tales of Origin:**
When Chris Genik, a M.Arch student of mine at Rice, asked me to do the Times Square Competition in 1983, we quickly realized we had two distinct approaches, as we were both storytellers. We decided to take the competition board and make it in a diptych, two stories/spatial tales (architectural images building sequential ideas, eventually Specifications for Construction and a Cast of Characters) of where our ideas originated, like a Genesis of an idea thus we termed *Two Spatial Tales of the Origin* of our response; a Dialogue. This was a joyous frictional fictional exercise, we smiled a lot and won first prize on Time Square awarded by the Head Librarian of NYC, later Yale President, and second and third prizes in other urban competitions. We were on a role/roll.

page 7

5. Carl Sagan, *The Dragons of Eden: Speculations on the Evolution of Human Intelligence* (Random House, 1977).

page 9

6. Waldman's paraphrasing of two of four primary elements of architecture, Earthwork and Framework/Structure, from Gottfried Semper's *The Four Elements of Architecture and Other Writings*, trans. Harry F. Mallgrave and Wolfgang Herrmann (Cambridge, 1989).

7. **Landscapes of Aggression:**
Lessons of the Lawn ends with an essay on the 8/11 White Nationalist Invasion in Charlottesville revealing Landscapes of Aggression, suggested by David Turnbull.

8. A paraphrasing of a passage from Pliny the Elder's *Natural History*, eds., John Bostock and H. T. Riley, book XXXVI, chapter 24 (Taylor and Francis, 1855), referring to the strong roots of fig trees that may grow underneath marble and stone construction and damage or destroy them.

9. **Lightness and Exactitude**: Two of the five literary qualities Italo Calvino identified in *Six Memos for the Next Millennium* (Harvard University Press, 1988), a series of lectures written by Calvino but never delivered due to an untimely death.

page 10

10. **"What could be more modern than the archaic?"**
From Sanford Kwinter's essay *African Genesis*, recalled from his lecture at University of Virginia in 2004.
Sanford Kwinter, "African Genesis (A Presentation)," *Assemblage*, no. 36 (1998): 25–41. https://doi.org/10.2307/3171363.

11. JEF7REY HILDNER's 2020 book *VISUAL EF9ECTS: Architecture and the Chess Game of Form & Story* (The Architect Painter Press, 2018), which was also included as part of the epilogue of *Connective Tissues* by Peter Waldman (2020).

page 11

12. **Long Day's Journey into Night:**
An early 20th-century play by Eugene O'Neill, for which Waldman did the stage sets as an adolescent at Gray Gables and about which he wrote his senior thesis while at Princeton, inspiring later the more mature mindset of a lunatic. It inspired both the diurnal and nocturnal dialectical responsibilities of the architect.
Eugene O'Neill, *Long Day's Journey into Night* (Jonathan Cape, 1982).

page 13

13. **An architecture of almost nothing**: A term of Scott Bernhard, Rice student who worked with me from 1988–1990, now Tulane faculty in architecture.

14. **Hullah**: A rural vernacular term for a cleaved shallow valley of cleared pastoral land at the Forest Edge in the Piedmont. Also spelled *hollow*, *hollar*, and *holla* in different regional dialects.

page 26

15. **Terra incognita**: unknown land or territory, in Latin.

ACT TWO

page 49

1. Michael Benedikt and Kory Bieg, eds., CENTER 21: *The Secret Life of Buildings* (Center for American Architecture and Design, 2018).

2. John Brinckerhoff Jackson, *The Necessity for Ruins, and Other Topics* (University of Massachusetts Press, 1980).

page 51

3. *Connective Tissues* is the title of Peter Waldman's previous publication featuring the work of 10 Kenan Fellows, the terminology that defines his teaching pedagogy, and the guiding framework of the collaborative spirit of *In Search of Spatial Scripts*. In *Connective Tissues*, Waldman writes that "The greatest lesson is Jefferson's belief in collaboration across generations as the proof of citizenship for this nation founded at the frontiers of Arcadia." (*Connective Tissues*, XI)

4. Practices that engage in this outlined pedagogical approach that were studied include both architectural and landscape architecture practices. Architecture practices include Bruner/Cott's work of repurposing former mill buildings at MASS MoCA. Landscape architecture practices include Julie Bargmann's D.I.R.T. Studio and her pioneering approach to industrialized land in projects including Urban Outfitters Headquarters, and Latz + Partner's work at Duisburg Nord Landschaftspark in Germany.

5. Architects have historically ignored the importance of site context, including landscape realities and material weathering. In the context of the Packard Plant, there was a 2014 competition titled "Reanimate the Ruins!" While the brief called for retaining original elements of the plant, the winning entries show an abstracted site: one that is repackaged as shiny and brand new. Academic practices such as Stan Allen's 2016 Venice Biennale installation "Botanical Garden" address the need to view the site as a landscape and T+E+A+M's 2016 "Detroit Reassembly Plant" project addresses opportunities to reuse building materials, yet both proposals highly stylize and abstract its proposed fragmentation and material reuse.

6. In a conversation between Patrick Sardo and Jock Reynolds on October 3rd, 2024, Reynolds stated that David Ireland didn't want to "obliterate the history of things." This phrasing encapsulates Ireland's approach to art that highlights the material realities of objects, artifacts, and surfaces. *Wasteland Spolia*'s approach of reusing and preserving degraded materials aligns with Ireland's pedagogy in both principle and creative expression.

7. The concept of defining an American Spolia is adapted from Aleksandr Mergold, assistant professor in architecture at Cornell AAP. His practice focuses on a contemporary interpretation of spolia. His forthcoming publication *Toward an American Spolia* makes the case for "the spoliation of the American 20th century." *Wasteland Spolia* builds upon this existing discourse.

page 55

8. Source for spoliated columns: Dale Kinney, "Spolia from the Baths of Caracalla in Sta. Maria in Trastevere," *Art Bulletin* 68, no. 3 (1986): 379–397.

page 67

9. In Robert Pepperell's "The Posthuman Manifesto," *Kritikos* 2 (2005), he states that "complex machines are an emerging form of life" in the first section titled "General Statements." Much of this manifesto aligns closely with the philosophy of the project and how it interprets the relationship between human and technology.

10. While not the first to use the term, Liam Young's definition of the "Post-Anthropocene" helps to align the project to an era of our civilization that may or may not exist. Benjamin Bratton first defined the Post-Anthropocene in this context in "Some Trace Effects of the Post-Anthropocene: On Accelerationist Geopolitical Aesthetics," in *e-flux* 46 (June, 2013), and was later expanded on by Liam Young in "Machine Landscapes: Architectures of the Post-Anthropocene," a special issue of *Architectural Design* 89, no. 1 (January/February, 2019).

page 69

11. Most fulfillment centers are currently designed with a 52-foot column grid in both directions, which permits four dock doors between each grid line for maximum efficiency in material and number of docks for inbound and outbound shipping. The structural design of future fulfillment centers will be dependent on many factors, but most likely will be driven by how the internal operations shape the shell of the building around them.

12. The upper floors of multistory fulfillment centers are fenced-in storage areas where small robots bring tall "pods" of goods to the fence for humans to pick an item out. The items are organized into different pods through a highly complicated algorithm, and the items that are purchased most often tend to be located closer to the fence. This creates a gradient of desire from the center of the floorplate being the least ordered while the edges are the busiest with more orders and more items being picked and replenished. This layout changes depending on trends, holidays, and even weather.

13. Fulfillment and shipping companies have different building designs to fill different roles in their logistics network. The size and availability of building plots, highway, train, and plane networks, local labor availability, and customer demand all inform what size and type of building a company may want to build in that area. Prototypical templates are first designed as generic plans that are updated and changed to meet local building codes and unique site conditions.

page 71

14. Current data center design principles feature raised floors and drop ceilings to move air, water, and wiring out of the way of the path for human workers to maintain the servers. These design principles could be the same if humans are replaced with robots, but massive changes to server design and layout could change the way that the mechanical systems are laid out and how the robotic maintenance workers manage day-to-day operations.

15. The use of machine learning tools and large language models requires far more energy than typical internet use and data storage, which has drawn significant concern. In September 2024, Microsoft announced it would be using the Unit 1 reactor at Three Mile Island nuclear power plant to offset the 800+ MW of power used by data centers in Illinois, Virginia, and Ohio. Other companies fund the construction of solar farms or work directly with energy suppliers through power purchase agreements to ensure consistent, and occasionally renewable, energy for their data center facilities. Unfortunately, this huge increase in power demand may also require nonrenewable power plants to remain open for longer to keep up with demand.

page 73

16. Tarla Rai Peterson, "Jefferson's Yeoman Farmer as Frontier Hero A Self Defeating Mythic Structure," *Agriculture and Human Values* 7, no. 1 (December 1990): 9–19. https://doi.org/10.1007/bf01530599.

page 75

17. In the early 20th century, modernist architects became concerned with how buildings might play a role in improving or deteriorating human health and hygiene. Architects were reacting to the disease and death caused by tuberculosis and other air-borne diseases that wreaked havoc through Europe and the rest of the world. Alvar Aalto's Paimio Sanatorium might be one of the most prominent of this era, with large expanses of glass and a sun deck to ensure each patient had access to clean air and natural light, once thought to be the cure for tuberculosis.

18. The CHIPS and Science Act became law in 2022 and aims to incentivize semiconductor manufacturers to invest in fabs in the United States. The goal is to create jobs, invest in US-based manufacturing, and ensure that the US stays competitive in the global technology market. The bill also aims to ensure that the United States has a steady supply of microchips in case of worsening geopolitical conditions in Taiwan, South Korea, and Israel, where some of the largest semiconductor manufacturers are located.

19. "The Engineer's Aesthetics and Architecture" is the title of the third chapter of Le Corbusier's seminal 1923 book *Towards a New Architecture*, trans. Frederick Etchells (Rodker, 1931).

page 88

20. In a conversation between Patrick Sardo and Jock Reynolds on November 6th, 2024, Reynolds spoke about David's very social nature and the tight-knit community of artists in the Mission District in the 1970s and 1980s. Reynolds emphasized that he, David, and others were always working together, helping each other get new opportunities, and sharing materials and techniques.

21. Constance M. Lewallen, *500 Capp Street: David Ireland's House* (University of California Press, 2015), 14.

page 89

22. In a conversation between Patrick Sardo and Jock Reynolds on November 6th, 2024, Reynolds connected David Ireland's work to the Arte Povera movement, one that focused on inexpensive everyday materials, unconventional artistic practices, and an emphasis on change and dynamism.

23. Karen Tsujimoto, David Ireland, and Jennifer R. Gross, *The Art of David Ireland: The Way Things Are* (Oakland Museum of California; University of California Press, 2003), 35.

24. Ibid, 58.

page 91

25. This is an excerpt of a letter David sent to his sister Judy in the form of a book titled *David Ireland's House* (1980). The rest of the letter can be found at SFMOMA's blog, Open Space. https://openspace.sfmoma.org/2017/05/the-david-ireland-house/.

page 95

26. **The Human Comedy** refers specifically to William Saroyan's 1943 fiction on Ulysses Macauley in Ithaca, California, telling the same frictional tales some call recurrent

ENDNOTES

dualities initiated by Gilgamesh, Homer, Cervantes of the genesis of place, and an eschatology of resilience which is the contemporary relevance of the Lawn. The full original quote: "After a moment he smiled the smile of the Macauley people—the gentle, wise, secret smile which said Yes to all things."

ACT THREE

page 105

1. Megaron refers to a ninth-century BCE Archaic building type: e.g., the Tomb of Atreus, before the Hellenic age in Greece, which hybridized caves and tents, now with combined walls and columns, in didactic harmony of the heavy and the light, the open and the closed, of the public realm and the private retreat. With columns out front, making a porch, there also were posited columns inside around a brazier permitting an aperture in the roof.

page 131

2. Seen in Plate XIX.

page 139

3. *The Architecture of Time*, University of Pennsylvania, Philadelphia, November 14–15, 2024.

page 143

4. John Brinckerhoff Jackson, *The Necessity for Ruins, and Other Topics* (University of Massachusetts Press, 1980).

EPILOGUE

page 163

1. Parcel X was featured in Yukio Futagawa's *GA Houses* 51 (March, 1997).

page 165

2. "Replacement" by WG Clark is a short essay shared with students in his Elements of Design class and it is also in the book *Place Matters: The Architecture of WG Clark* by Robert McCarter (ORO Editions, 2019)

page 171

3. **The Eric Goodwin Memorial Pavilion/Passage** (2004), completed by Peter Waldman as studio critic and Sam Beall, Jennifer Findley, and Justin Walton as Design-Build Team.

page 173

4. Peter Waldman was a Brunner Fellow of the American Academy in Rome in 2000 where he developed a collage-focused research project titled *Deep Frieze: Studies for a New Facade for Villa Aurelia*. Several photos of these large material collages are included on page 101.

ACKNOWLEDGMENTS

I acknowledge Mathide Nancy Claudina Davila Carpio from Arequipa, Peru, who inspired our first and last dwellings: *The Parasol House in Houston* in 1981, and this last encampment *Parcel X in North Garden* in 1994.

I also acknowledge our daughter Beth Davila Waldman, a multimedia artist and cultural activist in the Bay Area, who introduced me to David Ireland's *House as Museum* the Summer of 2023 first as a catalytic oasis and then appreciated as a *deus ex machina* for this enduring spatial script of here and now and then and there. In retrospect, on the Solstice of 2007, I recall Beth introduced me to Rebecca Solnit's *A Field Guide to Getting Lost*, which continues to reinforce my appetite for *Both Sides Now*.

I now acknowledge my first dean at the University of Virginia, Harry Porter, who as a Landscape Architect, inspired me to transfer from Rice to this vital School, which he radically and ethically grounded to prioritize the preconditions of the site in this our Piedmont Condition. *Parcel X* is a testament to this vision of Raphael's *The School of Athens* on both my pedagogy and practice.

I also acknowledge my millennial dean, Karen Van Lengen, who upon my return in 2000 from the American Academy in Rome, offered me the opportunity to teach a new university-wide humanities elective, *Lessons of the Lawn*, and promoted me to the William R. Kenan Professorship in Architecture. Then, in 2004, Karen Van Lengen challenged me to develop the *Eric Goodwin Memorial* as a design-build project with a fourth-year studio of undergraduates.

In the summer of 2024, it became clear to me that I needed to incorporate David Ireland's character more explicitly to haunt the stage sets of Parcel X and the Goodwin Pavilion as a post-script. That summer, my undergraduate teaching assistant Robin Xiao suddenly served as a requisite on-site digital wizard and was easily recruited as yet another collaborator. Over a week-long spontaneous charette, we created a spatial narrative in the final Six Vellum Diptychs, which now script the 28 PLATE sequence. Therein, David Ireland is staged between vellum scrims here and there, then and now. Herein, yet again I acknowledge my insatiable appetite to improvise with generational strangers.

Finally, I acknowledge *The William R. Kenan Foundation* for my ongoing Research Support for the past 25 years, which made possible *LESSONS FROM THE LAWN* (2019), *CONNECTIVE TISSUES* (2020), and now *IN SEARCH OF SPATIAL SCRIPTS* (2025).

Needless to say, I acknowledge my generational gratitude across five decades to family and familiar students and colleagues, Karen Van Lengen and WG Clark, and two perfect strangers Ann Hamilton and Henry Moss who were introduced to me by Sofia Kuspan and Patrick Sardo without whose generosity and endurance this project would not have been possible.

PHOTOGRAPHY CREDITS

Front Cover: Patrick Sardo (2023)
Back Cover: David Turnbull (2018)

500 Capp Street Foundation page: 85

Yujin Cao: page 84

Mimmo Capone: page 101

Robert Corser: pages 21–22

Jean-Pierre Dalbéra: L'entrée de l'université d'architecture IUAV (Venise) (https://flickr.com/photos/72746018@N00/29945676542) available under Creative Commons Attribution (CC BY) 2.0 Generic License (https://creativecommons.org/licenses/by-sa/2.0/): page IX

Fabrice Florin: The House—Conceptual Art (https://www.flickr.com/photos/fabola/albums/72157665384593068/) available under Creative Commons Attribution (CC BY) 2.0 Generic License (https://creativecommons.org/licenses/by-sa/2.0/): page 83

Yukio Futagawa (*GA Houses* 51): pages 25, 27, 29

Sofia Kuspan: pages 53–55, 57–59

Kirk Martini: pages 42–44

Jock Reynolds: page VI

Patrick Sardo: pages 9, 10, 26, 28, 29, 30, 87, 88, 90

Ben Small: pages 5–6, 95

David Turnbull: pages 162–176

Beth Davila Waldman: pages 87, 89

Justin Walton: page 34

ORO Editions
Publishers of Architecture, Art, and Design
Gordon Goff: Publisher

www.oroeditions.com
info@oroeditions.com

Published by ORO Editions

Authors: Peter D. Waldman, Sofia Kuspan, Patrick Sardo, David Turnbull
Contributors: Ben Small, David Ireland
Forewords: Ann Hamilton, Henry Moss, Karen Van Lengen, WG Clark
Editor: Jake Anderson
Book Design: Patrick Sardo
Project Manager: Jake Anderson

10 9 8 7 6 5 4 3 2 1 First Edition

ISBN: 978-1-961856-82-0

Prepress and Print work by ORO Editions Inc.
Printed in China

ORO Editions makes a continuous effort to minimize the overall carbon footprint of its publications. As part of this goal, ORO, in association with Global ReLeaf, arranges to plant trees to replace those used in the manufacturing of the paper produced for its books. Global ReLeaf is an international campaign run by American Forests, one of the world's oldest nonprofit conservation organizations. Global ReLeaf is American Forests' education and action program that helps individuals, organizations, agencies, and corporations improve the local and global environment by planting and caring for trees.

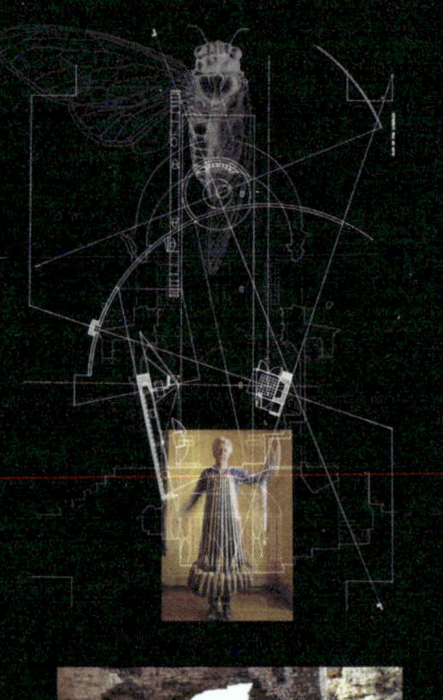

<table>
<tr><td>1</td><td rowspan="2">5</td><td rowspan="4">7</td></tr>
<tr><td>2</td></tr>
<tr><td>3</td><td rowspan="2">6</td></tr>
<tr><td>4</td></tr>
</table>

ELEMENTS: 1–4

1. Lunatics and Surveyors: David Ireland with *Broom Collection with Boom* (1978-1988) and Parcel X Composite Plan, Tempietto section, and cicada illustration from Ben Small's catalytic 2021 collage.

2. Nomad: Ruins in Tunisia (top) and *The Course of Empire – Desolation* by Thomas Cole (bottom).

3. Stage Set: 1920s East Boston lightbulb factory, now residence for two co-authors.

4. Stage Set: Parcel X and compass pier.

CONJUNCTIONS: 5–6

COMPOSITE: 7